Lightspeed Business

Find It, Fund, It, Build It
When There's No
Margin for Error

Lightspeed Business

Find It, Fund It, Build It When There's No Margin for Error

J. Neil Weintraut, 21st Century Internet Venture Partners
Christopher Barr, CNET

WILEY

John Wiley & Sons, Inc.

New York • Chichester • Weinheim • Brisbane • Singapore • Toronto

Published simultaneously in Canada.

This publication is designed to provide accurate and authoritative informa-tion in regard to the subject matter covered. It is sold with the understand-ing that the publisher is not engaged in rendering professional services. If professional advice or other expert assistance is required, the services of a competent professional person should be sought.

Library of Congress Cataloging-in-Publication Data:

ISBN 0-471-41972-9

Printed in the United States of America.

10 9 8 7 6 5 4 3 2 1

Contents

Foreword

3G Start-ups

Starting a successful business is a dream that eludes more than two million frustrated overachievers each year. Every entrepreneur searches for a smart guide or an experienced mentor to help shoulder the heavy lifting of an Internet start-up. While start-ups are the El Dorado of opportunity, millions of smart, driven entrepreneurs fail to execute their ideas because they don't have a partner to lead them safely through the treacherous curves.

The usual avenues for advice turn into detours and dead ends. Business schools are poorly equipped to give sound instruction advice because expertise about Internet start-ups is too new to be included in the syllabus. Bankers, investors, venture capitalists, and wealthy individuals make assumptions and share opinions yet lack the tried-and-true experience of veteran entrepreneurs.

■ THE BEGINNING OF THE GOLD RUSH

Everyone got swept up in the Internet environment beginning in late 1994. Actually, the genesis of the Internet gold rush can be traced to the day NetCom, an Internet service provider (ISP), went public in November 1994. Investment bankers, such as myself at the time, had refused to take NetCom public because it failed all of the standards we had—it didn't have a management team, its business model wasn't proven, and it wasn't profitable. Prior to that time you needed four quarters of profitability, a proven management team, and a clear, viable business model if you wanted to go public.

NetCom went public despite the fact that all of the prominent investment banks passed on it. The day it went public, the stock doubled—and that's the day the world changed. We went from the first generation of start-ups right smack into the second. All of a sudden it seemed like the rules had changed, and so we all wanted to just jump in. Or to put it another way, the fear was that if you didn't jump in, you would be left behind—and then you were dead.

And so began the gold rush. Although NetCom was an ISP, it just went out and raised a ton of money in the public marketplace and created a sexy stock. From a customer vantage point, NetCom was viewed as a hot company—you wanted to use its product. The next thing you knew, PSI, another ISP, felt it had to compete against NetCom; and although PSI didn't have management, didn't have profits, and didn't have a proven business model, PSI went public and raised a bunch of money. And we were off to the races.

■ BIG OPPORTUNITIES ATTRACT ENTREPRENEURS, EMPLOYEES, AND INVESTORS

When the Internet emerged in a big way in 1995, opportunities materialized for new businesses that applied technologies—such as Web browsers (there were more than a dozen in 1995), search engines, streaming media, Internet service providers, and digital photography—around which they then built their own businesses. Since the end of the second generation of start-ups (post-2000), the trend has been toward start-ups that create technology that they then sell to enterprises that use the technology to run *their* business.

Gone are the days of businesses built on the promise of attracting "eyeballs." That was the idea of attracting masses of users that you would later find a way to monetize. One of the many flaws in that thinking was that the traffic volume was transient—users came only because you had the lower price. Another flaw was thinking that those businesses could continue to monetize the traffic and that

Table F.1 Start-ups through time.

	1G	Generation 2G	3G
Years	1970–1994	1995–2000	2001 and beyond
Era	BC—Before commercialization	AN—After NetCom	AD—After dot.com crash
Time to IPO	5 years	2 years	3.5 years
Rules	Growth with profits	Get big fast (grow at all costs)	Get profitable fast (grow within costs)
Neilism Model	Create technology that can be sold to Wal-Mart—computers, information technology, components to run the business better	Apply technology that competes with Wal-Mart—e-tailing goods and services, online stocks, B2B exchanges	Create technology that is sold to mainstream companies
Market Valuation	$300 million	$2 billion	$600 million
Market Opportunity	1 million users	50 million users	100 million users
Business Environment	Pre-Internet	Wired Internet	Wireless, broadband, Internet incorporated into businesses
Business Behavior	Forecasting	Rapid experimentation	Experiment and implement without forecast

by getting users with a one-time acquisition fee those businesses could then sell products to the users at a profit in the future. But it didn't pan out that way. Markets had too many competing entrants. It also turned out that the centralized-supply-chain model of e-commerce is not superior to the bricks-and-mortar model. The idea was, "OK, we'll have everything in a central warehouse so that we'll have all these economies of scale," as opposed to having the inventory at each corner drugstore. The online retailing venture ended up being a disaster for hundreds of companies.

■ THIRD-GENERATION START-UPS

The environment for start-ups changed dramatically in 2000. Valuations were driven down by the drop in the availability of capital from the public markets. Early-stage investors, once dripping with cash, were more reticent about putting money into unproven ideas. The year 2000 ended the second generation (2G) of start-ups, and, like a phoenix emerging from the ashes, the third generation (3G) began. This new generation is dramatically different from the two preceding generations (see Table F.1).

Lightspeed Business: Find It, Fund It, Build It When There's No Margin for Error conveys useful hands-on instruction on how to get a 3G start-up launched quickly and on a trajectory to make it big. The two main themes are (1) we're now in a new era for start-ups and (2) there are new rules appropriate for this new era.

Lightspeed Business will boost 3G entrepreneurs in their quest for building successful start-ups. Readers will discover:

- How to distinguish a winning start-up opportunity from a loser.
- How to construct an attractive business offering, including how to convey the value proposition.
- How to build a bulletproof organization that can succeed quickly.
- Everything they need to know about equity—what it is, how to get it and keep it, and how to put it to work.
- Strategies on how to survive and thrive.

J. Neil Weintraut and Christopher Barr

Acknowledgments

This book was made with contributions of hard work, insight, and guidance from many talented experts. Martin Grossman supplied his prodigious speed, smarts, and energy; Alicia Neumann, Bradd Graves, and Mark Glaser assisted with style, grace, and timeliness. My friend Eric Knorr was always there with a calming voice and rock-solid confidence. I thank them all. There is one person who deserves special appreciation; without Sally Zahner's dedication and perseverance *Lightspeed Business* would never exist. Thank you, my dear friend.

Christopher Barr

Introduction

■ THE EDGE OF SUCCESS

Since the advent of the Internet in 1995 and *because* of the dot.com meltdown in 2001, the opportunities for true start-ups—and the entrepreneurs, employees, investors, customers, partners, and competitors behind them—are greater than ever before. According to the MoneyTree Survey by big-five accounting firm PriceWaterhouseCoopers, some 5,000 start-ups will launch in 2001 alone.

■ HOWEVER, FEWER THAN ONE START-UP IN 10 WILL SUCCEED

Although start-ups are well publicized, how to make them successful is not. And success, of course, is actually the reward and, hence, the reason for creating a start-up in the first place. Start-ups fail for any number of reasons, although most don't succeed either because they were doomed from the start or because they started well but stumbled under the very burdens of growth in success. Others failed because they were not sure what to do and so did many things, but not one thing well enough; or else they were on the track to success but got overrun by competitors who were better able to grow.

Based on the recognition that there are three fundamental conditions that push start-ups to the *bleeding* edge of success, this book identifies what to do—and what not to do!—to make a start-up one of the 10 that *does* succeed.

■ THREE FUNDAMENTAL CONDITIONS OF A START-UP

Start-ups are businesses that *grow* BIG, fast, and profitably in an environment of pure and perpetual escalation—and they do this with scant resources. These are the three fundamental conditions of this special type of business we all call a start-up: (1) *hypergrowth*, (2) *escalation*, and (3) *scanty resources*. Start-ups exist under these three conditions only because the very behavior and rewards that distinguish start-ups from other types of businesses follow from these conditions. Pushed, respectively, to the unrelenting and escalating edge of growth, innovation, and execution, a start-up's success is on but one path on this razor's edge. Anything else is failure. This path to success is on the edge.

Having a business plan that has been referred to a venture capitalist, for example, versus sending a business plan directly without a referral is the difference between getting a meeting and ending up in the paper shredder. The former is on the preordained path; the latter, of course, is not. Building a product with the feature that customers care about is on the preordained path; building a product with *more* features is not. The former gets customers; the latter gets the same customers but ends up consuming more than the absolute minimum resources. A business selling boring technology to large corporations is on the preordained path, whereas, despite popular impressions to the contrary, a business selling sexy electronic games to teenagers *is not*. Hiring a world-class chief executive officer (CEO) who can attract world-class vice presidents is on the preordained path; having vice president executives who will work for someone who is a good founder but a weak CEO is not.

■ A TYPICAL SUCCESSFUL START-UP

Through growth, innovation, and execution, a successful start-up creates a new market. It takes on an endless flow of new entrants five at a time, attracts $30 million of venture capital and a world-class executive team, and grows to $150 million of annual and profitable revenue. Within five years a successful start-up will have 1,000 employees, thousands of customers, and a $500 million valuation. Within a decade, it will be on its way to a billion dollar business. From Cisco to Yahoo!, all successful start-ups followed this precise growth-innovation-execution path, even though they were in different industries; all of the start-up failures, from incubators to dot.coms, diverged from it.

■ SIX RULES

By following six rules—focus, fit, form, lead, simplify, and make attractive—success-enlightened start-ups succeed not only because they ride this path, but also because *they*, rather than the market, set the path for others to follow. They become the edge of success.

1. Focus on the new things that matter, and do them better and faster (i.e., innovate) than anyone else.
2. Fit the offering and the start-up's business to its environment, and benefit from that environment.
3. Form the organization, offering, equity, strategy, trajectory, and numerous other components of a start-up to their natural order at the edge.
4. Lead customers, employees, and partners.
5. Simplify pricing, contracts, hiring, and products to the point where simplicity is actually a reason customers do business with the start-up, and the business operates more efficiently.
6. Make the offering, employment, investment, and partnership opportunities organically attractive to customers, employees, investors, and partners; don't merely try to attract customers with whatever the start-up happens to have.

In combination, these rules guide a start-up to become the edge because with them a start-up gets *better* with scale, does more with less, and extracts the details of innovation. It delivers innovation faster, while customers, employees, and investors that the start-up didn't even have access to before seek out the start-up proactively.

■ ACTIONS OF SUCCESS-ENLIGHTENED START-UPS

These rules, in turn, guide the few actions that a start-up needs to take. They guide with what not to do by eliminating the multiple directions that can tie a start-up in knots, and they explode the misguided wisdom that can lead them astray. Specifically, the top four actions of success-enlightened start-ups are:

1. *Starting start-ups that can succeed.* Although just about any technology business that starts is popularly viewed as a start-up, *successful* start-ups start with *six* essentials—(1) a BIG, early, and healthy opportunity; (2) a "gotta-have" offering; (3) attractive founders; (4) a bootstrapping franchise; (5) moderate capital needs; and (6) no baggage—or they won't get started at all. The first action any start-up, or its entrepreneurs, should take is deciding if it has the right stuff and then organizing these six essentials.

The upshot of this action is that electronic games, personal messaging, or any other consumer business does not have these essentials and, hence, is not a start-up to start. Start-ups are substantially only businesses that provide technology business tools to large corporations.

2. *Running the business with one goal: to raise the next round of capital.* Raising the next round of venture capital is not just one of many things that a start-up does; it is the goal that overshadows everything else. By running the business to this goal, not only will the start-up be successful, but it will also have the ability to fight another day, and its actions will exactly align with the ways and the things that help the rest of the business.

3. *Hiring.* People *are* the ability, the innovation, and the scalability of any business. They are the edge of success. And start-ups are merely the catalyst and the container for them. So start-ups perpetually ride, if not perpetually push, the edge of business by hiring more and better people—perpetually. Hire high, hire "hirers," and hire now. Go!

4. *Following the answer to the question, "What successful business do I look like?"* Because the path of success is the same for every start-up, the best and all-but-effortless answer for every question of how and what to do isn't in a textbook; it can be found at successful start-ups. What price do I charge for my product? What is a good public

relations agency? When will the business turn profitable? The answers to these and virtually all other questions about running a start-up come from the successful start-up that a new one looks like. Forget spreadsheets, start-up boot camps, consultants, and yes, even books. Pick your comparable successful company and look up its facts at the finance section of www.yahoo.com. It's that easy and that good.

The thriftiness of these actions embodies the spirit, the very Zen of start-up success—a scrappy make-shit-happen, get-it-done, us-against-the-world, paranoid-confidence, merit-wins, push-the-edge, and hold-it-together mindset that customers love, competitors fear, and, most important, makes a start-up win.

J. Neil Weintraut

Part One

Anatomy 101

Chapter

The Anatomy of
a Start-up

NEILISM: If your feet are cold, put on a hat.

Today is the perfect day to begin the journey of launching a sensational start-up. Although the rules changed in the spring of 2000 and the timeline to an initial public offering (IPO) has been extended by an additional 18 months from the heydays of 1998 and 1999, there are zillions of brilliant ideas yet to be conceived, and there are billions of dollars waiting to be invested. Investors are being much more rigorous about choosing which start-ups to fund today, but the potential pot of investment capital has never been bigger.

■ WHO WANTS TO BE A BILLIONAIRE?

Everyone wants to invest in companies that have the potential to grow into the next eBay, Yahoo!, Cisco, or CNET. Whether you call it clicks and bricks or clicks and mortar and whether it's in infrastructure, enterprise, broadband, or wireless, it doesn't matter where you build your business as long as it is technology focused and embraces Internet technologies. This book focuses on building outstanding technology-related start-ups because technology offers the greatest opportunity for nearly infinite growth. Run your business right, and the payoff potential is massive.

For evidence, just look at the riches amassed by the entrepreneurs in *Fortune* magazine's rankings of the 40 Richest under 40. Ever since it was first published in 1999, the list has been dominated by millionaires and billionaires who earned their fortunes with technology or Internet companies. This includes David Filo and Jerry Yang of Yahoo!, Jeff Bezos of Amazon, Pierre Omidyar of eBay, Rob Glaser of Real Networks, Rob DeSantis of Ariba, Paul Gauthier of Inktomi, and Marc Andreessen, formerly of Netscape and now of Loudcloud.

Of course, you don't have to be younger than 40 to launch a start-up! According to *Forbes* (November 16, 2000), Andrew McKelvey (65) of Monster.com, Broadcast.com cofounders Mark Cuban (44) and Todd Wagner (41), and Joe Ricketts (59) of AmeriTrade have all joined the rich-people-over-40 club.

What characterizes all of these people best, however, is not their net worth but rather their drive to build companies that change the world. If you asked these entrepreneurs what drove them and sustained them through the years of backbreaking work it took to realize their visions, they'd be unlikely to tell you that it was the money. To be a successful entrepreneur, you must have a passion for your idea and a consuming drive to make it a winner. And this is more true than ever in this third generation of start-ups.

■ IT'S THE USERS, STUPID

Why technology and the Internet? To twist a campaign slogan from an ex-president, it's the users, stupid. The spread of technology products and the growth of the Internet have increased dramatically the access to large markets. The growth of users since the commercialization of the Internet in 1995 has been meteoric. According to Nua Internet Surveys, the number of Internet users in the United States and Canada has grown from 18 million in 1995 to more than 150 million in 2000. That's an increase of more than 50 percent each year (see Figure 1.1).

And even though the growth rates in the United States and

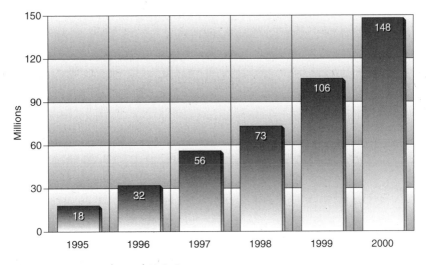

Figure 1.1   Number of U.S. Internet users.

Canada are sure to slow down as those markets approach saturation, the growth outside the United States is expected to grow at a huge rate. Worldwide usage has grown quickly since 1994; and if the growth continues even at a smaller percentage than in the past, there will be more than 1 billion Internet users worldwide by the year 2004. To go from a few million users to more than a billion in 10 short years is a stunning achievement (see Figure 1.2).

■ THE NATURE OF THE NET

So what is it about the Internet that makes it such an extraordinary new environment in which to start a business? In some respects, start-ups all share some similar characteristics whether they operate in a traditional environment or in the Internet environment. But the Internet adds dimensions that materially change the game:

- *Speed:* The Net moves at a speed an order of magnitude greater than traditional start-ups.
- *Instant access to huge markets:* It offers near-instantaneous access to potentially millions of users.
- *Customer-centric mindset:* The combination of speed and au-

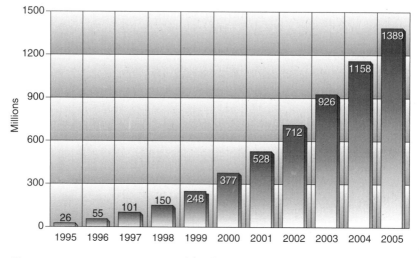

Figure 1.2 Internet users worldwide.

dience reach gives the customer unprecedented power. If your business can quickly attract an audience of millions, then so can your competitors. You can lose an audience as quickly as you gain it if you don't offer the best value to the customer. On the Net, the customer rules.

• *Interactivity and measurability:* The Net's interactive nature makes it possible for a business to quickly reach users on both a mass level and an individual level and to use customer feedback to precisely measure its impact on those users.

■ THE LIGHTSPEED ECONOMY

Technology and the Internet have created an economy that spins at a rapid pace. It's what we call the Lightspeed Economy. For example, purchase deals between one company and another that used to take days, weeks, or months to consummate now conclude with a single mouse click. Capital can be raised quickly when a start-up innovates a new solution that becomes essential to the success of a business. Equity, in turn, propels start-up businesses at rates limited only by their ability to attract employees. As shown earlier, enormous markets are accessible instantaneously. Online collegiate bookseller BigWords, for example, sold books to 150 universities within two weeks of launching on $50,000 capital in 1998, only to close two years later because it couldn't build a profitable enough business.

Opportunities appear on the horizon at an astonishing rate. Business models and value propositions defining entire industries can change with a few lines of code—whether hypertext markup language (HTML), Java, or extensible markup language (XML) computer code. And it wasn't too long ago—namely pre-Internet—that publishers charged for their information; during the dot.com heydays they paid portals and syndications to feature it. Now some are beginning to charge again.

Instant markets, customer feedback, and market morphing make experimentation rampant. Four11.com started as a "yellow pages" of e-mail addresses; but as that business topped out, it launched a free e-mail service in a month. The upshot? Yahoo! acquired Four11 for $92 million (now worth many times that) for its e-mail service, which powers Yahoo!'s e-mail to this day.

■ IN THE LIGHTSPEED ECONOMY, IF YOU CAN, YOU MUST

In markets that harness the Internet, shifts can occur between market leaders and fledgling upstarts virtually overnight. AskJeeves.com went from being an auxiliary search capability to Yahoo!'s competitor within six months. Similarly, fortunes mercilessly change instantaneously based on brutal merit. CDNow, a music distribution company, and Peapod, an online grocery store, each went from industry-defining-icon status to bankruptcy as customers and capital instantly flowed to upstarts with only marginally better value propositions. CDNow was eventually rescued by German conglomerate Bertlesmann, and Peapod was rescued by Dutch giant Ahold as Webvan crashed and burned.

The marriage of technology and the Internet created the Lightspeed Economy—an economy in which small differences have big consequences in a blink of an eye. New start-up offerings have access to more than 100 million customers overnight and can quickly attract the customers vital to the business. For example, Kmart-affiliated BlueLight.com signed up 1 million unique customers to its

Totally Free Internet Service within 14 weeks of its December 1999 launch.

Customers will defect to an even marginally superior offering with no more effort or consideration than a single mouse click. Comparison engines, such as MySimon, that enable the customer to click on the best option across hundreds of vendors prosper by exploiting this capability and behavior. Similarly, fortunes turn into failure as quick as superior offerings arise—CDNow and Peapod went from industry darlings to bankruptcy as customers and capital flowed to the next new thing as readily as water down a waterfall. Indeed, the only constraint on the velocity of a business in the Lightspeed Economy is the pace at which businesses can attract employees and customers.

■ THE ORGANIC START-UP

This new environment has produced revolutionary rather than evolutionary changes. So while some fundamental principles of start-ups haven't changed over time, technology and the Net have changed the world dramatically enough to make the start-up a whole new creature.

What are the common lessons to draw about 3G start-ups? Just as a common human nature runs through all human beings, all 3G start-ups share a common nature, whether they're consumer plays like Yahoo! and eBay or business-to-business (B2B) ventures like Cisco and Ariba. These companies appear to be very different from one another, but they all hew to a natural order. For example, a successful start-up's operating margins, equity lineup, and organizational structure all fall into common designs. And if they don't at first, over time variations tend to converge to a natural order.

To succeed as an entrepreneur in this environment, you need to understand the organic nature of a 3G start-up—its components, its characteristic behavior (its "human nature"), and its stages of development. And while the start-up is considered as an organic entity unto itself, it is also part of the larger organic structure of the Lightspeed Economy. Your start-up doesn't operate in a vacuum. Its success also depends on how well it interacts with other companies within the Lightspeed Economy.

■ ANATOMY OF A START-UP

What is the nature of a 3G start-up? What are its common character-istics and behavior, its defining nature? A successful start-up is more than the sum of its parts, to be sure, but without these six compo-nents, your start-up will never take its first step:

1. Opportunity
2. Offering
3. Organization
4. Strategy
5. Equity
6. Technology

These components are united by three fundamental principles that govern the start-up's behavior, both within the company itself and within the larger Lightspeed environment. Think of these as the systemic principles—the central nervous system, if you will—that penetrate and command every aspect of the start-up, that provide overall command and control:

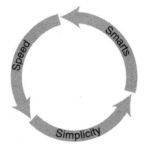

When all six components converge in an organic whole and operate according to these fundamental behaviors, the start-up is targeted for the success zone. We'll delve into each of these topics in detail in individual chapters. Then we'll detail the stages of devel-opment of this 3G organism—the five stages every 3G start-up goes through as it develops from infancy through adolescence and on to being a mature company.

But first, a brief overview of the essential components:

➤ Opportunity

The opportunity must be big. There are millions of ideas for businesses, but the market opportunity must be compelling enough to attract paying customers, great employees, and serious investors. With instantaneous access to millions of people, entrepreneurs will fail if they go after an opportunity that's too small or one that's yesterday's news.

3G start-ups mandate a business that will generate at least 50 percent gross margins. Business plans for e-tailers, for example, will be ignored by most investors because of the lack of success of such big names as Pets.com, Eve.com, eToys.com, and even Barnesand-Noble.com. A primary reason for these failures is that the gross margins for e-tailing are so low to begin with that there isn't enough margin to compensate for further erosion due to marketing and other variable costs.

Start-ups that begin with the potential for high margins, such as eBay, Yahoo!, JDS Uniphase, and CNET, have a much greater chance of creating a profitable business.

➤ Offering

If entrepreneurs create a compelling offering and then continue to innovate, its success is guaranteed. Sounds simple, but it's not. A start-up's offering must be new, important, obvious, and immediate. It won't succeed with a deferred benefit if it communicates to customers, for example, "Sign up with our service, give us all this information on how to personalize it for you, and over the next two months we'll learn about you and then you'll get empowering personalized advertisements." While the concept may actually have value, customers and investors aren't going to connect with it.

However, sometimes even when you win, you lose: You may have a seemingly innovative offering that, at the end of the day, just won't make it. Eve.com, a purveyor of beauty products over the Web, began in June 1999 and by mid-2000 had many paying customers and had hired more than 150 employees. Eve eventually reached a point where it could sell and ship products profitably—something even Amazon couldn't claim at the time.

But Eve closed in October 2000, citing "dramatic shifts in the market." What happened was that it couldn't scale its offering to make it a thriving business. On the day it closed, the company issued this statement: "Over the past several months the company improved gross margins and reduced costs to the point that Eve delivered orders profitably. However, this was not enough to overcome the lack of sufficient scale. After examining every alternative, the company regretfully concluded that liquidation is the only viable option."

So even though Eve got customers, hired great employees, and was on the road to overall profitability, it was a failure. Beware of scenarios where even when you win, you lose.

➤ **Organization**

If you want to win, if you want to have fun, if you want to learn, if you want to get better every day, your start-up will need a world-class organization. At the beginning of the life cycle, start-ups are organizations first, ideas second. Success will be determined by the quality of the organization in countless ways, especially in how fast you can grow.

> The single biggest mistake you can make when starting up or running a company is hiring the wrong CEO. And that could be yourself!
>
> —*Steve Kirsch, serial entrepreneur and founder of Infoseek, Propel, and Frame Technology.*

There are three main rules for a successful organization:

1. Start hiring immediately!
2. Make sure the people you hire are themselves adept at hiring, because over the course of a year everyone in the company will wind up hiring at least one person. By geometric progression some people will wind up hiring as many as 10 people. And indeed, the founders of the company—if the company is successful—will effectively have hired 200 people, on average.

3. Devise the structural model of a successful organization. This structure of people, personalities, and purpose is so critical to the future success of the start-up that this model is explained in depth in Chapter 4.

➤ Strategy

The fundamental strategy for start-up success is to run your business to raise the next round of capital. This advice may sound like it's too narrowly focused on the funding part of the start-up equation; but besides guiding you in funding your business, this strategy will also keep you on the path to success in building and running your business.

While other advisers may suggest that you wait and get a few more things completed before you raise more capital so that you can then raise it at a higher valuation, we believe there is a preferable way to succeed. In a 3G start-up, you're better off getting some money to get to the next funding milestone. It also turns out that by reaching your milestones, you'll automatically be focusing on doing only what will make you a successful business, whether it's building a working product, building your organization, or attracting your initial customer(s).

Of course, another fundamental strategy is to get out in front and run like hell!

➤ Equity

The most misunderstood aspect of a start-up is equity, and many people approach equity backward. Most entrepreneurs tend to focus on venture capital or fund-raising when they should really look at equity as an essential tool of the company that is used to attract employees, partners, and venture capitalists.

Because any one share of equity affects the ownership of every other share of equity, equity should be managed as a system, rather than handled as shares issued in isolation. Overgranting ownership to one constituent comes at the expense of the others; ownership is a zero-sum—or 100 percent sum—game. For example, a smart CEO being recruited to a start-up in the midst of a financing round, knows that a financing dilutes the ownership of all shareholders, and will ask for higher ownership than normal to offset the dilution. The prospective CEO is correctly looking at equity as an overall system that must be managed over time, rather than as just a point number. Indeed, equity needs to be managed as a system to orchestrate the right balance between the players. If you mishandle the equity equation, you'll create big problems for your company down the line.

➤ Technology

While it's permissible to outsource parts of your technology needs, such as designing the company Web site, the technology choices you make are critical to your start-up's success. If you are a technology company, some of your choices for platforms and tools will be made for you. But if you are first assembling your team and technology platform, keep in mind that if you choose products and services that are not commonly used, it may be difficult to hire programmers and software engineers to support them in the future.

■ BEHAVIOR/NATURE OF A 3G START-UP

➤ Mindset

There is a Zen-like mindset that is common among the leaders of winning start-ups. This intensely focused mindset ties together the strategy, the fundamentals, and the organization to produce an unstoppable business. A focused mindset will let you play the competitive environment to your advantage. For example, when thinking about raising money, often the thought is to just raise a predetermined amount of capital. But in truth, capital abounds. So instead of taking the attitude that you should just do good things with the business and that will make the money come, we say run your business in a way that attracts capital. It's a critical difference, a nuance, where you say, "I'm taking it to the next level. I'm going to do things with my business that make it particularly appealing to capital."

➤ The Knee Bone's Connected to the Thigh Bone

No more, no less, these are the atoms and bits that make up a start-up. They are all connected and they all work together. Like the Neilism at the beginning of the chapter says, "If your feet are cold, put on a hat." In other words, these components interact as a system to create a successful start-up.

That old saying indicates how your body works together in order to protect itself. The way a human body works, most of the heat that is generated can be lost through the head. By putting on a hat, the heat loss stops and the entire body, including the feet, warms up. The same concept is true for start-ups. All the components work together, and the start-up won't survive if the different building blocks don't support each other.

■ THE THREE S's

The six start-up components are united by three operating principles: speed, smarts, and simplicity. These seemingly basic principles will affect the success of your start-up.

➤ Speed

The primary principle you'll learn is that speed succeeds. This book will show you how to use the fundamental principle of speed to make your start-up succeed. It is a truism of the Internet that it runs on its own speeded-up time, which is roughly equivalent to dog years. To succeed on the Net, entrepreneurs must move quickly or they'll be roadkill. If you run your start-up right, you can even create your own speed so you actually do things to make yourself faster. Speed doesn't mean writing programming code faster; it means doing things in such a way that you actually get the better results sooner.

➤ Smarts

Are you ready to lead a start-up? Most would-be start-ups are finished before they start. Failures lack even the critical mass to ignite a trajectory to success. Accordingly, the first and critical step in pursuing a start-up is to determine if it is one of the few that has the right stuff; determine this so that either you avoid an ill-fated endeavor or, more important, you retool to make it successful.

There is no such thing as dumb luck in a 3G start-up. Smarts are fundamental because smarts touch every part of a start-up—from the founder to the employee, from the board to the financing. Start-ups that succeed have an abundance of brains that are put to effective use. At the core is the founder who must attract other people with brains. If a start-up has a lone-wolf entrepreneur who can't attract smart people, then that start-up is doomed to fail.

Successful start-ups prove this point about smarts. Pierre Omidyar, eBay's founder, hired Meg Whitman as CEO in 1998 with much success. Same goes for Yahoo!. Its founders hired Tim Koogle years before Yahoo! turned its first profit. Tim Koogle was obviously attracted by the founders' offer for good reason. Koogle has since been succeeded by another CEO, but he was essential to Yahoo!'s early success.

➤ Simplicity

Einstein said, "Everything should be as simple as possible, but no simpler." As a fundamental rule, simplicity will make a start-up's growth easier. In this chapter, you'll find examples of start-ups that have measured themselves with this high-level test: When analyzing a situation, if it doesn't look simple, then you don't have the right strategy. When entrepreneurs want to know, "Is this the right course of action?" we ask, "Is it simple?" The text will offer a number of examples of how to apply simplicity to your business.

■ FIT, ACT, ATTRACT

In looking over the range of start-ups, there seems to be no limit to the permutations of failure, whereas the forms and the formulas of success are so similar that it's amazing . . . or fundamental. Winning start-ups' origins, organization, behavior, sequencing, failures (yes, failures), and rewards, to name a few, are tellingly similar, even though their industries span a spectrum from million-dollar telecommunications equipment companies to free consumer media sites. At the core, successful start-ups all do three things: (1) They *fit* in the Lightspeed Economy. (2) They *act* with speed and smarts. And (3) they employ simplicity to *attract* customers, employees, and partners.

The Lightspeed Economy is the playing field of the start-up game. Start-ups must play by its rules merely to survive, much less to exploit this environment to their advantage. And what a special environment it is: friction-free, merit-based, self-reinforcing, and people-constrained. A competitive offering is but a mouse click away. One line of HTML computer code can undermine an entire industry, changing, for example, a subscription business model into a free advertising business model. Venture capital may be difficult to raise, but raising it is still easy compared to landing a great vice president of engineering.

This is an environment where speed—or more precisely lightspeed—wins. For starters, start-ups inherently lack the resources to do everything; so instead, they should do the few things that matter and do them faster than everyone else. But most profoundly and fundamentally, the friction-free Lightspeed Economy is an environment in which small actions compound into BIG consequences, and do so essentially instantaneously. These compounding spirals can either be upward or downward, virtuous or vicious, depending on whether the actions are smart or not smart. So the faster smart start-ups get geometrically stronger, bigger, and, yes, faster with each smart step—the fast eat the slow.

■ DEVELOPMENTAL STAGES OF A 3G START-UP

Now that we've mapped out the basic anatomy of a start-up and touched on its characteristic behavior and nature, we can chart the five predictable stages of development through which a 3G start-up goes, from infancy to maturity. And make no mistake: almost all start-ups follow this natural order.

Third-generation start-ups have five stages:

Stage 0	Stage 1	Stage 2	Stage 3	Stage 4
	Proof of	Define	Expand to	
Bootstrap →	concept →	market →	profitability →	Go public!

The overriding goal at each stage is to achieve the milestones that enable you to raise the next round of capital. Money is the life-blood of a start-up. If you have money, you at least live to fight another day. If you're not moving ahead, you're falling behind. The price of not hitting your milestones is being worse off than when you were simply selling the promise—you've proved failure. Avoid doing anything that gets in the way of achieving your milestones. For example, don't open a sales office when you're still building your prototype; or don't add a gee-whiz feature to the product if it doesn't gain you customers.

Don't forget the Zen-like mindset. By pursuing your goal of achieving your milestone, everything else you do will fall in line to support your efforts.

➤ Stage 0

The bootstrap stage is the very beginning of the start-up: You're living off credit cards, formulating plans, putting ideas for the business together, and making contacts. At the end of this stage you'll be capitalized in the most uncomplicated manner.

Stage	0
Age	0–6 months
Genus	Bootstrap
Number of customers	0
Number of employees	4
Capital requirement	$3 million
Valuation after funding	$12 million
Percentage of company sold to investors at end of stage	Sell 33 percent to get $3 million.
Funding stage	Series A
Milestones	• Create mockups. • Attract seed executives. • Talk to investors, attorneys, customers.
Goal	Attract next round of capital.

➤ Stage 1

The proof-of-concept stage is a period of rapid organization: You use the capital to create the prototype product or service, attract the first customers, sell your promise, and hire a few crucial employees. Whether you have seed-stage funding from yourself, friends, family, or angel investors, the goal of this and indeed each successive stage is to raise your next round of capital.

Stage	1
Age	0–6 months
Genus	Proof of concept
Number of customers	1 or 2 enterprise customers or 1,000 consumer customers
Number of employees	30 by the end of 6 months
Capital requirement	$12.5 million
Valuation after funding	$50 million
Percentage of company sold to investors at end of stage	Sell 25 percent to get $12.5 million.
Funding stage	Series B
Milestones	• Build a simple product for proof of concept. • Attract core employees. • Gain requisite customers.
Goal	Attract next round of capital.

➤ Stage 2

In this stage you take the feedback from your customers to build a stable version 1.0 product. At the beginning of this stage, you've raised $15 million to sustain you for the next year. You increase the number of customers and add employees, and you're working to raise the next round.

Stage	2
Age	7–12 months
Genus	Define market
Number of customers	10 to 15 enterprise customers or 200,000 consumer customers

Number of employees	60 by end of 12 months
Capital requirement	$20 million
Valuation after funding	$100 million
Percentage of company sold to investors at end of stage	Sell 20 percent to raise another $20 million.
Funding stage	Series C
Milestones	• Turn prototype into stable, go-to-market version 1.0 product based on customer feedback. • Scale up the number of customers. • Fill out executive ranks.
Goal	Attract next round of capital.

➤ **Stage 3**

As in the first two stages, you continue with product development, but now you're aiming for profitability. At the beginning of this stage you will have sold 20 percent of the company at a valuation of $100 million to raise $20 million. The business scales to produce $3 million of revenue a quarter, and you're very close to turning profitable. At the end of this stage you'll have an IPO to raise $60 million.

Stage	3
Age	13–24 months
Genus	Expand to profitability
Number of customers	100 enterprise customers or 2 million consumer customers
Number of employees	140 by end of 24 months
Capital requirement	$60 million
Valuation after funding	$400 million
Percentage of company sold to investors at end of stage	Sell 15 percent to raise another $60 million.
Funding stage	IPO
Milestones	• Develop product further. • Scale to produce $3 million in revenue per quarter without stunting growth. • Profitable by end of stage.
Goal	Attract next round of capital.

➤ **Stage 4**

This is the stage you've been working your heart out for. By the end of this stage, you'll be profitable, you'll have gone public, and you'll have a great company.

Stage	4
Age	25–36 months
Genus	Go public!
Number of customers	200+ enterprise customers or 2 million+ consumer customers
Number of employees	200
Milestones	• Introduce a second product. • Be profitable. • Go public!
Goal	Stay profitable.

■ THE NATURAL ORDER OF SEQUENCING

These five stages reflect the natural order of sequencing a start-up, not some arbitrary sequence. For example, Stage 1 takes six months because one month is too short to develop a product, attract the initial customer(s), and raise funds. And a year is too long because the competitive and customer markets change too fast. The successful start-ups all fall within these ranges of development. Follow this sequencing, and you'll stay in the success zone.

■ REFERENCES

More information about the right start-up elements can be found on our Web site: *http://www.lightspeed-business.com*

Bluelight: *http://news.cnet.com/news/0-1007-200-1581313.html*

Yahoo! Buys Four11, October 1997: *http://news.cnet.com/news/0-1005-200-322847.html*

Chapter

The Opportunity Must Be Big

NEILISM: Big opportunities attract entrepreneurs, employees, and investors.

You are living in a period of historic opportunity. While it may seem that all the prime locations in the Lightspeed Economy have been staked out already, virgin territory remains hidden in plain sight, and vast regions won't be colonized until new technology emerges. Of course, you could simply carve out a small parcel of the frontier that no one else has claimed, but you don't need the Internet to play it safe and create a viable little business. You want to grow a business that reflects the size of the opportunity—one big enough to attract venture capital.

Though investment has declined since the Nasdaq's infamous March 2000 meltdown, venture capitalists (VCs) keep betting heavily on technology-related companies. In 2000, they invested more than $103 billion in 5,380 companies, significantly more than 1999's $59.4 billion in 3,947 companies. Investment during 2000 continued to shift from content to managed services, from e-commerce to infrastructure; but still the money flowed at an average rate of $282 million per day.

Perhaps you've heard the clichés about what inspires VCs to invest in one company versus another—they want experienced managers, they want one company in each of several predetermined market sectors, they want a CEO whom they'd enjoy having a beer with. While any or all of these criteria may persist at a given time, in truth there is only one concern that dwarfs them all: VCs want to invest in companies that skillfully target big, fat market opportunities.

■ HOW BIG IS BIG?

In the movie business, blockbuster hits end up paying for the duds and the loss leaders. So it goes with a VC firm's portfolio. The idea is to bet big, because one big win can more than compensate for other investments that don't pay off.

The bottom line for hugeness is surprisingly solid: With few exceptions, VCs won't play unless they believe they have the potential to make at least $50 million. Or to put it another way, if your company can capture 10 percent of a $5 billion market and if a VC's profit equals 10 percent of your company, then it was worth the VC's time and money. If you're probing a smaller market or a smaller market share, don't bother looking for VC money. Your start-up won't get backed. And you shouldn't want it to be because you don't want to answer to VCs who've put money on a treadmill that doesn't have enough steps.

■ DETERMINING MARKET OPPORTUNITY

As you determine your prospective company's market opportunity, you'll have to pass several key tests:

• *Show me the profits.* Before the Internet seemed to change the basic rules of business, Wall Street valued public companies based partly on their price-to-earnings (P/E) ratio; that is, their capitalization divided by their after-tax earnings. Many second-generation (2G) start-ups went public before they had any real earnings to speak of, so the playing field shifted in the late 1990s to a price-to-revenue model. In these pragmatic times, however, you must not only outline a plan for consistent revenue growth but also offer a plausible time frame for the profits those revenues will produce. Amazon was able to put that one off for years, but you can't.

• *The value of opportunity.* The valuation of your company will be determined in large measure by the size of its market opportunity. To take a negative example, Salon.com seemed like a winner at its inception—surely there was a sizable market for a literate, *New Yorker*–style magazine on the Web, particularly one that was free to users instead of 45 bucks a year. Unfortunately, the prospects for the success of such a publication actually appear worse online than off, even with 3.5 million visitors per month (and even though it avoids the paper and direct-mail promotional costs that account for the lion's share of a magazine's expenses). In 2000, the market cap for this company had dropped to less than $10 million, and its stock had sunk far enough to risk delisting from the Nasdaq.

• *The structural ramp.* The term *scalable* gets misused more than any other bit of start-up lingo. Everyone trots it out, but most VCs see right through attempts to graft it onto pitches where it doesn't fit. The most attractive start-ups have an "infinite ramp" built right into their structure as a business, and they can scale with no plateau in sight to stymie an IPO or to prompt analysts to declare a limited market cap. With its first-mover advantage and brilliant execution, Yahoo! provides a classic example: What could scale better than a search directory that serves as a user interface for all of the Internet? A great notion if you can get there first. Whatever you do, don't let the ups and downs of the market deter you from pursuing a good idea. Keep the constant market and environment fluctuations in perspective.

I believe that in 2000, roughly 200 million people worldwide have access to the Internet and they use it about 30 minutes a day. Over the next five years I predict the number of users

(continued)

will increase by a factor of five to more than one billion people. The usage will easily grow five times to about two hours a day. With a five-fold growth in users and a five-fold growth in usage, there is an underlying 25-fold growth over the next five years.

—*Bill Gross, CEO of Idealab*

Even if Gross proves to be overly optimistic, the message is clear: The game ain't over yet. In fact, it's only beginning.

■ THE CUSTOMER UNIVERSE

Part of your job in identifying a large market opportunity is to characterize exactly who your customers will be. For a consumer-focused start-up, you need to sketch a collective profile of the millions of customers who will use your product—and describe a surefire way to derive revenue and profits from their patronage. You'll have far fewer customers for a service that targets enterprises, but you will need to be more specific in detailing customer needs and the users within various organizations who will find your product and service worthwhile. The cost of customer acquisition continues to climb for most consumer ventures, so you may need to factor in an expensive marketing program to rise above the noise.

Even a compelling idea for B2B services, however, can fall short of attracting venture money. Recently, an entrepreneur pitched a panel of Silicon Valley VCs on new software to automate timecards for independent consultants. Most consultants still use paper and could really use a product like that. It's a fine idea, but how big is the market? The software may be valuable, but only to a small number of individual customers. To a VC this venture is simply not worth pursuing.

On the Web, remember not to confuse customers with visitors. Take Priceline.com, one of the most trafficked consumer sites. Once seen as a blue-chip dot.com, this name-your-price service—which deals mostly in airline tickets—has too many visitors that are "lookers, not bookers." In late 2000, Priceline's share price was off more than 90 percent for the year, top executives were jumping ship, and layoffs were underway. When Merrill Lynch analyst Henry Blodget downgraded the company's stock in November 2000, he dryly noted: "It has become clear that this is a much smaller business opportunity than we initially hoped."

■ SHARING THE DREAM

Investors are just one audience for your pitch. To build a great company, you need to attract quality talent, and that means offering equity that stands a good chance of being worth something. Everyone has heard about paper millionaires whose options have gone up in smoke; so selling this dream is harder than it was at the height of the boom of 2G start-ups. Once, just whispering that you had a hot dot.com idea was enough to seduce the ambitious. Now, the best people need to be convinced of your prospects with as much zeal and organization as you'll apply to capturing customers.

No one can prove in advance that a venture will be successful, but you can make it worth the risk. One way to close the deal when hiring top management is to offer what could be a "life-changing" incentive—which, according to the current trend for venture-backed companies, is an option package worth $10 million if the company enjoys a successful IPO.

If that seems extravagant, remind yourself of the hiring environment, and then consider the very small pool of people with the experience and ability to put your company over the top. Assuming your market opportunity is real, whom you snag for the top spots will decide more than any other factor your chances for success. For example, Yahoo! wasn't the only Web company that had the chance to turn huge site traffic into a big, moneymaking business—Disney, Lycos, About, AskJeeves, NBCi, and others had it, too. But only Yahoo!'s management has shown the wherewithal to turn millions of eyeballs into a profitable category killer.

But ultimately, you can't ask something of potential hires that you wouldn't ask of yourself. Is your idea compelling enough and is the opportunity truly big enough for you to quit a secure, lucrative job you enjoy? You're asking the best people you can find to take a significant risk. Putting yourself in their shoes and imagining them weighing the risk versus the return can give you real insight into the viability of your business idea.

■ HOW TO RECOGNIZE A BIG OPPORTUNITY

When the dot.com bubble was still inflating, you could identify a huge market, lay out your plans to grab a piece of it, and, with the help of projections that the Internet's rocketlike trajectory would continue, get funding.

Today, no one in his or her right mind would consider targeting, say, the $25 billion U.S. health-and-beauty retail sector and solicit money for an e-tailing dot.com that would supposedly take that market by storm. For one thing, there are now credible estimates from Gartner Group and Forrester Research that e-tailing will capture no more than 7 percent of the total retail market by 2004. So even if you miraculously captured 100 percent of online health-and-beauty sales, you're talking about a market opportunity of less than $2 billion. More obviously, trying to build a viable brand in this overcrowded space today would be madness, especially when you consider that pioneering health-and-beauty e-tailers Eve.com and Beautyjungle.com closed after massive investments couldn't resuscitate a bad business model. And e-tail veterans More.com, Drugstore.com, and PlanetRX.com are all sputtering or closed.

Clearly, you can't simply spin the dial, pick a big market, and expect immediate success. Even e-tailers spun off from bricks-and-mortar companies like Nordstrom, Kmart, and Wal-Mart had to postpone their IPOs indefinitely. VCs not only view new e-tailing ventures as nonstarters, but VCs now also scoff at ventures that merely add "dot.com" to an ordinary business idea. The top online players are already established; trying to grab market share away from them would cost a fortune in misspent marketing dollars.

Toward the end of the second generation of start-ups, even previous winners took big losses. Not only business-to-consumer (B2C) but also B2B pure-plays were under assault. Just consider the fortunes of the Internet Capital Group, the high-profile B2B venture firm, which has seen its market cap plummet from a peak of $60 billion in January 2000 to below $2 billion by December 2000. At the height of the B2B craze, you could simply point to multitrillion-dollar projections for B2B e-commerce, pick a fat industry sector in which to set up a B2B exchange, and say slyly, "If we get just a little piece of this market . . ."

Both B2C and B2B relied on incorrect assumptions: that consumers would abandon the strip mall in favor of the browser and that businesses would invest in integrating with B2B exchanges to reduce operating costs, even though they were also being asked to pay a tithe to trade with existing customers. Given the sudden and unexpected surge in Internet usage, media hype, and "irrational exuberance" among investors, those great expectations were, in hindsight, predictable. As it turned out, the opportunity was there—but in most sectors for a few first movers alone.

The lesson is clear: Look ahead. Today's established winners were the first to capitalize on the confluence of technologies that gave birth to the Internet. Currently, the money is flowing to the infrastructure and managed services companies that keep e-business humming. That space is crowded and should be approached by those who offer demonstrable innovation. If you really want to attract investor, employee, and customer attention, focus on the exciting new extensions to today's technology and Internet opportunities and plan a business that will capitalize on their cycles of explosive growth down the road.

■ TRENDS TO WATCH

If a technology niche suddenly seems hot, VCs move like a galloping herd. Take the rage of the year 2000: photonics. A generic name to describe systems that generate light, the term *photonics* was practically unheard of until, in late 1999, Nortel bought Qtera for its technology that enables fiber optic lines to carry signals farther without regeneration. Everyone knew that fiber was prerequisite to the next generation of the Internet, but few were aware how crucial it was to break the looming bottleneck problems inherent in high-bandwidth communications. The optical switching equipment and multiplexing techniques offered by such companies as Cyras, Photonex, and Brightlink Networks suddenly became indispensable solutions that, by the spring of 2000, were succeeding in garnering a flood of venture capital.

The strategy of "get in early" still works if you pick the right area. Here's a sampling of hot trends where it could make sense to get in on the ground floor:

- *Broadband applications and services.* According to the Gartner Group, one-third of households with Internet access will have broadband connections by 2004—and based on samples of existing broadband users, they will spend 20 times the dollars online as those with dial-up connections will spend. Among other things, a wave of rich-media B2C e-commerce applications and services that enhance the online shopping experience seems inevitable. Communications may finally mature to the point where Internet-protocol videophones become a reality.

- *Internet appliances.* Smart wired and wireless networked appliances in the home, from self-diagnosing furnaces to Firewire sound systems, are on their way. Not only the appliances themselves but also the infrastructure and the applications that manage them or connect them to manufacturers or utilities pose a significant opportunity.

- *Wireless everything.* Lackluster wireless application protocol (WAP) applications (apps), confusing standards, and the astronomical cost of licensing for the 3G spectrum make a usable wireless Web seem far off at the beginning of the decade. But immediate opportunities lie in wireless apps, extensible markup language (XML), and middleware that extend enterprise applications to handhelds, from time and billing to sales force automation. Wireless services that sense the mobile user's location, arriving in 2001, will create a global market for location-based advertising that Ovum predicts will reach $16 billion by 2005.

- *Interactive television.* High-resolution digital TV, which will finally enable the long-awaited convergence between television and the Internet, won't happen anytime soon (largely because cable operators will want to use the bandwidth for more stations rather than for higher quality). But according to Cahners In-Stat, over half of all households will have interactive TV by 2005, enabling e-commerce, video on demand, multiplayer gaming, and a host of applications no one has thought of yet.

- *Voice recognition services.* Voice-based businesses like Tellme, Quack, and BeVocal are only the beginning. Voice may turn out to be the input method of choice for all sorts of products ranging from wireless handheld applications to automotive products. VoiceXML will open up all sorts of possibilities for making existing applications and services voice capable.

This sampling of trends is intended to spark creative thinking. There's plenty of room for innovation in other areas—data security, marketing and management services, entertainment, analysis, enterprise middleware, outsourced e-business applications, and on and on.

■ SPIN-OFFS AND CARVE-OUTS

Over the past couple of years, big, established companies have seen the advantages enjoyed by quick moving start-ups, so much so that many have spun off new ventures or divisions. A number of companies have also created carve-outs—partial spin-offs where assets of large companies are put into nimble start-ups and the majority of the ownership in the new company is retained by the parent company. If you're in a position to lead the formation of a spin-off or a carve-out, consider the recent history of such ventures, many of which have followed the vagaries of the market's irrational exuberance.

Agilent, a measurement technologies company, spun off from Hewlett-Packard in November 1999 with one of the biggest IPOs in history and reported strong first-year results. And few doubt that Palm should have detached from 3com—Palm has a dominant position in an emerging market and has been an island in the storm for beleaguered investors in 3com shares. Siebel Systems, a large enterprise applications maker, started Sales.com in late 1999. It quickly secured funding as well as a strong management team.

Oracle, led by CEO Larry Ellison, is the parent of two spin-offs that make Internet appliance-like products: Liberate Corp, initially spun off as Network Computer in 1996, changed its name in 1999. Ellison spun off the other venture, New Internet Computer Co., in January 2000. Former CNET employee Gina Smith was named founding CEO.

Large telecommunications firms seem to spin out divisions frequently and often successfully. Nortel Networks, for example, spun out its low-end networking subsidiary, Netgear, in early 2000, not long after IBM did the same to its home networking division, Home Director. Lucent created corporate networking spin-off Avaya, although its stock immediately fell below its October 2000 IPO level.

As for examples of carve-outs, the bricks-and-mortar side of Barnes and Noble, the venerable bookseller, chose to carve out its Internet business back in 1997 and had an IPO the following year. Closer to home, CNET carved out its Snap directory-and-search service in 1998 in partnership with NBC. Wal-Mart Stores carved out Walmart.com, and even Microsoft created a carve-out with Expedia, its online travel service.

The bottom line is that the same rules apply to spin-offs and carve-outs as to bootstrap start-ups. A hot business unit may have every chance of success as a separate company. A blueblood parentage is helpful but guarantees little, especially when management lacks the street smarts for an entrepreneurial venture.

■ PICK YOUR PARADIGM

To help you bring your vision into focus, do what Hollywood pitchmeisters have done for years: Pick some smash hits and recombine them or at least put a different spin on them: "By 2005, our patented 40Gbps transducers will be on every cell tower. We'll be like a combination of Cisco and Level 3 for wireless interconnectivity." This practice keeps you externally focused and puts you in league with business models that may closely resemble yours. Right out of the gate, you are speaking a common language. And when you create a business plan, you can rely on at least some data that draws on the performance of existing models. There are millions of great ideas; and although particular sectors, such as e-tailing and B2C and B2B companies, go in and out of favor depending on the business environment, here are some ways of roping together big-name companies into a business-model typology:

• *The gazillion-eyeballs model.* Game over if you want to be another Yahoo!, America Online (AOL), ICQ, or Microsoft Network.

But there is plenty of investment money available for plans that can generate revenue and profits from current and future online traffic. Plans that are strictly traffic drivers and have no revenues, such as the early incarnations of ICQ and Napster, are not likely to be funded as quickly in the 3G start-up environment.

• *The e-business software model.* The innovator's playground, this vast area is home to all manner of developers, from Siebel (the most successful customer relationship management [CRM] company) to Vignette (the current leader in content management software) to WebMethods (the top purveyor of XML tools). Other winners include Ariba, Art Technology, BroadVision, Commerce One, Inktomi, Interwoven, i2 Technologies, and Vitria. In most cases, revenue accrues from both software licensing and aftermarket services.

Don't be dazzled by the application service provider (ASP) model, where providers lease software over the Internet rather than license it: Any software maker can decide to become an ASP; so focus on the functionality, technology, and services, not just the delivery method.

• *The content-driven model.* Original content ventures make money through advertising, referrals, commerce, subscriptions, licensing, or some combination thereof. But what does it take to make money? CNET Networks stands alone as a model for success, not only because it delivers ads to more than 40 million unique users per month but also because its referral system accrues fees for users that CNET delivers to technology-based e-commerce partners. Original content sites outside of technology tend to be labors of love or bloated, troubled ventures, like TheStreet.com, Quokka Sports, or Salon.com. Pay-per-view or subscription sites, like Hoover's or Northern Light, can work, but only on a small scale. You might find a niche, but don't expect to tap into an opportunity big enough to attract interest from outside investors.

• *The peer-to-peer (P2P) model.* Napster and Gnutella have gotten the publicity; but there's more to P2P than using the Internet to swap tunes from hard disk to hard disk, and there's still room for innovation here. The "distributed computing" angle—where businesses lease processing power and storage space from idle desktops—is getting attention. One of the proponents, Centrata, got backing from Kleiner Perkins. Ray Ozzie, the brains behind Lotus Notes, started Groove Networks, a P2P company. Redpoint Ventures admits investing in a couple of stealth P2Ps; and Marc Andreessen, of Netscape and Loudcloud fame, has dropped money into Infrasearch, a P2P search engine.

• *The e-market model.* Whether B2B or consumer-to-consumer (C2C), e-markets line up buyers on one side and sellers on the other and either take a share of every transaction or charge a subscription fee. In the consumer market, this usually means auctions; and eBay is still the only mass-market success story (though many companies run auctions as a sideline). In B2B, auctions and exchanges abound. But keep three things in mind about these businesses: (1) They work best when they address a vertical market. (2) There's room for one or two successful ventures in each vertical. And (3) big buyers or sellers may not join the party unless they get an equity share.

• *The e-tailing model.* This 2G model went down in flames. The biggest e-tailer, Amazon, is *still* losing money, as are other biggies— Buy.com, BarnesandNoble—and on and on. And don't forget the spectacular failures: Pets.com, Furniture.com, Garden.com, eToys.com, and so forth. The tide for 3G mass-market e-tailing is turning toward bricks-and-mortar retailers such as Walmart.com and VictoriaSecrets.com. Of course, you might find a niche that looks promising, but you must make sure that the market isn't too small and that the marketing costs aren't prohibitive.

• *The free service (or software) model.* This is another 2G model that won't have much traction in the third generation. Users get something for nothing: free ICQ chat software, free hosting on Geocities, free Internet access through Juno or NetZero, the ability to send an Evite free. Users pay no money, but they must often give up deep-profile information in exchange for the service, so they can be upsold via e-mail or targeted ads. Do the users buy? Only time will tell. Remember that ICQ had no revenue when it was sold to AOL in 1998 for $400 million.

• *The infrastructure model.* Somebody has to lay down the technology track on which the Internet chugs along. Cisco was smart enough to elbow its way into position as the leading router manufacturer when the Internet took off; manufacturers of optical switching equipment were the darlings of 2000, as were some of the companies that actually manufacture or lay the fiber. There's always room for technical innovation. If you have a way to do it dramatically faster or cheaper, and you can prove it, you'll get funding.

You can mix and match these models into any number of hybrids. So-called vertical portals, for example, often combine specialized content with an e-market and/or highly targeted advertising. And new models emerge all the time.

■ DO YOU HAVE WHAT IT TAKES?

You can pick precisely the right idea at the right time and plug it into exactly the right business model—but that doesn't mean you can pull it off. It's true: Successful entrepreneurs do tend to be zealots and very persuasive personalities. Now that the stakes have been raised, and the money has tightened, there's no room for the halfhearted.

Do you have the self-confidence to walk into a room full of skeptical investors and employees and make your idea come alive? Do you have the diligence and experience to nail down a business plan, or at least a detailed model, from beginning to end? Do you have the charisma to recruit the best people, the flexibility to change direction when necessary, and the strength to stay the course when others hammer on your judgment? If you have a great idea, the first people you should hire are those who are good at what you can't do well. But they can't make up for a lack of leadership qualities at the top.

There's no shame in finding a partner who has the management experience to be CEO if you'd be better off as, say, chief technical officer (CTO) or even vice president (VP) of product development. The hardest thing of all is to assess yourself as rigorously as you would your business plan. If it helps, get honest opinions from people you trust. You owe it to yourself and your future employees to decide as objectively as possible where you fit in the founding team. And if you don't think you're quite ready to lead a start-up, then go work for one to learn what it takes!

Chapter

Create a Compelling Offering

NEILISM: No good idea goes unpunished.

It sounds so simple, but a lot of people falter right at the starting gate. Why? They fail to offer their customers a compelling offering. A start-up must provide a product or service that is new, important, obvious, and immediate. In the fast-changing Lightspeed business environment, you have only about four months to transform your idea into an actual product. If you spend a year doing focus groups and market research and keep rewriting your business plan on every whim, you're dead. Because no good idea goes unpunished, you'll quickly have competitors whose mission is to put you out of business.

■ IF YOU CAN, YOU MUST

Because your window of opportunity is four months, you must be focused and decisive in the early stage. Time to market is the prime advantage of being a start-up. If you have an idea that you want to ponder for half a year, you might as well forget about it. On the Internet, if you can, you must—because if you don't, someone else will.

Winning start-ups aren't the ones that outthink the competition; they're the ones that outexecute the competition. With technology and the Internet, an idea has very little time to evolve. It has to happen *now*. Companies that are first get more money, and it snowballs from there. To get into the start-up space and succeed, you need to be bold, to move fast, and to produce action.

For example, Epinions.com was founded in May 1999 by a group of Internet veterans from Yahoo!, Netscape, America Online, and @Home. Within a few weeks, the product-advice site had raised $8 million in funding from venture capitalists; and by June 1999 the first site prototype was complete, and the company had signed its first partnership. Epinions.com was the subject of a lengthy *New York Times Magazine* article titled "Instant Company." By August, the company had launched a preview of its product. Now that's lightspeed.

Here's what Po Bronson, who penned the piece for the *Times*, wrote about Epinions: "In 12 weeks, the amount of time it might take an average person to decide what kind of hedge to plant in the backyard, they built a company from scratch. An instant company, or what is being called in Silicon Valley a 'second-generation' Web company."

Now is the time to build a third-generation Web company.

■ TODAY, THE CUSTOMER RULES

Technology and the Internet have brought customer interaction and engagement to a new level. If certain shoppers at a large department store received better deals than other customers did, you might never have known about it. But when Amazon started charging repeat customers higher prices for digital versatile discs (DVDs) than it was charging new customers, an online shopping club called DVDTalk.com quickly figured it out, and the press reported the story widely. Amazon was only looking for a way to maximize revenues; but when its practice became public, some customers were furious.

This incident notwithstanding, Amazon has always been a leader in customer service because it knows too well that the customer rules on the Internet. Your offering must provide an immediate, obvious benefit. It won't succeed with a deferred benefit that will help customers down the line. For example, you might think there is value in telling customers: "Sign up today with our service, reveal the products you are in the market to buy, and within two months we will personalize the service. Soon you'll get money-saving offers suited to your particular interests." But customers and investors can't connect with it immediately. Give them value they can see, taste, or touch, rather than simply squeeze more advertising impressions out of them.

Remember: Customers are not in the business of buying your product. They aren't going to bed thinking about your product—it has to be compelling to draw users to it. Give the customers something they care about, and treat them as if they were your mother or father. Don't make them angry. Pamper them whenever possible, and show them the appropriate consideration. Keep them in the loop when making changes that will affect their experience on your site.

■ THE FORMULA FOR A COMPELLING OFFERING

Wouldn't it be nice to have a checklist for all the things that make a 3G start-up a success? In these incredibly competitive days, you'll need a checklist to stay a step or two ahead of the competition. You might not be able to check off every attribute on the list, but you should have most of them checked off if you want to make it big. And if you can't check off even one item, you're probably riding a losing horse.

Checklist for Your Offering

- ☐ New
- ☐ Important
- ☐ Obvious
- ☐ Immediate
- ☐ Exploits the Internet

Now let's take a deeper look at these attributes so you'll understand just what is meant by a "compelling offering." Remember that you are playing the ultimate balancing act: speeding to market with your innovative idea while staying focused like a laser on the customer and a fast road to profits.

➤ **New**

Marketers love to say their product is "New! Improved!" more than any other expression. On the Internet, marketers have found that the word *free* promotes the highest clickthrough rate on banner advertisements. But let's leave the "free" concept aside for a moment and focus on "new." Technology and the Internet have revolutionized business, and one of the most intriguing aspects is that it's all new. Sure, the Net has been around in various forms since the late 1960s, but it wasn't a place for business until the mid-1990s. Imagine this: In 1990, the idea of buying anything online in cyberspace was science fiction. During the 1999 Christmas shopping season alone, people bought $7 billion worth of products online.

By the end of the 1990s, the online retailing sector was saturated with hawkers of pet food, electronics, computers, and more. And many e-tailers were forced to close up shop for lack of money as investors have realized that most e-tailing ventures would never be able to turn a profit. In this third generation of start-ups, you'll need to set yourself apart with a new idea. Simply adding the word *online* to an old idea won't work this time around (e.g., selling books *online*, a fax service *online*, party invitations *online*). And *e-tailing* is the kiss of death for a 3G start-up.

For you to claim the mantle of a truly New Idea, either your start-up's value proposition must create a whole new business in a previously nonexistent sector, or you must take an existing idea and create a new value proposition. Companies that created entirely new businesses on the Internet include Yahoo! (online directory), eBay (online auctions), and ICQ (instant messaging).

Although Yahoo! had some competition early on, eBay and ICQ basically owned the market for their services and had no existing competitors for some time. eBay could then grab a huge market share in online auctions, making it *the* place to auction goods. This is a crucial point: eBay got to market fastest with a new idea and became difficult to topple because of a huge early-mover advantage. ICQ took the idea of e-mail communication and added a new value proposition (speed, immediacy) and created a new market. So now, instead of instant messaging supplanting e-mail, the e-mail and instant messaging markets coexist.

Fast Followers

Being first to market is no guarantee of success. Contrary to popular wisdom, Amazon was not the first bookseller on the Internet. There were at least three booksellers already established on the Net. Same with Dell Computers and Cisco Systems. Dell Computers, which started in Michael Dell's University of Texas dorm room as PCs Direct, was following the established mail-order model. He didn't invent mail-order PCs, he just built and sold them better. And Cisco Systems didn't invent routers, but it found a way to perfect them. Just being first isn't enough. These companies succeeded because they were brilliant fast followers.

➤ **Important**

The Internet is adept at delivering timely information to people right when they need it. As long as servers are up and connections are working, many Web sites and e-mail services have succeeded by providing just the right tidbit of information at the right time. For instance, the InfoBeat e-mail service will let you sign up to get e-mails tailored to the sports teams you follow. So the day after your favorite college basketball team played its rival, you would get an Associated Press (AP) story on the game, along with a box score—all conveniently delivered to your e-mail inbox.

This e-mail contains information that is *important* to the customer; it is not an irrelevant e-mail about all the college basketball teams that played last night. The key to success is offering something the customer actually wants and needs. In the second generation (2G) of Internet start-ups, entrepreneurs rushed to offer everything under the sun to consumers, from jewelry to furniture to pet supplies. Now you must focus on offerings that will fill a need for the customer, whether the customer is a consumer or a business.

One great example of an important offering comes from Akamai, a start-up conceived by Tom Leighton, a professor of applied mathematics at the Massachusetts Institute of Technology (MIT). Leighton wanted to help end the "World Wide Wait," and so with the help of a top researcher he developed a set of algorithms for intelligently routing content over a network of distributed servers—without relying on centralized servers as most other sites did. Akamai built itself quickly as a back-end technology company for other Web sites, serving rich streaming media or applications for everyone from CNET and iVillage to Intuit and NBCi.

Just how important was its service? On November 7, 2000, election day in the United States, Akamai helped serve streaming video and audio for CNN.com, which experienced record traffic on that day (6.3 million unique visitors). In this case, the visitor was going to CNN.com for the important information (election results—little did any of us suspect it would be weeks before we'd finally get them!), while Akamai was performing its work behind the scenes, making sure that all the media feeds were operating under that enormous strain. The visitor was unaware of the back-end operation; but for CNN Akamai's service was mission critical. Akamai was founded in August 1998 and by late 2000 had 2,800 corporate clients and a market cap north of $5 billion.

➤ Obvious

Just as a television commercial needs to make its message clear and understandable in a small time frame, start-up founders need to have a clear message to give to potential investors, employees, partners, and the media. Is your offering obvious? Would your grandfather understand it? Of course, your grandfather might not immediately understand the concept for eBay; but if you told him he could auction off his antiques to people all over the world, he'd understand its power.

Make sure you can explain your business in a few sentences. If you have to spend time, money, and energy explaining the service or the product, then you'll have a tough time attracting financing, employees, and customers. And more important, those blank looks you've been getting as you describe your offering might be a clue that your idea is too complicated.

Whether you're in telecommunications, wireless, infrastructure, content, or any other sector, you have to clearly explain your business proposition to customers, investors, and, yes, your grandfather. If they nod their heads and understand your idea, you're probably on the right track. If their eyes glaze over and they have no idea what you're doing, then it's not obvious.

➤ **Immediate**

The customers must receive the benefit immediately or they won't stick around. If you ask someone to register for your site and the registration is eight pages long, it's going to take a lot to get most people to stay. That's why many sites offer sweepstakes for free gizmos (digital camera, Palm Pilot) in order to entice people to give personal information and register. But seducing people into registration might not make them coveted return customers. Your offering should not be predicated on delayed benefits for customers.

Instead, focus on an *immediate* benefit—something they can sink their teeth into right away. For Google, it's searching the Web thoroughly; for About.com, it's searching the Web with the help of human expert guides; for AskJeeves, it's asking a question in plain English.

But some start-ups are so focused on cutting-edge technology that they put up barriers to customers. One example of a technology that sounds neat but in fact has offered less value than meets the eye is voice-over Internet protocol (IP). The idea was that people could use the Internet, and its packet-switching IP, to make free or cheap long-distance calls. This sector has produced many start-ups with much fanfare, but there's a reason everyone and his or her brother isn't using the product: You have to buy a different telephone in many cases. Barriers like the need for new equipment, having to dial extra numbers, and poor-quality transmissions have doomed it in its early stages. Voice-over IP is a technology whose time will come, but it's just not here yet.

➤ Exploits the Internet

If you were starting a business based in a shopping mall, you would make sure the business made sense in a mall, for instance, selling jewelry and not farm equipment. Because you're starting a technology-based business, you need to make sure that your business is a good fit for the environment. What we've learned about today's 3G environment is that its primary characteristics are its hyperspeed and its customer-centric nature.

So make sure your offering exploits the medium of the Internet and doesn't just recycle an old idea from another medium. Similarly, the way you do business on the Net will have to be new. Some of the old business concepts still apply (being profitable, spending money wisely), but there are new rules you'll need to learn to live by.

➤ Speedy: "Get out in front and run like hell."

How much value is there in last month's winning lottery numbers? Not much. And when you run on Internet time, new ideas become old in the blink of an eye. Why is this? Because in many sectors of the Lightspeed Economy, there are few barriers to entry. Anyone can set up a similar business and offer lower prices; and in one mouse click—boom!—you've lost your customers. So speed is of the essence.

Speed has other important qualities: It can give you markets before there are any competitors, like it gave eBay and ICQ; and it gives you the edge on raising capital so you can hire more employees and gather more speed. If you are first to market, all you have to explain to venture capitalists are your business opportunity and your offering. If you are second, you have the added burden of explaining how you're going to overtake the leader. So if you have an idea, run with it, get it to market, hire the right people, and jump in with both feet.

In designing your offering, look for the "lowest viscosity" solution—the one that offers the least resistance and utilizes the Net's fluidity. If you are giving away a free cable-modem service and you ask your customer for 10 pages of personal information, you'll lose quite a few people along the way. But if you limit your request to one long page of information, you will likely get more customers, grab more market share, and get the ball rolling much faster. Speed wins every time.

Another aspect of operating at lightspeed is the way your business model will change over time. America Online (AOL) was once just a dial-up service provider. But when it changed to a flat-price, all-you-can-eat model in order to compete with ISPs, it needed revenues quickly; so it started charging merchants and other start-ups to be featured on its service. This revenue stream quickly became a big part of its business. And as the company changed its business model, AOL ended up doing business with companies it had previously viewed as competitors—others in the online content business and even others who provide online access (for example, Microsoft).

So when you draw up your business model, remember that on the Internet your entire raison d'être might disintegrate in a nanosecond. Change is the only constant because hyperspeed shifts the landscape, bringing new competitors, new partners, and new customers faster than you can imagine.

➤ **Focus on the Customer**

To survive competitive challenges in this environment, you also must have another weapon in your arsenal. Remember, today the customer rules. Why is this? Look at a bricks-and-mortar comparison. Say you're shopping at Macy's for a particular stylish handbag. You see exactly the one you want, but it's much more expensive than you thought it would be. If you traipse around town to Saks and Neiman Marcus, you might not find the same handbag; and by the time you get back to Macy's, the bag might be gone. So you buy the bag at Macy's. The bricks-and-mortar barrier is that you're in the store now and it's a pain to shop around. But on the Internet, product-comparison engines make comparing prices a breeze.

Simply put, the Internet puts the customer in the driver's seat because the customer can find your competition in the click of a mouse. So how do you turn this fact to your advantage? Customers will inherently follow the offering with the best value proposition. Because the Internet lets virtually anyone reach a vast audience immediately, a company with a new idea can lure away your customers in an instant. Make sure your offering addresses the customer's needs.

The key question to ask yourself in creating and innovating a compelling offering is: Does it benefit the customer? Don't load up your service with extraneous features that offer gee-whiz technology but don't benefit the customer. Microsoft is infamous for loading its software products with hundreds of features even though most people only use a tiny portion of those features. If you are creating an Internet application, you want the opposite of Microsoft-style software: something simple, sleek, quick, and easy to download. Focus on delivering what the customer really needs, and you'll win.

■ ALL TOGETHER NOW . . .

To create a compelling offering in the Lightspeed Economy, keep these five concepts in mind: new, important, obvious, immediate, and Internet savvy. Watch the marketplace and learn the hard-fought lessons from the failures and the successes of others. But keep your eyes on your own business at the same time—you need to be focused on creating an innovative business that will make its own lasting impression on the market. You can do that by avoiding bad attributes of start-ups (see Table 3.1).

The problem with some of the bigger consumer e-commerce players has been that their offerings really aren't new. Amazon's most important value proposition is not online ordering, as many people think, but rather the offline delivery of goods. That delivery mechanism has created an infrastructure of inventory, distribution centers, and real estate—ironically, the very *bricks and mortar* that most of these companies were supposedly shunning. These Internet companies are facing the same business constraints as their offline brethren: huge infrastructure costs and a business that doesn't scale well.

Webvan, the now defunct grocery delivery service, planned to expand with 26 distribution centers to saturate the market; but in 2000 it had to scale back its nationwide efforts in order to cut costs. Ultimately, even that didn't rescue Webvan. In the second genera-

Table 3.1 Good versus bad attributes of start-ups.

Good	Bad
New	Old idea revisited but without adding value
Important	Marginal, limited market
Obvious	Takes time and effort to explain
Immediate	Delayed benefit
Internet	Shovelware simply ported to the Net from another medium
Quick to market	Developed over long period of research
Customer-centric	Great technology with no significant customer benefit

tion of start-ups, the rule was hypergrowth at all costs; in the third generation, the rule is growth *within* costs.

■ START-UP JUDO: EITHER INNOVATE AND IMPLEMENT—OR ELIMINATE

Now is your chance to earn a black belt in start-up judo. This concept is based on the martial art of judo, where instead of countering an opponent's force, you turn it to your advantage.

Here's how it works. Let's say you've succeeded in creating an offering with a winning value proposition. That's great, but it's only the beginning. Creating the best offering is an ongoing process of innovation: experimenting to see what works and then either implementing a winning change or eliminating a bad idea quickly and moving on. If you are a success, we guarantee you'll soon have competitors making it their mission in life to best your offering. To stay alive, you must constantly innovate your offering. Instead of responding to a competitive challenge by erecting a barrier, you should focus on how you can use this new development to create an even better value proposition.

eBay offers a good lesson on this point: At one point, meta search sites starting crawling eBay and other auction sites in order to give users an aggregated list of items. eBay initially resisted this because the company saw it as a threat to its business and even initiated a lawsuit against BiddersEdge, hoping to block the searches. But eBay got smart and developed an application programming interface (API) that opens up its auction services to third-party companies interested in developing products for eBay customers. As a result, eBay gets to extend its business with the help of interested and innovative partners, and it gains an additional revenue stream through the licensing of the API.

To win in start-up judo, you might collaborate with the competition ("coopetition") or at least use their weaknesses to make you stronger. And most important, you must innovate your offering based on the principles outlined in this chapter, and implement them with the greatest of speed. And everything that lies outside your area of focus must be eliminated.

■ REFERENCES

Epinions: *http://www.epinions.com/about/index.html?show=history*

New York Times Magazine: *http://www.nytimes.com/library/magazine/home/ 19990711mag-tech-start-up.html*

Amazon: source: *http://news.cnet.com/news/0-1007-200-2703210.html*

1999 sales: source: Jupiter: *http://www.jup.com/companypressrelease.jsp? doc=pr001113b*

Akamai: *http://www.akamai.com/html/nr/press/press185.html*

Chapter

The Organization

NEILISM: Start-ups are not ideas or innovations, they are organizations first.

In 1994, back in the early days of the commercial Internet, Time Warner's Pathfinder and Yahoo! launched around the same time. Pathfinder was well financed with tens of millions of dollars. It had more computers than it knew what to do with and it had a global franchise of proprietary content, such as articles from *Time* and *Fortune* magazines.

Meanwhile, Yahoo! was born in a dorm room by Jerry Yang and David Filo. Yahoo! originally ran on borrowed computer time at Stanford University and a total of $3 million in venture capital funding. Yet Pathfinder was a colossal failure and Yahoo! was a legendary success. The difference? The people. Your organization—and the people in it—determines whether your start-up is the next Yahoo! or the next Pathfinder.

■ PEOPLE ARE CRUCIAL

The organization is critical to your success for so many reasons. It is a common fallacy that because the Internet runs on computers and tasks are automated a business can scale without increasing the number of employees. The people you hire are crucial, especially at the beginning of the start-up lifecycle.

Size does matter. A big organization can support a larger customer base, a richer product set, and more partnerships than a small company can. The dry reality is that the size of a business—the number of customers and the amount of revenues—is directly proportional to the number of employees. And to get big, you need the right people.

The skills, the talent, and the experience of the people you hire play a major role in your success. The better the organization, the more leadership it produces in many regards, including crazy-like-a-fox smarts that play the environment, its competitors, and its industry to its advantage. The stronger your people and the smarter and more creative they are, the more innovative your product will be and the more it will impress customers. The more experience they have will reflect positively in avoiding rookie mistakes.

The people you hire are the golden elements that will make your start-up a success because they are the ones who will create and execute your plan. Not only that, the organization is the greatest expense, consuming as much as 80 percent of your cash, so you want to get your money's worth!

People are the core of a successful start-up. You cannot create a great company without great people. I used to think that with the right managers we could recruit people from all over; we could train them, provide them with skills, and then compete. We would build a big company. But it doesn't work that way.

Let's put it in terms of a sports analogy: You're a team and you're going to compete with 20 other teams. Even if you have the best coach, it won't matter if you don't have the best players. Say, for instance, you take inexperienced kids right out of high school who have never played the sport and throw them straight into a game. Even if you have the best coach, you're still not going to win.

—*Steve Kirsch, founder of Infoseek,*
Propel, and Frame Technology

■ YOUR FIRST JOB IS TO HIRE!

Employees are critical, yet it's difficult to find the time to recruit. Recruiting preoccupies and taxes a start-up during the first two years of its existence—so much so that it may feel as if you are in the recruiting business. But get used to it: Make hiring a top priority.

A start-up cannot hire fast enough. And remember that the hiring time takes longer than simply the lead time to hire. From the time a candidate accepts the offer, it'll probably be several more weeks before he or she is on the payroll, much less up to speed. Without the right people, your start-up is doomed to fail.

> When I say hiring should be the priority, that means hiring *is* the priority. Entrepreneurs don't always understand the importance of this. For example, if we decide at a board meeting to hire a certain person, then I expect the entrepreneurs to pay their full attention to it. I don't want to hear at the next board meeting, "Well, we traded calls." My response is, "Give them your cell phone number and your admin's number. And when they call, you somehow talk with them. Don't tell me you're in another meeting. This is what's most important."
>
> —*J. Neil Weintraut*

■ HIRE NOW!

Consider the following math: A start-up on a success track will grow to 150 employees within two years. Each employee is selected from a pool of, on average, five interviewed candidates. And each of these candidates is interviewed, on average, by two different employees, or founders, of the start-up. That means that merely to grow its business, a start-up conducts more than 600 interviews in its first year!

Moreover, the lead time in hiring is typically three weeks for an entry-level position, three months for a director-level hire, six months for a VP, and nine months for a CEO.

■ HIRE HIGH!

The organization is a start-up's ceiling on the seemingly infinite business opportunity; the higher the ceiling, the higher the opportunity horizon. So that means whom you hire is just as important as how quickly you hire because each executive can affect the performance level of another one. An unqualified CEO, for example, can frighten off seasoned vice presidents from even joining in the first place. If a green CEO ends up hiring vice presidents who are, in turn, green, these new vice presidents have a tendency to hire down so as to not threaten their roles. Poor hiring can start a vicious cycle. As a result, start-ups should always hire as high on the excellence scale as possible and then try to hire even higher. Your success horizon, if not success itself, depends on it.

■ HIRE THE HIRERS!

The hiring imperative is partially alleviated by hiring people who either bring other people with them or have the ability to markedly enhance the hiring process. This is yet another reason to hire high, because the higher an employee is, the more likely it is that he or she can hire more people faster. Like it or not, you will find that hiring is the most important and time-consuming activity that an entrepreneur does. Hiring, then, should be treated as a fully accountable job, rather than as a secondary task.

Each candidate interview should have specific objectives established, often queued from the last meeting. Is it time to probe into salary requirements? To answer a question that surfaced from the previous interview? Or is the goal to resolve all issues, so as to set up an offer? Know what you want to accomplish before the meeting begins.

You need to set up for success. Set up not by just letting an interview process unfold as it will, but rather by leading candidates down a trail to closure. Notably, drive the discussions to a point where a desired candidate is morally committed to the position; then make the offer. In other words, both skunk out and resolve any issues that actually do remain, and then put the onus on the candidate to acknowledge that there are no more issues and that he or she is interested in the position—lead the candidate to take ownership of the position. Then the only answer to an offer is to accept. Set up for success by making success the only option.

■ HIRE LIKE—AND HIRE WITH—PROFESSIONALS

Professionals, such as third-party employment firms, recruiters, headhunters, and skilled human resources managers, should be engaged for all hiring activity. A professional increases your hiring capacity, expands the candidate pool, facilitates the process, and serves as a trusted go-between in broaching sensitive issues or in simply syncing up communications. However, engaging professionals does not mean that the responsibility of hiring has been transferred or even alleviated. Instead, you will need to manage the recruiter just as you would an internal report, and you will be just as involved with interviewing candidates as before. Engaging professionals is not for the purpose of alleviating work but for getting better results.

■ HIRE WITH EMPLOYMENT AGREEMENTS

The legal commitments of employment are actually straightforward if employment agreements are handled correctly. You can avoid a lurking time bomb—not just in terms of the employee but even of outside investors—if you set up your agreements appropriately. Since you're probably not a hiring expert yourself, have the human resources counsel at your law firm set up the practices and written documents associated with hiring. Offer letters, for example, should explicitly include "at-will employment" and "nondisclosure" agreements, to name a few of the key topics. Conversely, nothing should be committed to or put into writing that has not been reviewed by employment counsel.

The War for Talent

It's so difficult to locate and retain great employees to help build your start-up that many companies resort to poaching from their rivals. You might find potential recruits working for your competitors, but beware of triggering a lawsuit.

- In 2000, Net2Phone, a start-up that enables telephone calls over the Internet, sued rival start-up Dialpad.com for hiring two of its business development executives.

- Giant retailer Wal-Mart lost a number of systems gurus to start-ups. In 1998 Wal-Mart sued Drugstore.com and Amazon.com. The companies settled in 1999.

■ DON'T SETTLE FOR SECOND BEST

Avoid letting mediocrity get infused into the system because it will spread like a plague. Mediocrity breeds mediocrity. Mediocre people are intimidated by excellence, so they discourage excellence from coming.

To succeed, you have to attract and hire the "A team." However, suppose you're trying to get an "A player" for a position, but either you can't get an A player or it's going to take three months. However, a "B player" is available now. What do you do? You hire the B player and explain the situation to her or him. For instance, you convince the person to start working for your start-up, and you say up front, "Look, our success is now your success if you're joining us. So you will want to be first in line to help us get an additional strong player that the company needs. We're hiring you so you can help us get this person." Admittedly, this is a tricky one to pull off. Even if it doesn't work, it's worth trying anyway because you'll be no worse off than if you didn't try it: You still need to fill the position. And, if the B player doesn't like this scenario, then he or she is probably not the right person anyway.

> The key to hiring is to hire people to the roles that they are skilled for and nothing beyond. And this is where you get into that tough-love type stuff. You have to be prepared to say, "No, I'm not going to give you a VP title. I want you to come here; we're going to work our hardest to recruit you because we think you're good; but the reality is if I give you a VP title, it's going to impair me from attracting other director-level people because they will not view you as a VP."
>
> —J. Neil Weintraut

■ ORGANIZED FOR SUCCESS

The best practices of successful start-ups always point back to the same simple organization chart. It's a flat model without a lot of layers of management. This allows an entrepreneur to have clear lines of communication with each department.

An entrepreneur must construct an organizational model, so create a matrix based on your needs as soon as possible. Start by listing all the people you think you'll need to hire and when you'll need to hire them. The hiring plan will come out of that. First, there's the founder, who is probably you. Then you'll need a CEO to lead the company. After that come vice presidents of sales, marketing, business development, engineering, operations, finance, and human resources, all of whom report to the CEO. One to four directors report to each vice president, and up to ten employees report to each director. Then you can drill down into each one of the departments.

At the end of Stage 1 you will have approximately 30 employees, and your organizational structure will look like Figure 4.1.

Six months later you will have doubled in size. The departments that have grown the most are engineering, sales, and marketing, and your organizational structure will look like Figure 4.2.

After two years you will have interviewed nearly 1,500 candidates and hired nearly 140 employees. Your organizational structure will look like Figure 4.3. Your start-up is now on track for spectacular growth, profitability, and an initial public offering (IPO)!

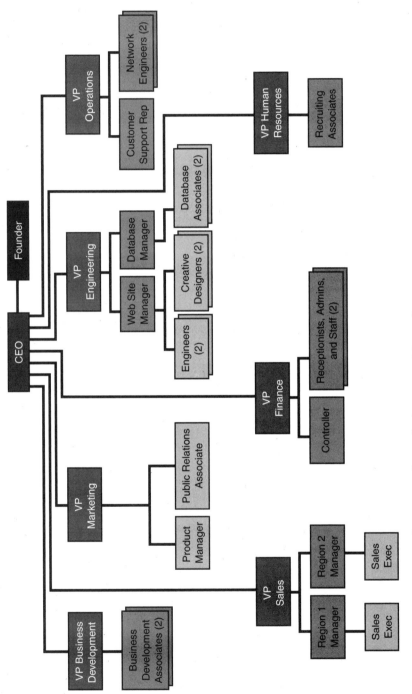

Figure 4.1 Organizational structure by end of stage 1: 30 employees.

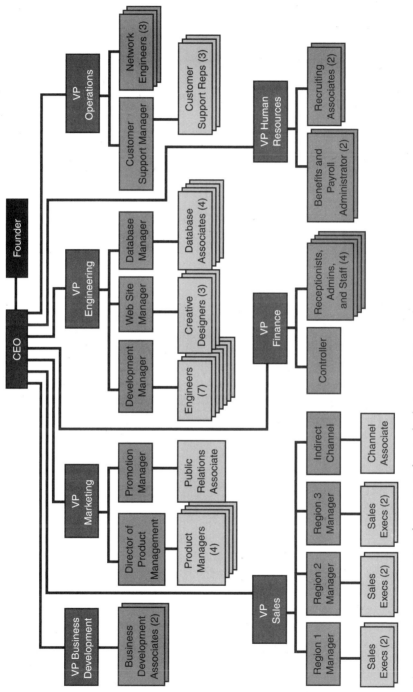

Figure 4.2 Organizational structure by end of stage 2: 60 employees.

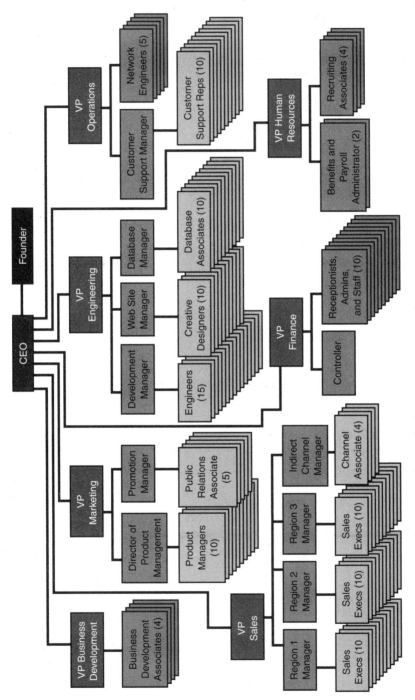

Figure 4.3 Organizational structure by end of stage 3: 140 employees.

∎ HIRING ESSENTIALS FOR A SUCCESSFUL ORGANIZATION

Building the Team

Don't have both a CEO and a president. Start-up companies are too small to split decision making up between a CEO and a president or a chief operating officer (COO). Additionally, split leadership occurs when neither person is the caliber of a success-creating CEO, so don't put yourself in that situation either.

Split decision making is a common flaw of start-ups because there are typically two or even three cofounders of a company. The cofounders tend to be egalitarian; they're reluctant to say who is boss. Those situations introduce problems: for instance, when you're hiring someone who asks who his or her boss would be, what do you say?

Remember, the strategic imperative here is to hire people. In the spirit of achieving that goal quickly, do not do things that slow you down. Having split leadership will slow you down. So you want just one boss.

Conversely, what will make speed? Having a clear leader who is, in fact, a leader. Similarly, all leadership responsibilities should be crystal clear. The marketing duties are clearly the responsibility of the marketing vice president, not of the sales or the business development vice president. If an executive is weak in part of his or her responsibilities, the wrong solution is to reassign responsibilities; the right solution is to find a new executive.

The management team is absolutely the most important thing in a company because a single person can't pull it off. You need complementary skills from multiple people, and you should look for true complementary skills—with a pull and tug—in the management team.

The very best businesses, ones that have been most successful, have almost always had two strong leaders that have

(continued)

a give and take with each other. They may have different outlooks, but they find a way to balance both of their separate opinions.

At Idealab! we look for smart people, but we discovered that smarts alone wasn't enough; so we started looking for smart and hardworking people. We found that was a good combination, but it wasn't enough. The next thing we started seeking was this quality of teamwork. Every one of these tasks at a start-up is bigger than a single person's capabilities.

We found that the final key to building success is adaptability.

What's important is not just a quicker pace but moving at a quicker pace in response to signals from your environment. Many people have a goal of doing the same thing for five years, but that's not going to work in business anymore. We believe that businesses need to be much more flexible and adaptive in their missions and in every aspect of what they do for their customers.

Adaptability turned out to be a key—and a more original—trait than we had expected when we started making businesses.

—*Bill Gross, founder, CEO, and chairman of Idealab!*

➤ Are You CEO Material? If Not, Hire One

One role that is characteristic of an Internet start-up is that of the founder: the person who focuses full time on the vision and the future of the company. The Lightspeed Economy is so fast and changes so quickly that we recommend you don't have the same person running the day-to-day operations and planning for the future. Usually the founder plays the visionary role, whereas the CEO is charged with executing the plan.

When hiring a CEO for a company, look at seven key criteria:

- Leadership ability and passion
- Decision-making ability
- Position on the issues
- Experience
- Intelligence and ability
- Trust
- Judgment

> A leader has a vision and can enlist others in that vision. He's passionate about his vision for the future. And he's got a credible plan to get there.
>
> —*Steve Kirsch*

Steve Kirsch was dead-on when he said, "The single biggest mistake you can make when starting up or running a company is hiring the wrong CEO. And that could be yourself!"

If starting a company was your way of becoming a CEO, then you might be on the wrong track. If you are someone who wants to be a CEO of a company but doesn't have the skills and experience to attract talented employees, then you'll fail. For example, when you interview VP candidates, you should realize they are scrutinizing you as much as you them. If as CEO you don't project leadership, inwardly the candidates will say, "You're not a CEO. I don't want to work for you." It is not the management who decides who will run your company; it is actually the employees.

Founders of successful start-ups have often chosen someone other than themselves for the CEO job (see Table 4.1). For example, Yahoo!'s founders, David Filo and Jerry Yang, brought in Tim Koogle early on (and replaced him with Terry Semel in 2001). eBay's founder, Pierre Omidyar, recruited Meg Whitman after two and a half years to take the company to higher levels. And Naveen Jain, founder of InfoSpace, waited more than four years before hiring Arin Sarin from Vodaphone

Table 4.1   CEOs hired by founders.

Company	Formed	CEO Hired
Yahoo!	April 1994	August 1995
eBay	September 1995	May 1998
InfoSpace	April 1996	May 2000

AirTouch, only to replace him a year later. Of course, there are numerous exceptions: Amazon's Jeff Bezos is founder and CEO; and Shelby Bonnie, CNET's CEO, was a critical player in CNET's growth almost from the beginning in 1993. Bonnie assumed the CEO mantle in 2000 when Halsey Minor left to form a new venture, 12 Entrepreneuring. There's no shame in recognizing that you may need to hire a CEO. In fact, it's an indication of smarts!

> ## Standardize Your Compensation and Make It Consistent

Which start-up can claim that its success came from rewarding its people less than the competitor does? The answer: not a one. A start-up's employees are its crown jewels; and treated right, they are loyal through even the worst of times. Excel in rewarding employees for their efforts and support, and you'll be paid back in full!

Reward takes the form of salary, stock options, and benefits that are granted in a consistent way across the organization. *Consistency* is the key word here. If you don't have a well-defined structure and set of standards for compensation, you'll introduce problems. Your compensation schedule becomes the basis for planning stock and cash budgets. This schedule will streamline board approval of hiring and grants, but most important, it preempts the adverse effects of inconsistent compensation.

Employees always find out how much the other people in the company are making. When that happens, it opens a can of worms, and then it just spirals out of control. It spirals when one of your employees comes to you and says, "I've got another offer from somebody else and the offer is at least as good as what I'm getting here. Plus I'm ticked off because you granted somebody else at my level more shares. So either you top me up, or I take this other offer." Well, when people find out that you're fungible on the amount of stock you'll grant, they'll all come and demand more! There is a solution. You standardize it—you standardize the compensation schedule.

—J. Neil Weintraut

Table 4.2 shows a prototypical compensation schedule for stage 1 and stage 2 start-ups. The compensation schedule allows for a 10 percent variance above and below an average target of salary and stock grants. This range enables the company both to match compensation to a candidate's specific circumstances and caliber and to stay within budget. Cash bonuses range from 5 percent to 15 percent of salary, based on individual performance.

These stock grants reflect the expectations in the early stages of a start-up, which in turn implicitly anticipate the typical dilution that inevitably occurs throughout the life of the start-up. A vice president of marketing, for example, typically requires as much as 3 percent equity when joining a start-up, whereas a comparable vice president of finance typically requires 1.5 percent. The difference in ownership granted at the time of hire is because the vice president

Table 4.2   Compensation schedule for stage 1 and stage 2 start-ups.

Grade	Salary	Stock Grants
CEO	$150K	8%–10%
Vice President	$150K–$200K	1.5%–3.0%
Director	$120K–$150K	0.1%–0.3%
Sr. Engineer/ Sr. Manager	$100K–$130K	0.05%–0.1%
Jr. Engineer/ Database Administrators/Sales Executives	$90K–$110K	0.03%–0.05%
Administrative	$50K–$70K	0.01%–0.02%

of marketing normally joins in the early stage, whereas the vice president of finance typically joins shortly before the initial public offering; and, hence, much of the original stock grants have been diluted. In the end, both the vice president of marketing and the vice president of finance wind up with comparable ownership percentages, although the vice president of marketing would own slightly more to reflect the earlier and longer involvement with the company. The stock grant examples are based on 1 million shares, so a VP would get between 15,000 and 30,000 shares.

We discuss stock options and equity in depth in Chapter 6.

Chapter

Start-up Strategies

NEILISM: The best way to be acquired is not to try.

Every start-up needs a game plan to get from prototype to initial public offering (IPO); and although start-ups fail in a variety of ways, those that succeed are amazingly consistent. They each develop a business strategy that takes advantage of this unique environment. To develop such a strategy, you want to think simple, understand your business environment, and create benefits rather than barriers in every aspect of your business. Follow these guidelines, and you'll attract the customers, the employees, and the capital that you need.

■ LEARN FROM SUCCESS

For an example of how two very different businesses followed a strikingly similar path to success, consider Cisco and Yahoo! (see Table 5.1). At first glance, they have entirely different business models: One is a consumer-oriented business, and the other is a business-to-business play. Yet on closer examination, both have employed similar strategies in defining and organizing their businesses and in staffing their top management ranks. And when you look at the investors behind these successes, it's little surprise that the same venture capital firm backed both companies. Draw your lessons from the proven success stories.

Table 5.1 Two different companies, one winning strategy.

	Cisco Systems	Yahoo!
Business Structure	A flexible network of of partnerships and integration with suppliers, contractors, and assemblers that allow Cisco to quickly pursue new market opportunities.	A flexible network partnerships and integration with suppliers that allow Yahoo! to quickly pursue new market opportunities.
World-class CEO	John T. Chambers	Timothy Koogle (now Terry Semel)
Clear Product Definition	Networking for the Internet	Broadcast media, communications, and commerce services for the Internet
Venture Capitalists	Sequoia Capital	Sequoia Capital

■ KEEP IT SIMPLE

In the fast-paced, friction-free Lightspeed Economy environment, there isn't time to implement a business strategy that involves either a lot of small changes or a single big, complicated change. For instance, one recent start-up pitched its idea for computerizing building management services, from utilities to cable access. Sounds simple, but, in fact, to implement such an idea would require braving a thicket of local government regulations. While addressing those rules is not an insurmountable barrier, the complication and the time involved require serious consideration. Small changes can have big consequences and can lead to phenomenal success or failure.

The best start-up strategies present a formula for *one simple change*. In this unique environment one small change can spiral into something huge, using less money and fewer people. By trying to make just one crack in a dam, you can move quickly and capture a market before anyone else wakes up to it.

America Online's Secret Strategy

Here's AOL's secret strategy for success: Make it really easy to sign up, and make it really hard to cancel. In fact, it's nearly impossible to cancel from AOL.

—*Steve Kirsch*

Take Napster. The company did one simple thing: It allowed everybody to look at everybody else's hard disk, everybody else's music library. It took a hard disk and opened it up to the Net, allowing instantaneous, effortless access.

Or look at HotMail. It blew away USA.NET, then the premier vendor of Web-based e-mail, by changing its business model from one of charging customers for the e-mail software to one of giving e-mail to customers for free and instead generating revenue by serving ads. USA.NET didn't have the technology in place to serve ads; so not only was it no longer attractive to its customers, but it also had no way to react quickly to this remarkably simple change! Needless to say, not many people today remember USA.NET, even though it's still in the e-mail messaging business.

Although it might seem a safer bet to take a scattershot approach and to try to do a lot of things at once and hope you succeed with at least some of them, you can easily spread yourself too thin. You'll succeed when you concentrate on achieving one thing. Challenge yourself. To design a product that attracts customers who pay you is a different strategy from that of the second generation (2G), when a start-up could grow without having to be profitable. React to your environment *as it is now.* In 2001, e-tailing is dead and wireless is red hot. Analysis: If it doesn't look simple, then you don't have the right strategy. If your company creates a good story, you won't have to go looking for funding. VCs will find *you.*

Give It Away for Free

Yossi Vardi, the prescient investor behind ICQ, devised a highly successful strategy for making ICQ into such a killer product: *(continued)*

"ICQ is an online real-time communications service. In 1996 nobody had ever offered a way for people to talk to each other instantaneously.

I came into the ICQ picture because of the financial motivation. I had a son who had not finished high school, and I was a concerned father. He wanted some money to start a company, so I gave him the money. Six weeks later I saw the demo for ICQ and I was astounded. I knew this was the biggest thing I'd ever seen in my career—and I've been doing start-ups for 31 years.

In the first version we considered four different business models:

1. Initially, we offered it free because we hadn't figured out what do with it.
2. We thought maybe we would sell the software.
3. We thought that maybe we'd have a subscription service where users pay a monthly fee.
4. We thought that maybe we'd create a service for the enterprise.

After a year we came to the realization that the value of the company was in aggregating users, so we decided to offer ICQ to a company for whom a persistent presence on the desktop was very, very important.

We began to embed features in ICQ that would make it appealing to the users a company like that would want to attract. In other words, we built it to sell it to another company.

My belief is that, even in today's environment, if you create something that has a wonderful user experience, that's unique, something that will grab the imagination of people so they will run and share it with their friends, you'll have a great asset. But you have to be smart enough to understand it. It's not enough to have a great asset for users. In order to maximize the advantage of the network effect, you have to give it away for free. If you charge for it, you will attract fewer customers; if you have to pay for promotion, then you'll have a burn rate.

Most of the offerings will fail. And most of what I personally sponsor will fail as well. But for me as a one-man VC, the question is: at the end of the day, what will be the total value?"

Yossi Vardi sold ICQ to AOL in 1998 for more than $400 million.

—*Christopher Barr*

■ SIZE UP THE ENVIRONMENT, NOT JUST THE COMPETITION

To create a strategy for implementing one small change, you need to do more than evaluate the strengths and weaknesses of your immediate competitors. You need to understand the entire market environment in which your company will operate and to assess how well your value proposition holds up.

Ted Leonsis, president of America Online's (AOL's) Interactive Properties Group, paints an expansive picture of AOL's business environment when he says, "Our biggest competitor is a sunny day." That's how you have to look at your competitive landscape—not just the existing competitors in front of your nose right this minute. Similarly, you need to look at your product as more than just a set of features and to analyze the customer need your product intends to satisfy. If you don't widen your vision, you run the risk of losing out to a competitor you didn't even recognize as a competitor.

What is the biggest threat to investment bank JP Morgan Hambrecht & Quist? It is not Goldman Sachs; it is actually *Red Herring, Upside, The Industry Standard*, or CNET. Sure, historically most of those publications were periodicals providing only general, less-than-timely technology information; but the Internet has made their news as timely, factual, and instantaneous as Wall Street's research. The boundary between these two traditionally unrelated businesses, investment banking and technology publishing, has disappeared. So while McKinsey consultants analyze Goldman Sachs or figure out how to steal an analyst from Morgan Stanley, reality presents a bigger threat: that their value proposition itself is morphing away.

Or look at Elcotel. A successful little company that makes payphones, Elcotel recently confronted a strategic challenge in terms of competition from cell phones. You wouldn't think that cell phones have anything to do with payphones, except that they do because people with cell phones no longer need to stop at pay phones. Elcotel responded to the challenge by adding features such as dataports to its payphones and credit card readers so users were not required to use coins. The company survived because it accurately assessed what it had to do to thrive in a new environment.

So evaluating your market and its environment is critical when devising your strategy. It's no longer enough to produce a comparative analysis for your business and its immediate competition; you need to imagine how your business changes your customers' lives and understand how your product or service fits within their world. Remember that the customer focuses on value, not products.

Think about your customers' alternatives. Even if you provide a superior product or service, you won't succeed if an alternative better fits your customers' needs. One example is the start-ups that offer free integrated e-mail, voicemail, and fax. The business plan sounds great, right? Customers face a seemingly great value proposition: They don't have to pay anything, and they can access it anywhere in the world because it's on the Internet. Why wouldn't they use it?

Well, they won't use it because when friends call and no one's home, they can't automatically leave a message. They have to call another number to do that. So although there are some undeniable benefits to the service, the alternative—a $20 answering machine—has a benefit that is more valuable: namely, simplicity. It fits customers' needs better.

For another example, suppose you are a cell phone vendor. Even if you know more about cell phone products than anyone and even if you sell them below cost, there's an alternative that's better. There's a cell phone company out there selling service *and* providing free phones. That company's got a completely different agenda. They're not trying to kill you; they don't even have their sights set on you. But they provide an alternative that better fits the environment. From the customers' perspective, a phone is no good without service; so as long as they're paying for the service, why not get the phone for free?

Many companies that come up short have failed to align themselves with their environment. Either the environment provides the customer with a better alternative, or the environment is changing and the company can't keep up. For example, when a market is expanding, a company needs to grow fast enough to keep up.

Analysis: If your business doesn't fit into and take advantage of its environment, then you don't have the right strategy.

■ DO WHAT YOU'RE SUPPOSED TO DO AND THE MONEY WILL FIND YOU

When it comes time to implement your strategy, focus on achieving your milestones and on creating benefits, not barriers. Find your success zone, and work in it!

It sounds simple, but by focusing on your milestones, you'll automatically eliminate extraneous or self-defeating efforts such as feature sprawl, wrong or mediocre hires, and nonpaying customers. By focusing all your efforts on reaching your milestones, you'll automatically limit your efforts by doing only what will make you a successful business, whether it's building a working product, building your organization, or attracting your initial customers.

To avoid feature sprawl, for example, look at whether the next feature that you're considering adding attracts more paying customers, the milestone that will in turn attract capital. If not, then skip it! CollegeClub.com learned this lesson the hard way. Originally designed as a communications resource for students, CollegeClub.com rapidly expanded to offer e-commerce, chat rooms, auctions, and other services. In the process of this expansion of the original value proposition, it acquired companies left and right, burned through its money, had to withdraw its IPO (scheduled for June 8, 2000), and finally filed for bankruptcy.

When running your business, focus on what's useful; don't get lost in details. Before you commit to an action, ask yourself, Does this help me raise the next round of capital? Remember, if you're not moving ahead, you're falling behind. The terrible price of not hitting your milestones is that you've proved failure. You're worse off than when you were selling the promise.

Avoid doing anything that gets in the way of achieving your milestones, including your funding milestones. Other books might tell you to wait and complete as much work as possible before you raise more capital because you can then raise it at a higher valuation. Well, there is a preferable way to succeed.

In this environment, you're better off getting money to reach the next funding milestone. Entrepreneurs and investors tend to focus on any one round in terms of the amount of money, the valuation, of that round. You see, over the life of a company, fund-raising is a zero-sum game. If you wait to raise money, you might get a little more at a slightly higher valuation; but raising less money at a lower valuation now allows you to raise more money at a higher valuation on the next round.

Yahoo! turned cash flow positive with $3 million in funding; Infospace turned cash flow positive on $2 million.

Make Your Business Appealing to Investors

The brilliant thing about today's environment is there's capital everywhere, right? So why not run your business in a way that attracts that capital? Notice, this is different than saying, "Well, just generally do good things with your business and by doing that, money will come." I'm saying, "No, go to the next level. Do the specific things with your business that make it particularly appealing to capital."

—*J. Neil Weintraut*

■ CREATE BENEFITS, NOT BARRIERS

One great strategy to attract what you need—whether capital, employees, partners, or customers—is to create benefits rather than barriers. The Lightspeed Economy is all about removing barriers, and the businesses that take advantage of this attribute will gain the edge.

➤ Attract Employees

When building your organization, do you have any barriers up? Have you hired the right people for the top jobs? This group is the core that you'll build from. This applies to every company. A band of vice presidents led by a CEO and a founder *is* the Internet start-up in its early stage. One of the things that's peculiar to a start-up is that success requires someone who works full-time on the vision of the business. That typically is the founder, like Jerry Yang at Yahoo!. Meanwhile, the VPs and the CEO have to attract and hire others and run the operation. You want all your people to be the best-in-class, so hire the hirers.

You have a lot of departments to fill out, and each one requires distinct skills. For example, no matter what type of company you have, there's some type of sales role. If you're a media company, you're selling advertising; if you're a B2B company, you have a direct sales organization that's pitching your service to the vendors in the industry. If you're an automotive parts exchange, you have to sell your service to the automotive parts companies.

So who's watching over sales? Is your engineer a good person to do it? Obviously not. But the marketing person isn't either—she's not a deal closer, she's more of an idea person. Or look at the difference between marketing and business development. Establishing partnerships can be viewed as an extension of marketing, but it's clearly a different role. Marketing focuses on the product itself and on the branding and the message. Marketing really targets the customer base, which is measured either in thousands or millions. Business development targets a dozen or so companies and focuses intensively on how to strike a deal that makes sense. The finance and administrative head is a numbers person. So you can see that there's a need within the company for each of these roles. Each is a distinct discipline and attracts a different type of person.

Don't put up a barrier to attracting good salespeople by having them report to marketing. Today's business environment is a network, as much of people as of machines, so when you build your organization, attract the VPs who attract others. The strength of the VP of technology isn't to code Java or to program a database, although he could do it if he had to. Rather, the VP of technology knows how to manage a project. He knows when the Web site development is off track. He might not know what the exact issue is, but he knows how to go to the people and address the issue. And he can attract programmers, who are very different from salespeople.

This is why the ideal scenario is to just go out and raid another company. You don't want just the VP of marketing; you want what's in that individual's wake—her best people. So hire the hirers. Hire the VPs who attract these people. When you remove barriers and create benefits for employees, they'll come to you, just as customers will.

➤ Attract Customers

Look at Real Networks for an illustration of how removing barriers can win you customers. The company offers products to stream media, but it was losing customers because it didn't offer a media player that included *every* format. Well, now Real Networks includes Windows Media in the engine, and it's doing better than ever. Although Microsoft is its archrival and the classic business approach would be to just slug it out with Microsoft and make the customers the pawns, today, the customer rules. Thus, the better strategy is to offer a complete media player to customers.

eBay is another company that started off relying on barriers but recently switched strategies to start focusing on creating benefits instead. A few years ago, it was fighting other auction sites tooth and nail, filing lawsuits, trying to stop auction software from searching its databases. Remember how it resisted? Well, now it is offering an application programming interface that enables other developers to more easily search eBay. It stopped blocking others and started attracting them—and more customers.

➤ Attract Partners

Take the same approach with potential partners. You want to attract them. For example, say that you want to partner with CNET or ZDNet. Everyday CNET Networks has a hundred start-ups calling and saying, "I have this new feature. Why don't you integrate it into your Web sites?"

And CNET or ZDNet says, "You know, we'd love to; but we're just so busy that even if we wanted to, we couldn't."

Well, what if you approach CNET or ZDNet in a different way? What if you call them up and say, "You do nothing, and I pay you money." That might get their attention—surprise, surprise! And partners such as Mail.com, Onebox, Trellis, and X:Drive used a similar strategy to great success.

It sounds pretty obvious, but before you talk to potential partners, sit back and figure out how you can put things together for them. You want to present a situation in which there's no effort for your partners yet enough benefit that they must work with you, so that the worst choice they could make is to not work with you.

➤ Attract Buyers

This advice applies whether you're working to build a stand-alone company or to be acquired. First of all, the best way to be acquired is not to try. If you build a stand-alone company, you're more attractive as an acquisition candidate; and if you don't get acquired, well, you're still a stand-alone company!

If you don't build a stand-alone company and your whole mission is to be acquired, the acquirer is going to know that. They're also going to know that if they don't acquire you, you're going to go out of business! So at best they're going to acquire you, but for much less money, or under less favorable terms, than you would want.

➤ Attract Capital

You also want to apply this idea of creating benefits, not barriers, to your equity setup. Is it attractive to an acquirer, or is it a hidden neutron bomb?

Say that a VC wants to acquire a start-up for his portfolio of companies. He would become livid with the type of situation where a start-up that he wants to acquire for $20 million has four people who all become fully vested if the business is acquired. In this situation, the VC might think, "Why should I pay $20 million when you're all going to leave? Even if you say you're not going to leave, the reality is that when you each have $5 million in your pocket, you're going to leave."

So the VC doesn't want to acquire the company; or if he does acquire the company, he wants to pay much less. Maybe he'll pay $4 million, to make sure the founders stay. Otherwise, all that company is doing is giving him the burden of hiring more people—and he *already has that problem*!

This situation shows perfectly why valuation analysis is over-rated. (Valuations will be explained in detail in Chapter 14.) Trying to value companies is a nonoperation. While you're sitting there doing your analysis, studying market penetration, the market is going to set the price. The VC is willing to pay $20 million for the start-up under specific conditions, and the price is ultimately determined by the equity structure. Something as obscure as accelerated vesting changes the valuation!

Don't do valuation analysis. Even though current business school practices include teaching students how to do it, don't bother! The market's going to set the price. No venture capitalist has ever in-vested in a company based on a valuation analysis.

It's like buying a house in California. Is the house worth $2 million? I'm sure that you can get some analysis that shows the asset recovery value if there were oil on the land or something. But if the reality of the market is that someone is willing to pay $2 million for it today, then it's worth $2 million.

Also, the great news is that by forgoing valuation analysis, you're avoiding work that you don't have to do, right? You don't have to do a valuation analysis, so don't. Remember that you want to stay focused and flexible.

■ GAUGE YOUR STRATEGY'S SUCCESS

Once you put your game plan into action, stop periodically and look at how well you're doing. If you have a strategy that includes some estimations in terms of customer acquisition milestones on x date, product shipment by x date, and revenue by x date, and those dates start slipping, then step back, see where you are, and what you need to do to fix things.

Steve Kirsch, the founder of Infoseek Corporation, explains that sometimes you're going to have change strategy. "The trick," he says, "is that you don't want to do it too often—you don't want to have a strategy du jour."

This means that you need to know when it's time to shift strategy somewhat, or to make a major shift and get everyone behind you. You need to know when you're doing something that's not getting you any traction against your milestones. "There comes a point in time when the rubber meets the road," Kirsch says. "If you've allowed the rubber to meet the road and you're not getting the traction you expected, then it's time to make some changes."

Halsey Minor Shifts CNET Strategy in a Hurry

CNET was incorporated in 1992 as a television content company with an online component to support the TV shows. That strategy exploded in 1995 when the Web elevated CNET's online strategy, and CNET developed into an Internet media company. During my first few years as CNET's editor-in-chief, we garnered a trophy case of awards from the Computer Press Association to the Webbys. But Halsey Minor, CNET's founder and then-CEO, realized that for CNET to reach the next level of success, he had to refocus the company's direction—and clearly and forcefully articulate the new direction in order to get everyone in the company moving in the same direction fast. And he knew his new vision would meet with some initial resistance, especially among the editorial staff. In January 1998, two months after launching Computers.com, Minor made an address to the employees of the company that took many by surprise.

He was brutally frank when he wrote: "I want to discuss [an] area where I think we have really missed the mark as a company. As we all know we are *almost* universally acknowledged to have the best editorial on the Internet. As a result,

(continued)

some people think our mission as a company is to do great editorial. It is not. As it turns out, great editorial is not a goal in and of itself. For us great editorial simply supports a larger mission of helping consumers and corporate buyers find and acquire the right products for their individual needs.

"So in 1998 we are not just going to create great editorial, we are going to substantially improve the process of buying computer products and services—that is part of the incredible potential the Web holds and what makes it so special as a medium. Computers.com clearly demonstrates this. I want *everyone* working to make this happen. It is not an editorial or a business issue. It is a user experience issue."

His message started a firestorm in the editorial departments, which prided themselves on creating great editorial. But Minor's message was clear—change your strategy now. Of course, the new vision he articulated did not mean that CNET was going to start compromising on its editorial quality, but rather that great editorial was a means to achieving the real goal: a great user experience. Every department responded and CNET indeed leaped to the next level, turning in a string of quarterly profits beginning in 1998.

—*Christopher Barr*

Look at all of the metrics of your business. What do they tell you? Look at them and use your interpretive powers to make assessments about what people care about, where you're making your biggest profit margin, and where you can improve. Then do it: day by day, week by week, watching your metrics. Two-way communication is powerful!

Bill Gross, CEO of incubator IdeaLab, said that he looks for management teams that use "sense and respond." "Adaptability is so important," he says, "because although you get feedback so much faster than before, that feedback is only useful if you actually adapt, if you actually change your business. A lot of people are resistant to changing their business. But being responsive is the key to being more successful than your competitors."

Chapter

Equity Is Ownership

NEILISM: There are only 100 percentage points of equity; there are always only 100 percentage points. No matter how many shares you issue, there will be only 100 percentage points of equity.

Equity! In a start-up, nothing seems to stir the blood and cloud rational thought more than the notion of equity. Often completely misunderstood, equity is the secret sauce of start-ups! If you manage it wisely, equity is the essential element than can be used to attract employees, partners, and investors. But before you can get it or use it, you have to understand it. Equity is ownership. It is a fundamental and unique asset of start-ups. It is fundamental because everything else that makes a start-up successful is attracted and motivated by equity.

Think about it: The employees who actually do the work are motivated and rewarded for their efforts, in no small part, by a share in the equity. The promise of getting equity is so tempting that employees of established companies have often jumped from high-paying careers to get it. The investors that fuel your start-up's growth with capital are buying shares of equity with that money. Even consultants and third-party contributors, such as your legal team, public relations experts, board members, landlords, recruiters, and other providers of specialized services can be attracted by and paid with equity. Because of its potential for upside growth, equity is the most powerful asset in your arsenal.

But far too few entrepreneurs understand how to make the most of equity. The mistakes that entrepreneurs make range from risking a round of funding while holding out for a percentage point or two difference in ownership, to frittering away 5 or even 10 percent of equity by wantonly granting options or by agreeing to business partners' demands for disproportionate percentages of equity (which, ironically, undermines the very value of the equity that they seek). Even a single misuse of your start-up's equity can push you out of the success zone, so it's imperative that you understand how it works and how to use it effectively.

Equity is a unique element for start-ups because start-up equity has a much greater upside potential than equity in other types of companies. Access to start-up equity is limited to individuals and corporations that have a material tie to the company—namely, employees, investors, partners, and service providers. Indeed, equity may be the only reason start-ups attract many of the essential things that will make them a success, such as venture capital and key executives. Equity is incredibly important, so don't screw it up!

■ IT'S OWNERSHIP, STUPID!

To use equity effectively, it must be measured as a percentage of ownership—not as a fixed number of shares—and managed as a system across all shareholders, as well as across the entire lifespan of the company.

Although most people commonly speak of stock in terms of number of shares, number of shares alone is meaningless; it's like having a stake in a vacation timeshare condominium without knowing what fraction of time that share represents. One month? One week? One minute? You need to see your piece of ownership in the context of the whole picture. Ownership is your percentage of the total number of shares.

Say you work for a company that's valued in the public market at $1 billion, and you happen to own 100,000 shares. If those are the only pieces of information you have, how do you know what your stock is worth? The answer, of course, is that you can't know. On the one hand, while 100,000 shares is twice as valuable as 50,000 shares, just knowing the number of shares alone doesn't tell you what percentage of the company you own. If, on the other hand, you know that you own 1 percent of the company, then you can determine the value of your ownership—namely, $10 million (1 percent of $1 billion). Alternatively, if you knew that the total number of shares issued by the company was 10 million, then you could determine that your 100,000 shares represented 1 percent of the company. These are two different ways to arrive at the same point: Think percentage of ownership, not number of shares. This is important because, as will be explained shortly, your percentage of ownership can change over the life of the company, even if your number of shares doesn't.

■ THERE ARE ONLY 100 PERCENTAGE POINTS OF EQUITY

Ownership is finite, whereas share count isn't. Ownership in a company always totals 100 percent. If you already own stock in a company and the company then issues more shares, that doesn't increase your ownership; instead it dilutes all existing shareholders' ownership to create room for new shareholders. Ownership is always a zero-sum game. For example, if a company issues 10 percent more shares, the new shareholders own that 10 percent, while the existing shareholders' stake is diluted by 10 percent (they used to own 100 percent of the company; now they own just 90 percent). Indeed, "going public" literally means issuing new shares. When a company goes public, it typically offers the public market 15 percent of the company. But that isn't a 15 percent block of stock that the company has been saving in its pocket; it's a new, additional block of shares. So the existing shareholders' stake is suddenly diluted by 15 percent. As the total ownership pie gets bigger to squeeze in the new shareholders, the existing shareholders' slices get proportionately smaller.

This is such an important concept that it's worth repeating the Neilism that begins this chapter: There are only 100 percentage points of equity—ever. Entrepreneurs, individuals, and, amazingly, even some professional investors fall for the fool's game of counting equity in number of shares. When a start-up is trying to attract a key hire, for instance, it can be tempting to offer that candidate a big chunk of stock even if the position wasn't budgeted for it. After all, you just need to issue some more shares, right? Wrong. Issuing more shares appears to be as simple as printing more money—but it's just as dangerous. You may succeed in snagging the engineering VP of your dreams, but her overly generous slice of the pie will come at the expense of all existing shareholders.

■ MORE VALUABLE THAN MONEY

Equity can literally be more valuable than money. Whereas cash has an absolute and unchanging value, equity is a dynamic commodity. It can compound hugely—in your favor if it goes up, or against you if it drops (see the sidebar "Tempted by Equity: A Cautionary Tale"). Equity is perhaps a start-up's most potent tool for creating success. It shouldn't be hoarded, but it should be used wisely. And equity should be handled as a system that evolves over time.

Try as many a start-up might to devise unorthodox equity schemes to get funding, an equity structure that's out of whack almost always follows one of two scenarios: Either the equity scheme rejiggers itself so that it ultimately converges to a time-tested, universal formula, with standard percentages going to various players; or the start-up fails. Out-of-balance equity can throw a monkey wrench in the best-planned start-up or spin-out. For example, companies need to use every bit of equity as a magnet—to draw other investors and to entice a first-rate management team. Even a large corporation that provides seed funding to a start-up or a spin-out could end up watching its majority ownership stake shrink into a minority position if the equity is unbalanced—and that's the good-case scenario. Just as likely, the spin-out's equity problems could dissuade future investors, dooming it altogether.

Misuse of equity can snowball. For example, a company that grants a generous 10 percent ownership to a vice president of marketing will likely soon encounter every other vice president demanding a similar amount, thereby diluting everyone's ownership. The lesson is to adopt the natural order of ownership from the start. Deviating from the natural order only introduces needless pain down the line, as equity inevitably converges back to the natural order.

Tempted by Equity: A Cautionary Tale

In 1999, Joseph Galli, former president of Black & Decker's power tools and accessories division, left a job that paid him a base salary of nearly $500,000 and a cash bonus of $600,000. He took a pay cut to work as president and chief operating officer (COO) of Amazon.com. His compensation package at Amazon included a base salary of $200,000, a $3 million signing bonus, and the option to buy nearly 4 million shares of Amazon stock for just under $60 a share. But Galli left Amazon in 2000 when the stock was trading for less than $40, about $20 below the strike price of his options, which rendered those Amazon options worthless.

Galli then joined business-to-business company VerticalNet in July 2000 as president and CEO. VerticalNet paid Galli a hiring bonus of $4 million and granted 3 million stock options at a strike price of about $50, which vested over a four-year period. VerticalNet's stock traded for less than $50 during most of Galli's tenure. When he left VerticalNet, that stock was trading below $6, rendering his vested portion of the 3 million stock options worthless.

Galli jumped ship again in January 2001, this time to Newell Rubbermaid. Will he be tempted by equity to jump once again?

—*Christopher Barr*

■ TYPES OF EQUITY

Equity comes dressed in different forms, but ultimately a start-up typically uses four types of equity: (1) common stock, (2) stock options for common stock, (3) preferred stock, and (4) warrants. Common stock is universally used by all companies (whether start-ups or mature companies). Options, preferred stock, and warrants are intermediate instruments that ultimately become converted into common stock in a successful start-up. Each type of equity has a number of attributes or rights, such as a purchase (or strike) price, voting rights, board rights, tax burdens, and liquidation preferences. The four types of equity dovetail with four different types of players: founders, employees, investors, and third parties, such as public relations companies (see Table 6.1).

➤ Common Stock

The founders of a start-up typically own equity in the form of common stock. This equity ownership is usually expressed as a percentage of the company based on ownership of a certain number of shares. For example, if a company with four founders has issued 5 million shares of stock, then each founder owns a quarter of the company, or 1.25 million shares.

Each share of common stock comes with a single vote. In a typical start-up the common stockholders, namely the founders, have the right to appoint one board member and to vote in the election of one or more other board members. The more shares one party owns, the more influential his or her vote will be.

Table 6.1 Four types of equity used by start-ups.

Type of Equity	Who Gets It	Attributes
Common stock	Founders	Vests over four years; has voting rights; no liquidation preference; tax burdens.
Stock options	Employees	Includes the right to buy stock at a certain price; vests over four years; tax burdens; no voting rights.
Preferred stock	Investors	Includes board seat per series; liquidation preference; tax burdens.
Warrants	Lessors, partners	Includes the right to buy stock at a certain price; no voting rights; has a vesting schedule.

The most distinctive attribute of equity granted to employees, namely common stock and stock options, is vesting. Vesting means that the individual earns the right to buy specified increments of the stock grant over a scheduled period of time, typically a four-year period, during the employee's tenure with the start-up. The primary intention of vesting is as an incentive to participate in the company's success over this vesting period. Having the opportunity to purchase equity in a growing company is a carrot and vesting isn't designed to penalize an employee or founder if they leave the company before the stock has vested, but rather to ensure that unvested portions of the grant remain available for that employee's replacement.

➤ Stock Options

Stock options are grants that provide the right to buy a specified number of shares of common stock at a specified price, known as the strike price. When you exercise your right to buy the stock, the options then convert into common stock. Stock options do not carry voting rights; common stock does. Voting rights become significant when there is a shareholder vote, such as voting for new board members or voting to sell the company. However, such shareholder votes are rare events in a start-up. As already mentioned, stock options are subject to a vesting schedule.

➤ Preferred Stock

Preferred stock is primarily granted to investors in a start-up. Although there are a variety of legal ways to frame it, preferred stock has three distinct attributes or rights: (1) preferred stock is owned rather than being subject to a vesting schedule; (2) each class, or series, of preferred stock typically includes the right to assign a board member; and (3) preferred stock has a liquidation preference, which means the holder has the right under certain circumstances (such as the sale or liquidation of the company) to recover his or her investment before investors holding common stock.

Then there are a host of other rights associated with preferred stock—typically, antidilution provisions, information rights, and registration rights—but these fall into the zone of legal arcanum. When the rights are handled properly, they are of little consequence to the business under normal conditions. So don't dwell on them now, but rather seek the guidance of legal counsel at the time you're negotiating an agreement.

➤ Warrants

Don't worry, stock warrants are nothing like search warrants. Warrants are the equivalent of options, but they are for nonemployees, such as leasing companies, business partners, and investors. Like stock options, warrants give holders the right to buy stock at a certain price. An example of a start-up using warrants to great advantage was Priceline.com, which, in 1998, granted 100,000 warrants to actor William Shatner of the original *Star Trek* television series. It was a win-win situation for both parties: Priceline got a high-profile spokesman without paying him cash, and Shatner got warrants on pre-IPO shares that ended up being worth millions of dollars.

➤ Simplicity

Regardless of equity type, the guiding principle in devising your equity structure is simplicity! Simple is just better. Furthermore, complex equity arrangements can manifest an underlying weakness, such as a lack of commitment by an investor. For example, if the start-up agrees to a clause in an investor's contract that says that if the company fails to meet a key milestone the investor will receive additional equity, then that investor's interests are suddenly at cross-purposes with the company's. What may seem like a benign or expedient equity arrangement at the time can put you in treacherous waters downstream. So keep it simple!

■ EQUITY AS A SYSTEM

We'll say it again: Ownership is a zero-sum—or 100 percent sum—game. What happens to any one share of equity does not happen in isolation; any change affects the value of every other share of equity. Equity is a system. And time and again it's been shown that all the successful start-ups have equity systems that adhere to the same design. The numbers are amazingly consistent. Founders get a specific amount of equity, as do employees, investors, and other financial backers. In devising your equity, follow the successful companies. Don't try to get creative with your equity—save those efforts for your offering. It's no accident that the successful companies all adhere to the same natural order of equity. The time-proven lesson is this: Manage your equity as a system rather than as shares issued in isolation, such as issuing all your equity in a single transaction.

The consequences of mishandling equity cannot be overstated. And there are two ways to misuse it: (1) deploying it incorrectly or (2) not deploying it at all. First, you need to deploy it, period. To hoard equity will doom you because you'll fail to do the things required to reach the success zone—namely, build your offering and attract investors and key employees. But the second way to mishandle your equity is to deploy it unwisely. For example, if you grant a disproportionate share of ownership to one constituent, you do so at the expense of all the others. A forward-thinking CEO who's being recruited to a start-up in the midst of a financing round will ask for a higher percentage of ownership than normal in anticipation of the funding, knowing that the financing round will dilute the ownership of all shareholders. That CEO is shrewdly looking at equity as an overall system that includes all investors over time, rather than as just the limited number at that moment in time.

Table 6.2 illustrates the typical start-up's system of equity, including its components and interdependencies. Equity must be managed as a system to orchestrate the right balance among all the players.

➤ Holders of Equity

Equity is a powerful tool when issued and used advantageously. There are multiple constituents who will want to hold shares of equity, yet equity should go only to those who will be motivated to perform by having it. This includes the founders, employees, angel

Table 6.2   Components of an equity system.

Holders of equity	Founders, employees, angel investors, venture capitalists, public stock investors, lawyers, public relations firms, leasing companies, board members, landlords, consultants, headhunters, and so on.
Time line	Three private rounds of financing, series A, B, and C, followed by an IPO; each round is staged in approximately 6-to-12-month intervals.
Dilutions	Stock grants, stock option grants to employees, equity incentives to business partners and investors.

and venture capital investors, public stock investors, lawyers, public relations firms, leasing companies, board members, landlords, and on and on the list goes.

➤ Time Line

A typical start-up will sequence through four rounds of funding, each following the other in roughly 6-to-12-month intervals: three private rounds of financing, Series A, B, and C, followed by an IPO. Meanwhile, the company grants stock options from a pool of stock options essentially continuously as it adds employees at a rate of two per week. Similarly, grants to miscellaneous business partners to cover business needs, such as equipment lease lines, public relations services, and executive recruiting, take their slices of the equity pie.

➤ Dilution

It is a fact of life that equity gets diluted over time. Granting stock, and thus, diluting ownership, is a routine part of business—forever! A succession of stock option grants to employees, equity incentives to business partners, and grants to investors promise to dilute ownership essentially every day of a start-up. Of course, the goal is that as the added employees and partners help to grow the business, the overall value of the company will increase and, therefore, so will all shareholders' value, offsetting the dilution. Still, early-stage VCs know, for example, that their original ownership in a start-up will be diluted by more than half by the time the start-up is a publicly traded company. This is why early-stage VCs require from 30 percent to as much as 40 percent of the company, as well as the ability to "top up" in subsequent financings.

■ CREATE AN EQUITY BUDGET

The upshot of the combination of interdependence of ownership, multiple constituents, and time is that equity should be managed top-down as a whole system—with a budget akin to a financial budget that manages cash.

Specifically, every equity grant needs to be considered in the context of the rest of the existing and future stakeholders. Viewed from the highest level, you need to budget ownership for employees, investors, and founders. In the first few stages of a start-up, investors will need to own 30 percent to 50 percent of the company, employees 20 percent to 30 percent, and the founders the remaining 20 percent to 50 percent (see Figure 6.1).

In the early stages of a start-up, the equity budget for employees is broken down even further. The CEO requires 8 percent to 10 per-

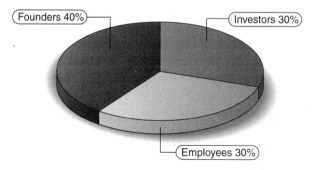

Figure 6.1 An early-stage equity budget.

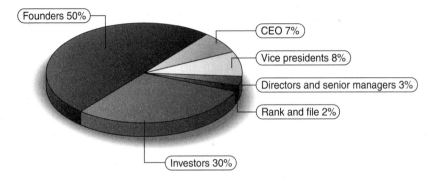

Figure 6.2 An equity budget.

cent of the employee budget; vice presidents get from 2 percent to 3 percent each; directors and senior managers get 0.5 percent each; and rank-and-file employees are budgeted at approximately 0.01 percent or less each (see Figure 6.2).

Stock options are a part of the pool in the overall equity system, but the stock options are not allocated entirely up front. Because a start-up will issue additional shares as a result of following the staged approach to equity, the option pool is set up for option grants that occur within the subsequent nine months to a year. Then the pool is topped up, typically in conjunction with each subsequent financing event. Additionally, the option pool category also includes option, stock, and warrant grants to nonemployees, such as public relations companies, recruiters, and consultants.

■ NATURAL ORDER OF OWNERSHIP

This natural order of equity sequencing is summarized in Table 6.3.

In the end, going public entails selling an additional 15 percent or more of the company, a fact that entrepreneurs often overlook. Employees wind up owning approximately 18 percent of the company, an amount that seems amazingly small considering that it represents more than a hundred employees, most of whom are now capable of launching their own start-ups!

The venture capital investors and other private investors wind up owning as much as half of the company, in part because start-ups need many investors. Also, the amount of capital that the private

Table 6.3 Equity percentages at each funding stage.

Stage	Founder's Equity	Private Investors	Employees and Others	Public Investors
0—Formation	100%	0%	0%	0%
1—Sell 33% of company for $3 million in funding.	42	33	25	0
2—Sell 25% of company for $12.5 million in funding.	28	48	24	0
3—Sell 20% of company for $20 million in funding.	22	57	21	0
4—Post-IPO—After selling 15% of company for $60 million.	19	48	18	15

investors have at risk balloons to colossal proportions over the life of the start-up. While the media may characterize VCs as greedy people, with front-page stories about a VC investment that returned 20 times its money in a year, most successful investments return a five- to sevenfold increase over a four- or five-year period. And the successful investments still represent a small fraction of the total investments private investors make. The majority of the investments will fail. The average VC firm will end up with reasonable returns of approximately 30 percent a year over the life of the entire fund.

The founders end up with whatever is left over after all the other people and companies necessary for the start-up's success claim their portions. The founders' amount is typically 18 percent. This percentage can be higher or lower, depending on the other resources needed or not needed to succeed. For example, a founder who is also a CEO can recoup 5 percent or more of post-IPO ownership that had been budgeted for an outside CEO. Or the founders' stake could be smaller because many start-ups need to sell or give equity to a major business partner, which can dilute the founders' stake by 2 percent to 5 percent.

One thing to keep in mind as a founder: While the size of your stake is shrinking, the value of your company and your shares is rising. Table 6.4 shows how the founders' stake would be valued over the course of the sequence.

■ PLAYING BY THE SYSTEM

If you want to succeed in a manner similar to other successful start-ups, the moral of the story is to let the natural order of equity steer your course. It tells you that venture capitalists need ownership percentages sufficient to produce the returns that will justify the amount of capital they put at risk. Similarly, the percentage of equity the natural order dictates for employees is the amount that's been proven time and again to be necessary to attract and retain good employees. And the founders require enough ownership to remain motivated—after all, success or failure ultimately rests on their shoulders.

To stay in the success zone, you must adhere to the natural order of start-up equity because it's the time-tested formula for balancing all constituent parts of the equity system. No single constituent should want more—or less—than his or her necessary share because to throw the system out of balance is to court failure. And 100 percent of nothing is . . . nothing!

Keep these guidelines in mind:

Table 6.4   Founders' stake at each sequencing stage.

Stage	Company Valuation	Founders' Equity Stake	Value of Founders' Equity
0	$0	100%	$0
1	$9 million	42%	$3.75 million
2	$50 million	28%	$14.15 million
3	$100 million	22%	$22 million
4	$400 million	18%	$74.8 million

- Above all else, keep the process simple. By keeping it simple, you'll make it easy on everyone involved, from the employees you hire to the partners you work with and especially to the private investors you want to attract. Using well-worn percentages, processes, and sequences will make it easier for others to understand your business and will communicate that you have a tacit understanding of and sophistication about the process. Equity is complicated enough already. So keep it simple.

- Make sure you consider the complete picture. Think about all the players you'll encounter over the life of the company: employees, investors (public and private), business partners, board members, landlords, headhunters, and other consultants. Approach it as a system.

- Use scenario analysis. Don't raise too much money too early. If you raise too much too soon, you'll be forced to sell a bigger piece later. Be sure to stage fundraising: 6 months, again in 6 to 12 months, and so on.

- Manage your equity like a budget, but don't hoard it. Deploy it in a proactive manner; if you don't deploy, you'll fail to attract the resources you need to succeed.

- Use a lawyer. Don't do all the work yourself because a lawyer can advise you on prevailing practices and can help you keep contracts standardized. And you'll get a better outcome with less effort on your part.

- No matter what you do, there is a convergence to a natural order. So instead of devising convoluted equity structures, spend your time building the company. Innovate your offering, not your equity!

- Also, if you sell too much equity too early, you won't own enough to make it worth your while. Owners need to own enough!

■ REFERENCE

Galli Leaves Top Spot at VerticalNet: *http://news.cnet.com/news/0-1007-200-4400127.html*

Chapter

Technology

NEILISM: Avoid building your platform on Microsoft products.

Which technologies should you choose to build your Web site infrastructure? Though your tech options are both more complex and more numerous than ever, the answer is much simpler than you may think. In fact, the most important factors in tech selection are not technological at all. Technology is not just tech, it's people, too. That's the good news.

The bad news is, in today's Lightspeed Economy you've only got one chance to get it right. Once you commit to a certain technological path and make the investment in the machinery, software, and people you need to hold it all together, there's no turning back. The time frame for getting your product to market, the cost of retooling, and the impatience of investors won't allow you to switch technological horses midstream. You want to get on a success track now in order to reap the benefits of a clear strategy that will pay dividends in the future.

■ THE VISION DRIVES THE TECHNOLOGY

Vision is the place to start. A clearly defined, relentlessly communicated vision provides a shared framework for selecting appropriate technology and helps team members settle legitimate disagreements concerning how best to architect your start-up's solution.

Vision is not a marketing slogan, such as "Quality is job one." It's a clearly articulated road map that defines your start-up—its mission, its customer, and its place in the overall business landscape. Your vision is the road map to where you want to go. Does everyone in your organization understand who your customers are and what they want? Do your people understand why what the customers want is important and why your offering is the best way to meet those wants? Does everyone understand the start-up's timetable and why it's important to stick to it?

If you can't quiz every employee in your organization and get the same answers to these questions, your people may be working at cross-purposes or surfing the Web looking elsewhere for more exciting work. More than stock options, beanbag chairs, foosball, or kitchens stocked with every imaginable kind of junk food, it's a shared vision that forges a team.

■ THE BUILDING BLOCKS OF A WEB SITE

When you first hang your shingle out on the Net, you may not need a high-bandwidth site that can serve up custom content to hundreds of users at a time without choking. But from the start you need to position yourself for the day success comes calling and your Web site goes from 100 customer visits per day to 100 visits per second. If your server sends most of these new potential customers a "page not found" error, you've just lost the marketing opportunity of a lifetime, and you won't get a second chance.

The components you need to run a large, interactive Web site are: (1) operating system, (2) Web server application, and (3) database application.

■ ISSUES TO KEEP IN MIND

➤ Flexibility and Scalability

One small change in the technology landscape or in the business environment at large can leave a gaping hole in your business plan, and you have to be prepared to respond immediately. You don't want to be boxed in by your technology and find yourself unable to compete.

That's what happened to USA.NET, the leader in outsourced e-mail until 1995, when HotMail began offering free e-mail. Suddenly the whole business model changed from one predicated on charging customers for the e-mail software to one based on revenues from advertising. USA.NET didn't have the technology in place to serve ads. So not only was it not attractive to its customers, it had no way to react immediately. It took USA.NET six months to respond to Hotmail's challenge. USA.NET is still alive, but the company lost precious market share because it wasn't prepared, and it never regained the market position it once had.

And just as you need to respond quickly to changes in your business environment, you also need to be ready for a big influx of customers—long before they show up. So even though your business may start out small, you need to build your technology platform so that it can scale upward with the success of your business.

CNET: Built to Scale

Jonathan Steuer was the information and technology architect for HotWired's Web site, which launched on October 27, 1994. In early 1995, CNET hired Jonathan to be the consulting architect for CNET's first Web servers. From the beginning, CNET's chief executive officer, Halsey Minor, was planning for an explosion of growth on the Internet and architected the CNET site accordingly.

Before Steuer arrived, CNET's Web site was hosted on two Silicon Graphics workstations. In early 1995, well before the public debut of CNET.com on June 24, 1995, Steuer moved CNET's Web site to Sun Sparc 10 and Sparc 20 servers that were running Solaris and the Apache Web Server—a more robust platform for growth. Meanwhile, CNET had been developing in-house a database-driven, content-management system called PRISM that would enable CNET

(continued)

to publish content quickly and cost effectively as the company grew.

"In 1994 and early 1995," Steuer recalls, "there were no tools, so everything had to be built by hand. Back then there was nothing to buy. At HotWired we had wasted a lot of money building everything by hand, so I convinced Halsey that the smart thing to do was to put the right infrastructure in place so that it could scale as traffic and users grew. So that's what we did before CNET launched with its database of reviews in 1995."

CNET built its core technology because it had to, initially. But Minor shrewdly realized that CNET was in the business of developing content, not software. To continue developing its software technology would have drained CNET's resources and focus from its core mission: producing great content that would attract customers. So once it was deployed, Minor quickly sold the technology to Web enterprise software developer Vignette, who went on to further develop it and market it as StoryServer. CNET then licensed StoryServer back from Vignette. The lesson in this story? Only build it yourself if you have no alternative—and build it to scale.

"As it turns out," says Steuer, "that's a lesson than can be learned even today. The people who are smart look for best-of-breed technology solutions, whatever that means at the time. If they cobble a system together based on an architecture that can last, they end up much happier because they have defined their production and workflow system and build it accordingly. The alternative is that you reinvent the wheel every six months while you fight with tools that might not exist [down the line] and processes that you never bothered to define precisely enough.

"Nowadays it wouldn't make sense to do it the way we did in 1995. If you want a content management system today, you don't have to build everything yourself like we did. Just go out and buy StoryServer, or DynaBase, or Interwoven TeamSite. There are five or six mature content manage-

ment products available and a bunch of system integrators who've implemented them ten times already."
—*Jonathan Steuer, vice president of eMarkets at Scient*

■ RELIABILITY AND AVAILABILITY

On the Internet you can lose customers as quickly as you gain them; so hardware or software failures that bring your Web site down can cost dearly. The online auction site eBay suffered a string of well-publicized "outages" beginning in June 1999 and continuing well into 2000 that resulted in lost revenue and a steady flow of negative publicity.

Microsoft's Web sites suffered a similar fate. In 2001, Microsoft.com, MSN.com, WindowsMedia.com, Encarta.com, Carpoint.com, and Expedia.com were largely unavailable to users for more than three days. This was especially damaging to Microsoft because the outages came just days after Microsoft announced a $200 million advertising campaign touting its software in competition with Oracle, IBM, and Sun Microsystems. The theme for the ads was "Software for the agile business."

The promise of the Internet is 24/7 availability, and customers don't care how or why your servers are down. They just know you're not living up to your end of the bargain. By the time you issue a lame apology for inconveniencing your customers, a good portion of them may no longer be your customers—they've already gotten what they need from your competitor.

➤ Make a Choice: Unix or Windows 2000/XP

It's a mistake to consider any one component in the Web server in isolation from the others; the failure of any one will bring the entire system down. What you need is group of products proven to work together well.

To simplify the situation only slightly, the Web server market is split into two mutually antagonistic camps: the Unix community, which tends to favor open-source, non-Microsoft products; and the Microsoft community, which favors only Microsoft products.

We'll outline the basics for both platforms, but the Neilism "Avoid building your platform on Microsoft products" tells you which side of the religious war we fall on.

Inside Information: What Is Your Competition Running On?

As suggested in Chapter 5, you can learn much by closely examining companies to which you are similar. This is especially easy on the Internet, where you can search for competitive information. Go to *www.netcraft.com* to find out what similar companies are using to run their Web sites. Click on the "What's That Site Running?" link on the front door, and on the subsequent page enter the URL of the site you're interested in. For example, typing in *www.amazon.com* shows that Amazon is running Unix (Solaris and Linux) and the Stronghold Web Server (a version of Apache that incorporates security for online transactions). Once you know what kind of hardware and software your competition is using, you can then do the analysis to decide if you should do the same. There's nothing like a little inside information.

➤ Configuration #1: Unix/Linux—Apache—Oracle

Many companies that put Internet technology at the core of their business overwhelmingly choose one of the many versions of this configuration. Because of knowledge of the operating system and reliable performance over time, experienced programmers and system administrators often strongly prefer some flavor of Unix.

Unix systems dominate the market for Web server operating systems, driving about 70 percent of Internet servers. This is due to its continuing superiority in mission-critical functionality (see Table 7.1), such as reliability, availability, and processing capacity, even when compared to Windows 2000 and XP, Microsoft's latest release of its Windows NT operating system.

Table 7.1 Web server operating systems: how they compare.

	Linux	NT v.4	Unix	Win2000/ XP
Stability	Excellent	Deficient	Excellent	Acceptable
SMP[1] scaling	Acceptable	Acceptable	Excellent	Excellent
Clustering	Excellent	Deficient	Excellent	Acceptable
High availability	Acceptable	Deficient	Excellent	Acceptable
RDBMS[2] size	Acceptable	Acceptable	Excellent	Acceptable
Ease of use	Deficient	Acceptable	Deficient	Acceptable
Plug and play drivers	Acceptable	Excellent	Deficient	Excellent
Technical support	Acceptable	Acceptable	Excellent	Excellent
ISV[3]/VAR[4] support	Deficient	Excellent	Excellent	Excellent
System management	Acceptable	Acceptable	Excellent	Excellent
Security	Excellent	Deficient	Excellent	Acceptable
Pricing	Acceptable	Acceptable	Acceptable	Acceptable

[1]SMP = Symmetric multiprocessing
[2]RDBMS = Relational database management system
[3]ISV = Independent software vendor
[4]VAR = Value-added reseller
Source: Gartner Group, Inc., *Linux, NT, Unix, Win2000 OS Comparison: July 2000.*

Commercial Unix refers to proprietary versions of an operating system (OS) such as Sun's Solaris or IBM's AIX. Commercial Unix systems tend to be more expensive than Windows 2000/XP systems; but most companies with large, interactive Web sites think the performance, reliability, enterprise experience, and depth of vendor support offered by the Unix systems are well worth the price.

Linux is a virtually free Unix system that is rapidly expanding, thanks to its reliability and a vast, fiercely devoted user community bent on improving the system. Linux vendors such as Red Hat are bundling this OS with most of the software you need to run a Web site, including the Apache Web Server, e-mail programs, and an Oracle or IBM database—at rock-bottom prices.

Apache is the most popular Web server, with a majority slice of the Web server market share. As with Linux, a devoted open-source community of engineers supports the continued development of the Apache project (*www. apache.org*). Apache runs on Unix, NT, and other OS platforms.

Oracle offers the most widely used, powerful, flexible, and scalable family of database products. The price you pay for this high level of adaptability is a bit of a learning curve. You definitely need a database administrator (DBA) who knows Oracle inside and out to get the most out of these products. Fortunately, Oracle experts abound, support is excellent, and selling your start-up will be much easier with an Oracle database at the back end rather than a lesser-known product.

➤ Configuration #2: Windows 2000/XP—Internet Information Server—SQL Server

This configuration holds less than 25 percent of the Web server market. Unlike Apache and Oracle, which run on just about any operating system, Internet Information Server (IIS) and MS SQL Server run only on Microsoft Windows 2000, XP, or NT. This configuration is favored by companies that have had a good experience with Microsoft products and that operate in an exclusively Microsoft environment.

Windows 2000, XP, and NT continue to trail the Unix operating systems in all mission-critical areas. NT has the upper hand only in the ease-of-use (graphical interface) and plug-and-play driver-support categories. IIS is Microsoft's Web server offering; it runs only on Windows 2000, XP, and NT. Engineers who have implemented IIS solutions describe it as a full-featured product. SQL Server is Microsoft's most powerful database product. Consistent with the company's overall marketing strategy, it's easier to set up than an Oracle database, but it lacks the depth of customizability that Oracle offers.

Engineers who have implemented a Microsoft-only solution also point out that it:

- Raises barriers to communication with non-NT servers.
- Doesn't scale well.
- Lacks processing power, making it a poor choice for large, high-bandwidth Web sites.

A Microsoft-only configuration appears best suited for intranets and static Web sites (sites that don't update often). Because traffic volume is low and the lack of performance and reliability in these environments are merely inconveniences, the cost and the ease of use have made sense to many businesses whose main business is not conducted on the Internet.

There are hidden costs to the Microsoft-only configuration. The hardware needed to run Windows 2000, XP, or NT is initially cheaper by half than that required by commercial Unix systems (though far more expensive than Linux or other freely distributed Unix software). And Windxows 2000, XP, and NT are universally acknowledged to be easier than Unix is to set up. But once you put it to work, you'll realize that the actual costs (monetary and otherwise) are much higher:

- *Poor scalability and performance:* It often takes multiple NT servers to do the work of a single Unix box, and to do it less well at that. And Windows 2000 and XP simply lack the raw processing power of high-end Unix machines.
- *The one-size-fits-all fantasy:* All real solutions are ongoing, custom solutions, solutions that allow you to respond quickly to *your* changing business environment, and that *your* people are going to have to develop and support. That translates into higher costs. The only company that can provide this level of service is your own. No outside company—least of all Microsoft—is going to take care of your tech needs.

What's the Best Midrange Server Software?

The Gartner Group compared four operating systems for Web sites. Gartner found that Linux has made much progress lately, primarily in functionality important to Internet infrastructure and Web server capabilities, including a greater selection of drivers, easier installation, and graphical user interface (GUI)-based front ends for Web administration and management. Gartner's comparison projects likely functional maturity through 2003 for Linux, Windows 2000/XP, and Unix.

Total Cost of Ownership

The bottom line is, which is cheaper: Unix or Windows 2000/ XP? Do the math: Hardware costs, software licenses, technical support agreements, prices of upgrades/service packs, costs of hardware upgrades, profits lost for every hour of downtime, personnel costs for recovering/recreating data lost due to product defects in the operating system and/or hardware platform required by your choice of operating systems, and personnel costs for systems administrators— these are only some of the factors that contribute to the overall budget resulting from your decision. It is not a trivial consideration.

—*John Kirch, Networking Consultant and Microsoft Certified Professional*

■ PEOPLE DRIVE TECHNOLOGY

Unless you're an expert technologist yourself, it's absolutely vital to have key technical people in place and to seek out their advice early on. Rely on these people to pull together the teams that will build and maintain the backbone of your success. You're going to have to support whatever technologies you choose with your own people. The pivotal position is vice president of engineering. This person heads up the software and programming side of things. This position combines engineering expertise with project management skills and marketing savvy. This position requires expertise in designing and developing networking, communications, transaction processing, and database applications.

The VP of engineering will:

- Oversee the selection, setup, and maintenance of the Web infrastructure.
- Define, develop, and deploy an information technology (IT) architecture that maximizes revenue, minimizes costs, and helps get and keep IT aligned with business goals.

- Ensure that all IT deployments are properly implemented, integrated, and supported.
- Have the expertise and experience to evaluate the trade-offs between the competing technologies. (Is Java's portability worth the performance hit? Or is the scalability of C++ worth the extra development time?)
- Build an engineering team. (Can this person attract and retain talent?)
- Plan and track projects to keep them on schedule and within budget.
- Make presentations and communicate with clients.
- Become the corporate expert on all trends and developments in IT that are relevant to business.

■ GETTING AND KEEPING DEVELOPERS

Developing a tight-knit team of core developers is not just the best way to assure your start-up's technological success, it's the *only* way. And not incidentally, should a larger company want to buy you out somewhere down the road, having a committed team that understands the system and having engineering architectures that fully support your offering make your start-up all the more attractive.

➤ Create Mindshare

Mindshare is a shared understanding of purpose and method that greases the development machine. Companies that have it run efficiently with a minimum of internal friction, making rapid progress; companies without it waste a great deal of time and effort developing toward contradictory goals and then trying to patch it all together into a product at release time.

Pitch your vision to your engineers as if they were VCs—because engineers are just as essential to your success. You're not simply hiring a tech grunt; you're hiring someone who can make or break your start-up.

Make sure anyone you hire shares your views about the market space and your value proposition, not just the feasibility and future of the technology you're using to implement it. The entire staff must be on the same page as far as what the company is doing, where you're heading, how you're going to get there, and when.

➤ It's Not about the Money

Money and a standard benefits package are always an issue, but never the most important one for talented developers. They know they'll get this package wherever they go. There are other ways to attract the best talent:

- *Keep software design simple and focused.* This requires constant effort. Caving in to constant pressure from marketing or engineering to add this or that feature has derailed many a software project. "Feature creep" tends to result from a company's internal politics and lack of mindshare and has nothing to do with getting a product to market.
- *Establish good practices among your developers.* Early on, get agreement on such things as common naming conventions and common documentation practices, then make sure they are followed. When one developer needs to incorporate another's code, they'll know where to find what they need, and you'll avoid petty arguments about unreadable code.
- *Match career goals.* Find out where candidates want to go in their careers, and make sure they're a good match for the position you're offering. This guarantees a high level of interest.
- *Establish a state-of-the-art development environment.* All developers want to work in a modern engineering environment, using the latest tools and methods.
- *Convey a sense of contribution.* Make sure engineers understand that the tasks you assign them contribute significantly to the success of the final product.
- *Provide a steady flow of challenges.* A recent survey of IT workers rated a challenging work environment as the most effective way to retain employees. In-house training, mobility within the company, and special projects are suggested as ways to meet this demand.
- *Avoid burnout.* Don't create the siege mentality so common

at start-ups. Don't make impossible demands and expect people to maintain 60-to-70 hour work weeks on a regular basis.

A Guide to Developing Good Development Habits Early

Software Project Survival Guide, by Steve McConnell (Microsoft Press, 1998), does a great job of detailing the staging, planning, and implementation of a complex software project, complete with checklists, clear guidelines, and pitfalls gleaned from the author's years in the software trenches.

➤ Markets Define Technology

Unless your start-up is creating a new technology, the market space your product or service inhabits probably has a standard (or emerging) set of tools and a built-in set of constraints. Are you building an application that will run in-house, on someone else's system, or on the Web? Do you need to deliver your product or service on different platforms? Here are some examples of markets that define the technology:

• *Web applications.* For a monthly fee, application service providers (ASPs) provide clients access via the Internet to an application they can use to manage a part of their business, such as accounting, finance, sales force automation, procurement and supply-chain management, and infrastructure services. A big part of the appeal of ASPs is 24/7 access to the application for input or reporting from any location. Because reliability, availability, and transaction-processing power are mission critical, the vast majority of these ASPs base their operations on platforms that have a history of being robust and practically fail-safe, such as Unix and Oracle. Many use Java and XML (extensible markup language) programming languages for messaging and data exchange with clients.

• *Client software.* This is shrink-wrapped software that customers install directly on their own computers. An example is the SAN Navigator product that solves a longstanding system administrator (sysadmin) headache: Sysadmins managing large networks that contain switches and other devices from multiple vendors currently have no way to monitor and diagnose their entire network at once. The SAN Navigator software provides a diagnostic view of the entire network—regardless of switch vendor. Because customers may be mixing Windows 2000, XP, or NT, Unix, or other OSs within their network environments, Java has grown in popularity as a reliable cross-platform solution.

- *Wireless.* The platforms for wireless and handheld devices and applications established in this burgeoning space are still being established. The technologies run the gamut from C++ to wireless application protocol (WAP) to XML. Then there are application programming interfaces for the Palm operating system and software development kits for the devices and wireless platforms you may want to address.

■ WHEN AND WHAT TO OUTSOURCE

The speed-to-market and profitability demanded by the 3G start-up environment all but guarantee you'll want to outsource some of your development. Outsourcing necessary but peripheral functions, such as documentation, doesn't just fill in gaps in expertise. More important, outsourcing lets you focus all your energy on your core business and lets you move faster. But only if you do it right:

- *Keep core technology development in-house.* This should be obvious. You can't remain competitive and you can't attract the best talent if you have to go outside the company for core technology.
- *Outsource tasks, not responsibility.* Always make a key, invested employee, such as your VP of engineering, ultimately responsible for the contractor's work. Contractors are in general qualified, competent, and very useful—even essential—but they are not invested in your success and may not be responsible for supporting the work in the future. For example, More.com outsourced its product development, which was built on Sun Solaris systems and an Informix database. Once the initial development was completed, the consultants implemented the product and then threw it back to the More.com staff to maintain. The problem More encountered was that it couldn't hire any Informix DBAs to work on it and take it forward.

A better choice is to build on the more industry-standard Oracle platform in the first place. Learning how to develop for Oracle databases is considered a career path, so you'll have a greater chance of finding people to further develop existing applications.

• *Don't assume anything outside your area of expertise is easy.* Another common mistake is assuming that a certain task, such as interface design, is easy, won't take much time, and can be done by anyone, someone in-house, in his or her spare time. No one, least of all developers, has the time to teach himself or herself a new discipline. This is a sure recipe for burnout.

■ REFERENCES

Philip and Alex's Guide to Web Publishing, by Philip Greenspun, (Morgan Kaufmann Publishers, 1999).

Software Project Survival Guide: How to Be Sure Your First Important Project Isn't Your Last, Steve McConnell (Microsoft Press, 1998).

http://www.netcraft.com/survey/

Computerworld: Survey: Above All Else, IT Workers Need Challenge, January 15, 2001: *http://www.computerworld.com/cwi/story/ 0,1199,NAV47_STO56335,00.html*

Gartner Group, Inc.: Linux, NT, Unix, Win2000 OS Comparison: July 2000: *http://www.gartnerweb.com/public/static/hotc/hc00091281.html*

Chapter

No Baggage

NEILISM: No uncles on the board.

If you've ever watched a cycling race, you've noticed that the bikers wear skintight clothes and ride incredibly lightweight bikes. You never see the racers carrying backpacks or wearing heavy coats even in the coldest weather. And there's good reason: They want to move as fast as possible. In building a lightspeed start-up, you should heed the lesson of the cyclists, and *carry no baggage.*

If speed, smarts, and simplicity are the keys to success in a start-up, then by necessity you must avoid any speed bumps that can derail you.

The technology and Internet start-up environment is about merit, and the stakes are high. To succeed, companies must hit the market with full-out force, leading with the best they can offer, or they are dead on arrival. Many start-ups include relatives or friends of the founder who serve either on the board of directors or in key executive roles. While this move is often of necessity—to get early funding or help from a trusted source—the founder must be certain that the "uncle" is qualified to serve the company in the long run and will not be a liability or will not present conflict-of-interest problems. The Neilism we use is: No uncles on the board. The unqualified uncle is taking the resources of the start-up and misusing them. For example, if the wrong uncle is on the board, then there isn't room for the right board member. This is baggage that you can't easily jettison.

■ GOOD UNCLES AND BAD UNCLES

We realize there are good uncles and bad uncles. Many publications have run articles on start-up founders even hiring their dads or moms to help. On the good side is the story of Globix CEO Marc Bell, who hired both his mom and his dad to work for the Internet infrastructure firm in New York. His father, Bob, was an experienced real estate lawyer before he signed on as executive vice president of business development. The younger Bell admitted to the *New York Times* (July 2, 2000) that "the dynamic was a little weird because my father was working for me. It required finding boundaries. There are definitely some tense moments, but there's no one you can better trust than family." When the company went public in 1996, both father and son became multimillionaires. Another example of a successful father-son pairing is Yossi and Arik Vardi. Together they created ICQ and sold it to AOL for more than $400 million.

However, for every Marc and Bob Bell or Yossi and Ark Vardi trumpeted in the press, there are dozens of examples of "uncles" brought in for monetary reasons early on, who later prove to be a burden for the company founder. And if you've got one of these bad uncles on your board, you're holding important board meetings with someone who might not have a clue. You might be deciding whether to make a deal with BEA Systems or with Vignette, whether to invest in technology or in an advertising campaign, while Uncle Louie is still trying to figure out who BEA Systems and Vignette are. Then you have a big problem: Your 3G start-up will die.

■ NO LEGACY ISSUES

Baggage also refers to any other legacy issues that can bog you down as you try to race ahead—from misguided fund-raising strategies to potential lawsuits. Let's say that an entrepreneur raised money from early angel investors at a $30 million valuation. So the entrepreneur figures that she is guaranteed a higher valuation with the next round of funding from venture capitalists. Wrong! Market conditions could change, and the next round of funding could be offered at a lower valuation. So then the entrepreneur has to go back to those early investors, spend weeks explaining why she must accept money at a lower valuation, and she might get sued in the process. A further potential ramification is that many subsequent investors will shun the deal because there is too much baggage. And if there's anything venture people hate in a deal, it's baggage.

In this chapter, we'll detail all the types of excess baggage that could slow you down in your quest to have the speediest cheetah of an Internet start-up. There will be plenty of "don'ts," but there will be just as many "dos"—advice on how to keep your company humming along at a brisk pace, avoiding obstacles (see Table 8.1).

Table 8.1   Common start-up baggage and solutions.

Baggage	Solution
Ill-equipped uncles on the board of directors	Appoint trusted, experienced board members.
Employees spread over multiple locations	Create a simple, centralized work environment.
Rock-star treatment for selected employees	Treat all employees consistently, regardless of rank.
Overreliance on angel investors	Let VCs set valuation of company.
Complex equity arrangements with early investors	Keep equity contracts simple.
Sketchy business practices that might be illegal	Avoid legal exposure; hire lawyers as necessary.
Stock options that vest inconsistently from employee to employee	Keep options deals consistent throughout company.
Starting salaries that are too high—you're burning needed cash	Keep starting salaries within the range used in the industry.

➤ Avoid Deadwood

Early in the life of your company, it might be difficult to get talented people to join you in your quest. This is not unusual, unless you're an established player with many contacts. So the temptation is strong to hire close friends and family who will show you loyalty and who will be known quantities. However, these people must be qualified, and you must build a merit-based environment. Otherwise, you'll end up with the dreaded deadwood in your organization. If you hire a bad uncle for your board, he will offer you no advantage and, indeed, will create a disadvantage for your company. Why? Because for every bad uncle you have on your board, your competition will fill that position on their board with someone who contributes value. And in the incredibly competitive Internet business landscape, any disadvantage can turn your e-business into a shuttered business in the blink of an eye.

Keep a keen eye out for rotten timbers, especially in the early days. If you put your cousin in place as the VP of engineering, don't be surprised when your engineering group is falling apart because you can't attract talent. Word spreads quickly in the Internet realm.

The key is to stay simple. Look at the example of Marimba, a start-up now focused on application deployment in enterprises. Until the company went public, there were only three people on its board of directors: founder Kim Polese, Ray Lane from Oracle, and Doug MacKensie from well-known VC firm Kleiner Perkins Caufield & Byers. With such a small but highly experienced board, Marimba was able to quickly change direction to become a successful B2B player, and it went public with a gung ho offering on April 30, 1999, that tripled on its first day.

Part of the problem with a bad uncle is that you might have difficulty removing a relative from the board. So either you retain someone who is not respected by employees, investors, and share-holders, or you have to dump a relative, who may never talk to you again. Worse yet, the fired uncle might feel disgruntled and block a crucial public offering or buyout by withholding his shareholder approval.

It's not unusual for a VC to request a change in the board of directors in order for your company to get funding. Venture folks like to nip a problem in the bud and will make sure that the board has solid contributors rather than deadwood. This is usually the time when you'll have to show your backbone and fire that close friend or relative in the name of furthering the goals of your company. The question is: Do you simply want to do a start-up, or do you want to do a *successful* start-up? To get to your goal, you'll have to prune the deadwood so the company can flower quickly.

➤ Keep It Simple: Innovate Your Offering, Not Your Organization

As we've said many times in this book, keep it simple. That means everything from a simple concept for your offering and a simple organizational structure to simple contracts for employees and even simple ways of doing your accounting. Why? Because complexity has a way of tripping you up in the long run. You will encounter countless obstacles on the road to success (see Table 8.2), so you might as well avoid creating your own roadblocks and tripping yourself up.

Table 8.2   Roadblocks to start-up success.

Roadblock	Consequence
Contracts with many exceptions, complexities	Difficulty getting future investors
An exec with more equity than he or she should have	Difficulty attracting funding in next round
Angel investors who take on VC roles	Investors who provide funding but no long-term, hands-on help
Promises to investors that "they'll get their money out first"	Broken promises when next investor demands his or her money out first
Too many early investors	Complications trying to reach all of them to get key decisions made
Withholding pay from employees	Legal entanglements that threaten new funding

The simpler your organization, the better. In the early days of your start-up, don't spread employees around multiple locations. Why not? Because doing so fosters poor communication and leaves some people feeling left out of the main hub of operations. Plus, you have to duplicate resources, such as conference rooms, office supplies, copy machines, printers, and support staff. Most important, multiple locations will end up splitting the focus of the top executives, who might lose the chance for face-to-face communication with key employees or with each other. When you're trying to be nimble, you can't have your SWAT team spread around the city.

➤ Be Consistent

Be sure to develop consistent business practices. It sounds easy in theory, but it's difficult in practice. The temptation to deviate is strong, but what seems like an easy one-time solution to an immediate problem can turn into a time bomb down the line. Make sure your contracts with employees, execs, and business partners are straightforward and consistent. Each deviation from your usual business contract requires a separate contract. So the next time you're trying to raise money, your lawyers will have to prepare 400 pages of documents rather than 40 pages. Not only will your legal bills go through the roof, but the prospective investor may decide that the deal is too complex to bother with.

When creating employee contracts, make sure not to give away the farm to one prospective star exec. You might think this person is the cat's meow, the perfect person who will attract other great employees and take your business to new heights. That could very well be true, but if you give this special "star" treatment—and a special contract—you are setting yourself up for trouble down the line. How so? Let's say you give this person 2 percent of the company. That might bring her on board, but it will make it harder for you to get funding at your next round because you no longer have that 2 percent of the equity to allocate elsewhere (see Chapter 14 for more details on the "natural order" of equity).

The job market in Internet start-ups has been incredibly tight, and companies are fighting tooth and nail for top prospects. So it's tempting to make exceptions to your rules for hiring people—offering stock options that vest earlier than dictated by the usual time-table or that accelerate vesting at acquisition. You might even want to offer stock options to your landlord or key business partners; but resist doing that. These are the types of contracts that will introduce complexity down the line, right when you're trying to sell your company to another firm or to the public.

All of these rules hold true for deals you make with business partners, suppliers, and service providers. Stick to tried-and-true business contracts that are simple, won't require hours upon hours of legal counsel, and don't involve giving away precious equity in your company.

Finally, use accepted accounting methods rather than trying to bloat the balance sheet to attract more capital or media attention. Amazon.com was investigated by the Securities and Exchange Commission (SEC) in October 2000 because of deals it made in its commerce network. Amazon made deals to sell other companies' items through its site but was often paid in equity in those companies instead of cash, including $145 million over five years from Living.com (now defunct). Amazon's chief financial officer (CFO), Warren Jenson, later had to warn investors that income from those deals would be much lower than had been reported. Amazon's stock was downgraded by analysts as a result. If you're getting paid in equity, be sure to report it as such up front—and not as cash revenues—so your shareholders will know exactly what's going on. This will save you from investigations and lawsuits in the future.

NEILISM: *Innovate your offering, not your equity.*

Getting funding for your start-up is important, but make sure to follow time-tested strategies for selling stakes in your company. Read through the prospectuses of successful start-ups such as Netscape and Yahoo!, and follow the trail of their equity. Are early investors asking for too much equity? Is there a natural order to the investments, or do they look forced or overly complicated? In other words, your funding should grow according to a fairly consistent formula; if you suddenly give an early investor an inordinately large chunk of equity, that's a signal that you're in a desperate financial situation and the investor is dictating the terms. In almost all successful companies, you'll see that the investments started relatively small and built up over time in a consistent fashion, until the IPO and beyond. If you're going to get creative, save it for your offering and your marketing campaigns. Your equity agreements should be straight-forward.

The Yahoo! Example

Yahoo! is one of the most successful start-ups in business history; and the two founders, Jerry Yang and David Filo, played it smart. Yahoo! started out with modest funding and grew at a consistent pace. They borrowed some computer equipment from Netscape's Marc Andreessen in exchange for a link to Netscape on Yahoo!'s home page. In early 1995, America Online offered to buy out Yahoo! for $1 million; but instead Yahoo! took $1 million in venture funding from Sequoia Capital in exchange for a stake in the company.

In February 1996, Yahoo! received a follow-up round of $5 million, with Reuters buying 2.5 percent of the company and Softbank, Ziff-Davis, Open Text, and The Capital Group each buying 2.0 percent. At this time, Sequoia had a 25 percent stake, and the founders still had about 21 percent each. Right before the IPO in April, Softbank upped its stake to 37 percent to help give the company more credibility; and to facilitate this, Yang, Filo, CEO Tim Koogle, and Sequoia sold some of their shares to Softbank privately.

On April 12, 1996, Yahoo!'s IPO soared from a $13 offering price to close at $33 on the opening day, making the founders multimillionaires—and eventually billionaires. Everyone up and down the chain of investors was satisfied with their stake and made out fabulously well.

➤ Angels versus VCs

Not everyone follows the same path to success in funding a start-up. Some rely on self-financing early on, while others go with angel investors or venture capitalists or even loans from banks. However, if you don't have a few million bucks lying around and you want to increase your odds for breakout success, you should make sure to take the appropriate investments from the right people at the right time.

Angel investors typically help your start-up with seed money, ranging from a few hundred thousand dollars to a couple million. This new class of investor became more prominent in the 1990s, when the stock markets soared and stock market millionaires were being minted by the tens of thousands. Be sure to use angel money frugally, and don't expect much hand-holding. Most, though not all, angels do not involve themselves in day-to-day matters, preferring instead to remain in the background.

One of the top angel investors, Ron Conway (whose investment group is actually called Angel Investors), explained the role of the angel in a 1999 interview with RedHerring.com. Conway has helped many start-ups, from Ask Jeeves to Broadvision to Concentric. "We're willing to help a company that needs less than $1 million. A top-tier VC won't even consider these companies. They've got bigger fish to fry. So who's going to fund companies that need less than a million bucks? As they are starting out, a million bucks is all a company needs to prove out its idea. And we mentor them through the process to the point where we're ready to introduce them to the VCs. You almost have to think of us as an assembly line, where at any one point we have about 25 of our companies in this pre–VC-funding mode, which is where we are really active. After they get VC funding and they get someone on their board, our activity tapers off."

While Conway is an example of a more dedicated and networked angel investor, many are just in it for a quick investment. It's true that we're probably a bit biased in the Angel versus VC discussion, but it's important to understand exactly what angels bring to the table—and what they don't. You shouldn't use angels in lieu of a VC because they generally don't have the same time commitment to the start-up—they won't see it through its full lifespan. For example, if you decide to get $100,000 chunks from 100 angels instead of getting one lump sum from a VC, you'll have a complex hierarchy of advisers, and few will give you the time and advice you may need.

Instead, let the VCs set the valuation of the company, not the angels. Since VCs usually have more experience in the entire life of the company, they'll understand exactly how to take the company to market. If you let early investors set the valuation and future investors don't agree, it can jeopardize future rounds of funding.

➤ **Equity Tip: Do the Math**

The best route to success is to go directly to a VC, but if you end up taking an angel round, use a bridge loan that converts as a function of the first VC round of funding. For example, when the VC puts money in, the bridge loan converts to equity at a discount (in the 15–50 percent range). So if the VC puts in $10 million and the loan is convertible at a 25 percent discount, then the angel gets $7.5 million in equity. But if the angel offers funding based on its own valuation of the company and then the VC values the company lower than the angel did, someone loses out. The VC won't pay that valuation, and the angel doesn't want to deal with the VC. No one winds up happy, and the funding is put in jeopardy.

Again, the key is to keep it simple, or you'll find yourself in a mess. The ramifications of complicating your equity are possible legal entanglements and protracted proceedings that happen right when your company needs to be running most efficiently. And that might delay crucial funding or a public offering.

■ **THE NO-BAGGAGE RULES OF EQUITY**

With everyone making a grab for equity in your company, it's important to remain conservative and to make smart decisions. Balance is the key, making sure each round of investors gets a fair deal without extracting too much in the process. Follow these six rules of equity to make sure you don't get tripped up with baggage that could burden your company's future:

1. Create a straightforward equity agreement. Remember, the new investor always sets the rules. Draft a simple three-page convertible loan document with an angel, not a detailed contract listing terms (leave that to the VC). Keep clauses as few and as simple as possible.

2. Don't promise any investor that he'll get his money out first. Why not? Because the next investor might demand to get her money out first. Keep all your options open, and don't bet your entire company on one round of funding.

3. Don't promise an investor more equity in the event the company misses its milestones. Let's say you promise someone that you'll give her a higher stake if sales numbers come in lower in the next quarter. That might entice the investor, but it puts her interests at odds with the company's—and then she is not a true investing partner. You want to be working together to meet all company goals.

4. Avoid complicating debt. Don't complicate debt in the early stages of your company. An angel investor might say, "I'll give you a loan, but I want my money back when your next round of funding comes in." That arrangement is dangerous because venture firms might shy away from a company operating under this agreement.

5. Keep the number of early shareholders to a minimum. Too many early investors can get unwieldy, making it hard to reach them and get approvals for key decisions—especially if they haven't had contact with the company on a regular basis.

Say your company is ready to take the big leap and go public. Existing private shareholders must agree to have their shares locked up for six months, so they can't cash out early. If one of these shareholders doesn't sign on, the next shareholder will be less likely to sign, and it snowballs. That might result in an underwriter bailing on the deal. The complexity of having so many shareholders can quickly devolve into minutia that eventually kills your start-up. You're spending precious board time worrying about issues like getting shareholders to approve 2,000 shares for a new employee instead of taking the company to the next level. The result: Right at the time when you need to be running your company at lightspeed, you're in quicksand.

6. Streamline your board. Your board of directors needs to stay lean and mean. If you have too many board members, it makes meetings, decision making, and getting required approvals much slower and more complicated. When it comes time for big decisions on funding, going public, and hiring key execs, for example, you want to act decisively—and promptly.

Avoid Legal Exposure

Some of the most common baggage a start-up will carry is legal expenses. While everyone can use some good advice, you don't want to spend all your time in counsel's chambers. Lawsuits have become a part of the fabric of American life, on a par with mom and apple pie. Let this story about iVillage be a cautionary tale for your start-up:

Right before the women's site iVillage went public in March 1999, two former executives sued the site, claiming that CEO Candace Carpenter reneged on promised stock options. The suits came just as the company was ready to go public, leaving the company unable to respond because it was in an SEC-mandated quiet period.

iVillage did end up with a successful IPO and settled the lawsuits quietly. What remains unknown is just how unsettling the lawsuits were to iVillage morale and how much they hurt both in public relations and in slowing the momentum of the start-up.

■ STAY LEAN

We hope the stories in this chapter will help guide you on the road to start-up success, keeping you traveling light. When you're trying to sprint to market, the last thing you need are complications weighing you down. Make sure to align yourself with good people who can advise you and help you make the smart decisions that will propel you forward.

Checklist for Staying Baggage Free

- ☐ Get professional guidance on prevailing practices so you'll avoid making costly mistakes.
- ☐ Hire a good lawyer to advise on contracts and legal and equity issues in a timely manner.

☐ Fill your board with experienced people to offer guidance on business, organizational, and operations issues. *No uncles on the board!*

☐ Use venture capitalists for advice on equity, valuation, operations, and business strategy. Don't rely too much on angels and early investors for advice outside of their areas of expertise.

■ REFERENCES

Bankrolled by an Angel: *http://www.redherring.com/insider/1999/1215/vc-vcps.html*

Mother, I'm the Boss Now; Internet Executives Hire Their Parents and Traditions Fall, Katie Hafner: nytimes.com archives; fee required, July 2, 2000

Dot.com Moms: *http://www.thestandard.com/article/display/0,1151,18523,00.html*

Biz Men Going to Work for Kids' Dot.coms: *http://promotions.nypost.com/04082000/04052000x/news/2214.htm*

SEC Inquiring into Amazon's Accounting Practices: *http://news.cnet.com/0-1007-200-3285391.html*

iVillage: *http://news.cnet.com/news/0-1005-200-1573129.html http://news.cnet.com/news/0-1005-200-338798.html*

Yahoo! example sources: Hoover's, and Electronic Information Report (Simba) December 1, 1995, found on WSJ.com Publication Library

Part **Two**

Start-up Fundamentals

Chapter

Speed Succeeds

NEILISM: Get profitable fast.

When you start up a technology- or Internet-related business, you're suddenly living on Internet time—which is roughly equivalent to dog years. Get used to it.

Internet time has not just speeded up all aspects of business, but it has also shrunk the margin between success and failure. It's only a slight exaggeration to say that either entrepreneurs must be roadrunners, or they'll quickly become roadkill. There's not much ground left in between anymore. And as the Neilism says, "No good idea goes unpunished." Roughly translated, that means that competitors soon spring up to copy every good idea. If you've got a winning offering, you can be sure other entrepreneurs are hot on your tail. So speed isn't just helpful, it's essential to reaching—and staying in—the success zone. And speed isn't just a mode of operating; it's a way of thinking.

If your idea is one that can't move quickly from shadow to spotlight, it may be worthy but not a good fit for the Internet economy. What a 3G start-up needs, even with the now-longer road to an IPO, is an entrepreneur able to leap several obstacles—financial, organizational, and technological—in a single bound. Time waits for no one. In an environment where capital is harder to find and investors are more impatient, you need to move quickly just to survive. Faster than a speeding bullet? Maybe not. But you have to be fast enough to dodge the bullets that will surely come your way. In the current start-up climate, speed may no longer be the only game, but it is still an essential factor in reaching the success zone.

Speed, Smarts, and Simplicity

In the second generation you just had to be fast. In 3G you need to be fast, you need to be smart, and you need to keep things simple. These three fundamental principles are requirements today.

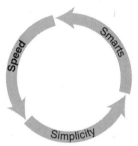

The spiral collapses if any one principle in the equation is missing. When these three parts merge in an organic whole, you can be sure that your start-up is targeted for the success zone.

■ WHY SPEED MATTERS

- The Internet immediately gives your business high-speed, direct, interactive access to a potentially huge customer base.
- Customers provide feedback instantaneously—and cheaply.
- Good ideas attract competitors fast.
- A competitor can steal your customers (not to mention employees and investors) as quickly as you acquired them. Another Neilism: "Your competition is just one mouse click away."

The "zero barriers" environment of the Net accelerates the process of innovation, competition, and, in fact, the business cycle itself to an entirely new level. Time may have been on the Rolling Stones' side, but it's not on yours. Or perhaps more accurately, it's not on your side if you squander it. But if you learn to turn it to your advantage, you'll find that it gives you a powerful competitive edge against your competition.

In 1995 when 2G start-ups such as NetCom and Netscape led the way to the commercialization of the Net, they quickly prompted the growth of a large pool of ready capital. This meant that practically any start-up could get funded, regardless of whether it had a viable business model. Ironically, there's even more capital available for 3G start-ups, but the threshold for getting funding is higher. Your value proposition must be viable, and no amount of enthusiasm or charisma will help you if it's not. Acquiring "eyeballs," for example, won't do you much good unless those eyeballs have dollar signs in them. The question that VCs, angels, employees, and, ultimately, the market will ask is whether your offering is capable of generating enough actual revenue within a reasonable length of time.

But what is a "reasonable length of time"? It may differ according to a start-up's particular circumstances. One thing is certain: It can't be too long, or you will miss your market opportunity. Let's put speed into the context of the new economic environment. Speed is an essential component in achieving your goals, but it's not an end in itself. The time line to an IPO has changed significantly since the dot.com crash of 2000 (see Table 9.1). In the third generation of start-ups, instead of living by the mantra of GBF (Get Big Fast), the new approach is GPF (Get Profitable Fast)! No matter what the business environment is at a given moment, any start-up must have a business model and a strategy that *fits* that environment.

■ SPEED FORCES FOCUS

A start-up that makes speed a key strategy says, "We can't hire enough people right now to create a product with all of the features it might include, but we can single out the one feature that customers want most and quickly build that one feature to gain market

Table 9.1 New speed rules for 3G start-ups.

	1G	2G	3G
Years	1970–1994	1995–2000	2001 and beyond
Era	Before commercialization of the Internet	After Netcom went public	After dot.com crash
Time to IPO	5 years	2 years	3.5 years
Speed Rule	Growth with profits	Get big fast—grow at all costs	Get profitable fast—grow within costs

share." Rather than just trying to do things faster, these companies do things in a way that makes them achieve their goals faster. This approach might be called "speeding to success."

Adding another neat but nonessential feature into a product that doesn't significantly help customers or make them more interested in buying your product actually slows you down. You'll lose time developing—and debugging—the extraneous feature. And you'll slow your customers down as well, because they'll have one more feature they have to learn to use. Because speed dictates that you focus your efforts, you're forced to build only the features customers most want and need.

Another bonus of the speed strategy's imperative to focus your efforts is that it'll be easier for you to communicate your value proposition to customers. For instance, if your offering consists of one essential thing that you do better than anybody, you can easily highlight that feature and create an entire ad campaign around it, as opposed to advertising a feature-laden offering that tries to offer something for everyone. Customers will more quickly understand who you are and the benefit you offer them. Speed forces you to take not just the shortest path to success but also the smartest one.

■ SPEED CREATES DEMANDS

1. *Action.* Speed demands three things of any business. You need to act fast to put an idea into action. Today's start-ups don't allow for

the months of planning common in a traditional, offline business—or for massive miscalculations that are months in the making, as in the case of Boo.com (see sidebar "Formula for Failure: Slowness Plus Stupidity"). If you're going to make mistakes in 3G, you'd better move fast and fail fast so you have the time and resources to correct your course.

2. *Agility.* Not only do you need to put your plans into action fast, but you also need to react nimbly to changes in your competitive landscape, the overall business environment, and new technological innovations—even your own missteps. You must constantly evaluate your position and be ready to turn on a dime, if necessary. Sometimes, smart speed means stopping in your tracks and making a 180-degree turn.

3. *Attraction.* Speed succeeds because it forces you to do the things that will attract customers, employees, and partners quickly. A great new offering with a visionary founder will attract employees, partners, and investors. These people and financial resources will in turn enable you to create products that attract more customers quickly, in effect creating an ever-increasing cycle of attraction—or what we call a "virtuous spiral." In the Lightspeed Economy, speed is the difference between attracting people and not attracting them at all.

Sense and Respond

When you're developing your business, ask yourself whether you're taking advantage of "sense and respond." Sense and respond means that you are effectively in touch with 100 percent of your customers. You can communicate with every one of them very inexpensively.

"Because of the Internet, all of a sudden you have two-way communication with all of your customers, which means you can do manufacturing-forward versus customer-backward development of your product. You can adjust the business based on real-time feedback. You can build Web sites or

(continued)

business processes that take real-time feedback and adjust the business based on what customers want. So the new way to do business is 'sense and respond' versus 'make and sell.' This responsiveness is key to being more successful than your competitors."

—*Bill Gross, from a speech, October 22, 2000,*
New York City

■ SPEEDY STRATEGIES

In this 3G environment, there are many strategies you need to adopt in order to thrive. Here are four strategies that use speed to help you achieve your goals:

• *Proactive—Create speed.* Understand that speed doesn't simply mean getting people to do the same work faster (that sort of speed doesn't offer you a competitive advantage—your competitor could do the same). Instead, creating speed means setting the bar higher for competitors, even redefining the competitive environment, and forcing them to react to you, just as Netscape did in its early days. Unfortunately, Microsoft outmarketed them (even competed unfairly, many would say) by improving Internet Explorer faster than Netscape improved Navigator and by giving Internet Explorer away for free. Microsoft acted with great speed and used its marketing muscle, fairly or not, to force Netscape to cry uncle. This is why one of the "New Economy's" poster children is now just another cog in the AOL Time Warner wheel.

• *Strategic Hiring.* Even though hiring may slow you down at the moment, strategic hires will be the key to moving fast and achieving your milestones, so you must hire the best people you can without spending too much time looking. Can't find the right people? Use headhunters. Pay referral bonuses. One way or the other, don't stand still. Keep moving toward the success zone. By speeding to success, you make your offering and your company more attractive to the best available talent. This is the "Attraction Economy." People leave start-ups for better ones, ones that will make a big impact and that will survive over the long haul. The days of employees jumping ship for any flash-in-the-pan are over. Often, not even simply offering them more money is sufficient incentive to lure great people to a mediocre start-up. But if they perceive your business as fast, agile, and dynamic, they will call you. Now more than ever, the companies that reach the success zone fastest will attract the smartest people.

• *Perpetual Experimentation*. Don't try to go from start-up to established operation in one fell swoop; experiment in smaller but faster steps. The first-generation strategy for creating an offering was to "build and distribute," meaning to conceive of an idea and go build the whole thing before presenting it to customers for feedback. Even software giants released extremely buggy products to a public who tolerated problems and who actually helped the manufacturer detect and fix bugs. 2G start-ups taught us to experiment in smaller bites and to constantly iterate. That's even more true in 3G.

• *Sense and Respond*. A powerful 3G strategy is, in Bill Gross's phrase, "sense and respond." In this approach, a company immediately starts talking to customers to get feedback, both before and during the design process. Customers can help you design your product in more ways than you can possibly think of alone, and they can point out more bugs than you can ever test for. As Bill Joy, Sun Microsystems' chief technologist, puts it: "Most of the smart people in the world don't work at Sun." In other words, no matter how many smart employees a company has (and Sun has plenty), they still represent a tiny fraction of the total pool of brainiacs out there in the world. So take advantage of all the smart people at your disposal— namely, your customers, partners, and anyone else—and get their feedback. Constant experimentation—trying a million different things, analyzing customer patterns, gathering information on user habits, asking questions, and so on—produces the little innovations that can add up to real success in marketing a new offering. This can provide a real competitive edge—if you do it fast. It will force competitors to respond to you. And if you act often enough and quickly enough, competitors will be too busy playing defense to ever catch up with or surpass you. This strategy is really a blend of speed and smarts. It's using speed to get to the right decisions faster than your competition.

Formula for Failure: Slowness Plus Stupidity

In the Lightspeed Economy, speed doesn't kill—sluggishness and stupidity do. Boo.com is a case in point. Its founders, Ernst Malmsten and Kajsa Leander, didn't know it, but Boo.com was doomed from the very beginning. Despite all of the press attention and the enormous piles of money investors threw at the online fashion play, Boo took too long to develop a Web site that actually worked. In fact, the company spent one full year building its site without testing it on customers. When it finally debuted, Boo.com bombed because it was too slow and cumbersome.

The Boo.com Web site was ambitious, but complex. It featured rich 3D graphics, multiple languages and currency conversions, and a host of other features, including an animated character called Ms. Boo, whose hair style (and color) kept changing at the whim of founder (and former model) Leander. All of these factors slowed down not only the site itself, but also any progress the company might have made in other areas more vital to its success. None of these features focused on what was needed to achieve success. Prior to its launch, no one at Boo.com bothered to test the site on prospective users who could have identified problems well in advance. Boo.com's launch was finally delayed from summer 1999 until the following November. Investors grumbled but could do little: Management controlled most of the board seats.

Another way in which Boo wasted time, as well as money and internal resources, was by developing much of its own technology in-house. Rather than save time by outsourcing efforts the customer would never see, Boo devised its own Internet platform and customer-fulfillment system from scratch. *Business 2.0* magazine reported that one investor who took a pass said, "It was like they were trying to build a Mercedes-Benz by hand."

■ SMART SPEED (BECAUSE TIME ISN'T ON YOUR SIDE)

Speed in entering the marketplace is essential. Moving quickly is always necessary when you're running on Internet time. But the much-vaunted first-mover advantage isn't always a guarantee of success. Sometimes it's better (and smarter) to be a fast follower.

While the ideal scenario may be to be an eBay and create a whole new market, with no competitors, fast followers can also succeed. For example, AskJeeves, a search engine with a difference (you can ask questions in plain English and get more-targeted results), became a search engine that could *make* a difference. AskJeeves did it despite entering a market in 1996 that already had more search engines—Excite, Yahoo!, and dozens more—than you could click a mouse at.

Another example of smart speed is Yahoo!. Why did Yahoo! succeed when so many others failed? Yahoo! used a combination of speed (the company's smallness was an advantage that enabled it to move nimbly) and smarts (it had bright people who were engaged by ideas). It also fit the environment (2G) within which it had to function, and it had a work ethic that became the norm in Silicon Valley (chain yourself to your computer until problems are solved). Also, Yahoo! was able to use the considerable charisma of its founders and a generous distribution of equity to attract smart people, including a CEO who could implement the founders' vision in a more mature, much larger organization. And when Yahoo! floundered in 2001, it quickly moved to replace Koogle with new CEO Terry Semel. In 2G, at least just to get funded, you didn't have to be smarter, just faster. Yahoo! anticipated the 3G environment by being smart and fast. It's this combination that will prove successful for start-ups in the current environment.

■ FASTER *AND* SMARTER

Here's an important part of what we mean by *smart speed*: It means you actually do smart things to make yourself faster. It doesn't mean your programmers write computer code faster; it means doing things that get better results sooner. We'll talk about this in more detail in Chapter 13, Scenario Analysis.

In addition to making you more agile, another way that speed leads to success is by helping you quickly clarify what works and what doesn't (see Table 9.2). If a particular project isn't coming together quickly enough, it may mean that the strategy behind it, rather than merely the execution, is flawed. Drugstore.com, for example, may find that not enough people really want to buy aspirin online and that the cost of shipping to individuals is much higher than traditional means of distribution, namely stores. If that happens, the company will have to quickly reevaluate its business. Your customers save you considerable time and money by voting with their mice. They will quickly teach you what works—and pays.

■ STAYING IN THE SPEED ZONE

Once your start-up has entered the speed zone, staying there is your next major challenge. It's all too easy to fall out if you lose focus.

Table 9.2 Success in the speed zone.

Creating Speed	Speed Killers
Sense and respond.	Build and deliver.
Building only what customers want.	Build what you *think* customers want.
Act and react quickly.	Slow down because of internal conflicts, poor execution, and inexperienced management.
Deliver products on time.	Take too much time in product development.
Quickly hire great people.	Hire on the slow track.
Do whatever it takes to reach your milestones.	Be complacent; miss milestones.
Make decisions quickly.	Take months to decide.
Close deals swiftly.	Negotiate for weeks.

Obstacles will always conspire to slow you down; and if you let them, they will. Review your situation periodically, perhaps every six months. If you wait longer than that, it may be too late to get back up to speed.

Even a seeming advantage, like having more funding than you need, can turn into a disadvantage that will slow you down—if you're not vigilant. If you have too much money to burn, you might spend far too much time developing your technology, only to find that someone else has stolen the market from you before you've even launched.

One such company was PowerAgent, which beginning in 1994 raised $15 million, more than enough cash to sustain operations for the time it would take to release its first product and become profitable. Their generous funding led to failure because it encouraged PowerAgent to initiate a massive development effort while ignoring the changes taking place in the market and the competitors that were ramping up and forging ahead of it. If you have a start-up idea and your plan is to spend the next year developing it, this is a recipe for failure. The sooner you can get something to market, the sooner you will get customer feedback that will let you respond to actual market conditions rather than to theories about the market and your customers.

■ DON'T DO IT

If anything your start-up initiates slows you down, *stop* doing it, whether it's developing new features, spending too much time in meetings, or attending too many trade shows or business conferences. If you don't, you are likely to slip out of the speed zone.

Whatever business issue you encounter, always ask yourself, "Right now, will the action I take speed us up, slow us down, or enable us to be faster in the future?" If it slows you down, don't do it. If it speeds you up, go at it, even amplify it. If it will enable you to be faster in the future, consider it carefully; and if you decide to act, make sure you strike at the right moment.

➤ Speed: Because Success Is Your Only Option

Successful start-ups are about speed, because at each step in the sequencing of your business, speed pays off big. Use speed to your advantage. Innovate your offering. Try something. In the Lightspeed Economy, feedback is immediate and inexpensive. If it works, you're in the success zone. If it doesn't, you have the time and the resources to do something else. Besides, in the current environment, if you can, you must!

Keep in mind that if you don't use speed to your advantage, it won't matter in six months—either your start-up gets to the next stage or it becomes the living dead. And most important, use speed to your advantage because everything else follows. Doing things in a way that makes them fast also both makes them right for other benefits and achieves the business goal.

➤ Keep Goals in Focus

What, exactly, *is* the business goal? Where are we speeding *to*? Remember that a key strategy in thinking about your business is to define your goals and work backward. The goal of a start-up is to attract people—customers, employees, investors, and partners. Growth of a business is nothing more or less than attracting more and more customers. Speed not only attracts more people more quickly, but in the Lightspeed Economy speed is the difference between attracting people or not attracting them at all.

In this third generation of start-ups, the obstacles to success are greater than ever. Budding entrepreneurs will no longer be able to sketch out a business plan on a napkin and be funded overnight by greedy investors who are too busy making deals to ask questions. And because the margin between success and failure is so slim, the need for speed is even greater. As the Neilism says, "Success is the only option."

Why Smarts Make
All the Difference

NEILISM: Mediocrity breeds mediocrity.

Contrary to the claims of the envious, there is no such thing as entrepreneurial dumb luck. The "millionaire next door" may have been in the right place at the right time, but he likely got there with a great idea and hard work. And it takes smarts to build on that initial success and stay in the game. Smarts are fundamental to success because true business intelligence touches every part of a start-up—from its founders to its employees, from choosing the right board of directors to implementing the right financial strategy. Start-ups that succeed have leaders who use their heads, while continuing to move quickly to press—and to enhance—the market opportunity within their grasp.

The speeded-up, connected environment of technology and Internet-related businesses has heightened the self-reinforcing quality of smarts: Smart actions can quickly compound to propel a start-up into the success zone. Conversely, unsmart moves can just as quickly propel you out of it. And operating in the success zone is really a combination of making the smartest decisions, which are usually the simplest ones, and moving quickly to execute them.

Speed, Smarts, and Simplicity

In the second generation (2G) you just had to be fast. In the third generation (3G) you need to be fast, you need to be smart, and you need to keep things simple. These three fundamental principles are requirements today.

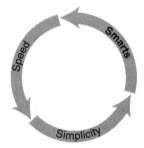

The spiral collapses if any one principle in the equation is missing. When these three parts merge in an organic whole, you can be sure that your start-up is targeted for the success zone.

■ A PERSON WHO AIMS AT NOTHING IS SURE TO HIT IT

Defining just what *smarts* means in this context of a speeded-up, connected environment is a challenging proposition. After all, we all like to think we're smart. But put into practice, smarts is an elusive mix of qualities. It means having the clarity of mind to make tough choices quickly, acting on a combination of information and intuition, marketing your idea with savvy and style, developing key business relationships in the shortest possible time, and being able to turn on a dime when circumstances demand it. These kinds of qualities reflect the sum total of your experience, your personality, and your ambition. Above all, you need to have what the first President Bush famously lacked: the "vision thing." Like the anonymous saying in the heading of this section says, if you don't aim at anything you're guaranteed to hit it. Knowing where you are going is the most important step in getting there. It focuses your attention on doing only the most necessary things you need to do to enter the success zone.

Here in more detail are some of the key factors in developing start-up smarts.

■ SMART LEADERSHIP

At the core of this concept is a founder who is able to attract other smart people. If a start-up depends on a lone-wolf entrepreneur who can't attract colleagues as smart as or smarter than he or she is, then it's doomed to fail. But smarts is about more than having an off-the-charts IQ. It's about more than reading all the right books or having a degree from Harvard Business School. Smarts is about shrewd judgment. It's about making the best possible decisions in the shortest amount of time. Smarts is about having an unquenchable passion to build a business and the ability to communicate that passion to others.

Take a look at successful entrepreneurs for role models. From Thomas Edison in the nineteenth century to the entrepreneurial pioneers of today, there are thousands of men and women who have focused all their energy and brainpower on a nascent company and brought it to life. Think about Jim Clark, founder of Silicon Graphics, Netscape, and Healtheon (now WebMD); Sandra Lerner and Leonard Bosack, founders of Cisco Systems; Steve Case, founder of AOL; Jeff Bezos, founder of Amazon; Steve Jobs, founder of Apple Computer; Marc Andreessen, founder of Netscape and Loudcloud; Kim Polese, founder of Marimba; Scott McNealy, founder of Sun Microsystems; Larry Ellison, founder of Oracle; and, of course, Bill Gates and Paul Allen, founders of Microsoft. Each entrepreneur used smarts to make his or her start-up succeed.

Larry Ellison and Bill Gates provide good examples of start-up smarts in action. Gates was certainly in the right place at the right time, but he was also smart enough to capitalize—in more ways than one—on the opening IBM left to the then-embryonic Microsoft by giving Gates a free hand to relicense MS-DOS, the operating system that began Microsoft's rise to U.S. (and global) business dominance. Gates was smart enough to see a window of opportunity open and then squeeze through it before anyone realized he was doing it.

Sometimes known as "the other billionaire" (as opposed to the less flamboyant but better known Gates), Ellison was smart enough to recognize the opportunity in the unglamorous database business and to make his company a cash cow that more exciting companies would come to envy. According to Bill Rosenblatt, writing in the *Unix Insider*, like Gates, Ellison took advantage of a monumental IBM mistake. "For Ellison," writes Rosenblatt, "IBM's missed opportunity was the now-standard relational database model and its associated programming language, SQL."

Relational databases aren't as exciting as the "killer apps (applications)" in other areas of high tech, but they are critical to the performance of businesses, large and small, around the world. IBM, a monolithic corporation, took its time developing database applications and languages; Oracle beat them to market by being smart enough to see speed as the key factor in capturing a market that was hungry for solutions.

Rosenblatt attributes Ellison's success to "fuzziness"; and this quality is a great example of the kind of smarts this chapter advocates: "The computer field is a curious dichotomy of solid and fuzzy," says Rosenblatt. "The solid part has been there from the beginning: It consists of things like engineering, materials, precision, processes, skill, science, and facts. But at some point, fuzziness began to creep in—things like gut instinct, creativity, elusiveness, hype, rumor, FUD (fear, uncertainty, and doubt), and wishful thinking. Larry Ellison was one of the first people in the computer business to give fuzziness a prominent role in the way his company worked and how it dealt with its customers. Thus, he changed the industry forever. Ellison knew instinctively that in a world where everything changes constantly and there's far too much information to assimilate, much less validate as fact, the right kind of fuzziness is a serious competitive advantage."

Of Gates and Ellison—both of whom have their critics—Ellison's fuzzy smarts are closer to the model of leadership appropriate for a 3G start-up. Ellison's brand of smarts consists of self-reinforcing moves—such as using speed to unseat a much larger, more powerful rival and thereby redefine the competitive landscape—that can spiral a company into the success zone.

■ SMART PEOPLE

You hire smart people quickly because that in itself is the smart thing to do. Why? Because they in turn attract other smart people. Smart people sense opportunity and are eager to join others who are smart enough to see what they see. As you can imagine, this strategy creates a self-reinforcing set of actions that propels a start-up toward its goals. The start-up becomes compelling and generates a momentum of its own; and soon investors, employees, and customers gravitate to it.

Always hire the smartest people you can find. It sounds self-evident, but it can be tricky in practice. In a start-up you're so busy expanding and running your business at lightspeed that it can seem more expedient to just hire the B player for a position that needs filling fast. After all, that person seems fine—not exciting, but competent enough. But beware: This solution to a short-term problem will create a bigger long-term problem. As soon as you start injecting mediocrity into the organization, especially in key roles, the sharp people lose confidence in their leaders. They become less attracted to the business. Conversely, the mediocre people tend to be intimidated by excellence, so they discourage excellence from joining the company. Avoid introducing mediocrity into the system in the first place because it spreads like a virus. Like the Neilism says, "Mediocrity breeds mediocrity."

➤ A Recruiting Problem Is Really a Company Problem

A quick way to know you're not hiring the best people is if you have trouble recruiting new talent. Over the past few years, lots of companies listed as one of their top challenges hiring high-quality employees. To be sure, in the 2G environment even the best companies found recruiting to be highly competitive, but the best job candidates are always going to end up working somewhere—and it's always the best companies that get them. A recruiting problem is actually a company problem. For example, say the company can't attract smart vice presidents. With all other things being equal, meaning the pay is competitive and the equity package is attractive, then either the company's story isn't compelling enough or the company's CEO isn't strong enough to attract smart VPs. To turn this trend around, you have to be smart enough to pinpoint the problem and address it fast. Unsuccessful companies fail to do this. They march along complaining about how tough it is to hire, and they fail to see the situation as a symptom of a bigger problem. Smart start-ups will identify and solve the problem with alacrity.

When a start-up is having problems recruiting and the entrepreneur thinks that offering more stock options will solve the problem, that's almost always wrong. Not only can that hurt the start-up (see Chapter 6), but it also misses the point. The problem isn't stock options. If the company has a good business idea—and the smarts to communicate it—then it has a good story, one that will have people clamoring to climb aboard. Employees want to work for companies they are excited about (and that they feel are likely to succeed over the long run); and employees tend to make fewer demands—monetary or otherwise—than they would with companies they don't really believe in. If the entrepreneur simply throws more equity at the problem, the smart job candidate will still turn it down, recognizing that scads of equity in a mediocre company is still a losing proposition. What you need is a better product offering or a better CEO—or whatever the problem is—not an offer of more equity.

➤ Trickle-Down Smarts

The smarts of the people sitting on the board of directors can make a huge difference, too. Start-up boards of directors are not like those of traditional companies that have big names on the board but are less operationally focused. Often populated by advisers (such as VCs) with experience building businesses fast, the start-up's directors are key players in a start-up's success strategy. If the entrepreneur is smart and chooses them wisely, these people aren't cronies. They aren't fat cats with more money than brains. And they aren't friends and relatives given seats to fill out a list or to repay an early financial favor. Your board of directors can—and should—be one of your best resources in building a successful company.

In the start-up universe, the board meeting is a catalyst for success. It's a regularly scheduled event used to address strategic issues facing the company. You're assembling some of the smartest and most experienced minds you can find, and you're asking them how to solve problems and address issues vital to the company: "Do we spend money on advertising? Should we spend more money on new hires? What are customers really interested in? What are the three most important things we need to accomplish in the next 90 days?"

The purpose of the board meeting is not merely fiduciary oversight. The purpose is also to help you execute as smartly as possible and to anticipate problems *before* they become problems. Your board is as important as the programming code that makes your Web site function. In fact, it may be more important. It's critical to remember, however, that you should never lose control of the board. The CEO makes company policy; the purpose of the board is to advise the CEO. If you invite VCs onto your board and they take control, that's a signal that both you and the company are in deep trouble. A good VC will not even think about intervening unless a company in its portfolio is in danger of going under or is fundamentally flawed.

■ SMART MOVES

In the fast-moving Lightspeed Economy, the business model you began with may turn out to be wrong months or even weeks after it seemed as if it was going to work. The environment changes quickly. One year e-tailing was in vogue. Then it wasn't. In another year it was broadband. No can predict with certainty what will work or what turns technology and business trends will take. But smart entrepreneurs spot the trends and act on them more quickly.

For instance, ad-based consumer Web sites that were smart anticipated that they would need to retool their business models long before the limitations of that model were clear to most people. One such start-up is Ditto.com, a visual search engine that quickly realized that its real market was in licensing or selling its technology to other Web sites as a business-to-business (B2B) offering. Another example is OneBuild, which began as an online exchange for materials procurement in the construction industry. The company quickly realized that its business model was not scaling quickly enough and switched to building private exchanges for construction industry giants—the very companies that had questioned the viability of its earlier business model. OneBuild now calls itself an e-market enabler for the construction industry. Major construction industry players such as Bethlehem Steel and Butler Builders quickly backed OneBuild in its new incarnation.

Acting on anticipated problems, challenges, and opportunities is never easy. It requires taking action on something that hasn't actually happened yet. A start-up must make educated guesses about the market, based on experience and judgment, and about what is likely to happen when it implements its plan. "Smarts" means anticipating changes in the market and then acting to correct any problems that arise after the offering is launched.

This is not to say that the discipline of picking a goal and staying with it isn't a good thing. But it is absolutely necessary to be adaptable and flexible as the ground begins to shift beneath you—as it always will in the Internet terrain.

Jeff Hawkins, who invented the Palm Pilot (and later Handspring's Visor), has a habit of making smart moves. In 1999, *U.S. News & World Report* told the story of how Jeff, when he was developing the Palm Pilot (and rapidly running out of capital), made the smart moves that turned Palm into one of the most successful start-ups in history. James Lardner, writing in *U.S. News*, described how the Newton, Apple's attempt at marketing a pen-based, handheld computer, had failed miserably, despite Apple's stellar track record in selling hardware. "Hawkins, by contrast," he wrote, "was a nobody—a software guy who had branched out into hardware because nobody else had been willing to build the device he had conceived."

Under pressure to add a number of features, Hawkins reimagined handhelds as "connected organizers" without the bells and whistles that made what were essentially small PCs too complicated for the market. He knew the value of the product was in its simplicity, so he stayed with his vision, resisted the advice he was getting to load it up with features—like sound—and instead positioned the Palm Pilot as an extension of the PC, rather than a replacement. With the advent of the Palm, professionals in all areas of business could easily take critical information from their desktop PCs with them on the road. Suddenly Hawkins's idea began to take off.

As Donna Dubinsky, Hawkins's partner at both Palm and Handspring, tells it, "I think the real breakthrough in thinking was to say, 'Let's stop thinking about this as a little miniature computer and start thinking about it as an accessory and complement to the PC.' As soon as you started thinking of it as an accessory to the PC, you started designing a whole bunch of things very differently."

According to *U.S. News*, "Palm could lay claim to the most successful product launch in consumer-electronics history. It has also played a major role in igniting a backlash against computer complexity."

Get the Girls, and the Boys Will Show Up

In the start-up world, the elements of speed and surprise are two key advantages that fledgling companies have over established players. And one frequently successful strategy is surprising the market by defying the conventional wisdom. One company that is having more success than anyone might have anticipated is Vault.com, a job board with a difference. Vault had enough smarts to successfully enter an already crowded field with a gutsy new idea. Turning on its head the notion that the customer rules (the customer being the employer), Vault created a chance for disgruntled employees to dish it out to their employers in a highly trafficked message board section: "Company X is stupid because . . ." Start-up Y will never succeed because . . ."

Vault is a New York-based company started by a gruff entrepreneur who pushed just the right button to gain attention from thousands, perhaps millions, of employees who were not happy where they worked. Most observers would naturally think that a successful offering in this space would have to be respectful of employers—they would, after all, be paying to have jobs for their companies posted on the Web site. The last thing you would think they'd want to do is patronize a site where people were railing about how much their employer sucked. Most observers, as it turns out, would have been wrong!

This is because conventional wisdom is often wrong. And

(continued)

Vault was smart enough to understand and act on this insight. The Vault innovation became an almost cultlike obsession for some users. Great numbers of people enjoyed seeing the nasty things employees were saying about their companies—and others—and saw it as a means of judging company morale and making their own decisions about which companies were good places to work.

The appropriate Neilism is: "Get the girls, and the boys will show up." Employers will post jobs on the sites that attract the most users. Vault attracted a lot of readers, particularly those who were likely to be interested in changing jobs. If you needed to hire people, you'd want to be there. And that's what has happened. Vault captivated the imagination of the market and tapped a latent desire people might not even have known they had. It's a simple value proposition: "Come here and say where it is terrible to work." Vault spent very little money creating content for the site because the content is generated by end users who actually feel empowered by doing it. The measure of its success is that employers call Vault, not the other way around. Vault doesn't even need a direct sales organization. They have gotten off to a great start and are headed for the success zone.

■ SMART STRATEGIES

Smart people often devise clever ways to reach their goals. Here are a few tried-and-true ideas of smart strategies.

- Surround yourself with smart people and listen to them.
- Install a hands-on, operationally experienced CEO early on.
- Choose board members who can identify problems for you before they manifest (hint: your uncle is probably not the right person for this task).
- Assemble a smart management team—people who are smarter than you are in particular areas.

- Be externally aware—know your business and how it fits into the larger business landscape.

- Pick a successful company to emulate—and emulate it!

- Adopt the best practices of successful start-ups.

- Look outside your current competitors to anticipate challenges from other types of businesses—this is where sea changes usually come from.

- Experiment and innovate—identifying dead ends quickly enough is the next best thing to avoiding them entirely.

- Be customer-centric—your customers can help you find just the right path to success if you listen to them carefully.

■ IT'S ALL SPIRALS: THE COMPOUNDING EFFECT OF SMARTS

As always, speed and smarts work together. When enough of the actions designed to take you into the success zone converge, what we call a "virtuous spiral" is created. Speed and smarts are two of any virtuous spiral's most important elements. Hire people fast, and they can hire more people, and your company will grow the way it needs to grow to succeed. This is fast and smart. Hire A players, and they will hire other A players. These are the people who will make your offering the best it can be. And a great offering makes your company more successful, which in turn attracts more A players. And on it goes.

Of course, not all spirals are virtuous. The vicious spiral everyone has heard about will hurt your start-up as much as a virtuous one will help it. For instance, C players will hire other C players. If you hire low, those hires will hire even lower. Soon, that mediocrity will show up in your offering, affecting your ability to attract customers and, therefore, the health of your business. With a mediocre business, you won't attract the top talent. Or say you're not disciplined in applying your compensation schedule consistently throughout the company. Employees will inevitably find out how much the others receive and will ask for more. If you give it to them, then others come and ask for even more. And downward goes the spiral.

■ SMARTS IN THE 3G ENVIRONMENT

The post-dot.com era of start-ups has added another layer to the definition of *smarts*. Smarts means taking the long view with your business (even while *acting* quickly, as the Lightspeed Economy demands), taking pride in working smarter and harder, and being more patient in terms of waiting for the work to pay off. In other words, the smart, successful entrepreneur is the one who fits into this new environment, who's in it for the long haul, and who has the passion to build a strong, successful, important company.

■ REFERENCES

The "Other" Billionaire: *http://www.unixinsider.com/swol-06-1999/swol-06-bookshelf.html*

How Palm Beat Microsoft: *http://www.salon.com/21st/feature1998/09/17feature.html*

PC Rebels Are Gaining: How Jeff Hawkins's Palm Pilot Changed Computing: *http://www.usnews.com/usnews/issue/990322/22comm.htm*

Chapter 11

Keep It Simple

NEILISM: *"Einstein said, 'Everything should be as simple as possible, but no simpler.'"*

The best ideas in the Lightspeed Economy are the simple ones. If it takes you too long to explain your business to venture capitalists, journalists, employees, prospective customers—or your mom for that matter—it's probably too complicated to succeed.

If you don't keep things simple, you can't move fast, and, by our definition, you're not being smart. This imperative extends to every part of your business: your offering, your organization, your business model, your strategy, and your equity. Always ask yourself before you make a decision, Is this the best, most direct way to go? Is it uncomplicated? Is it the quickest way to jump from one business milestone to the next? If what you're doing doesn't meet these criteria, then you are likely to find yourself on the outside of the success zone looking in.

But let's be clear about what we mean by *simplicity*. Simple is not the same as being "simple-minded." In fact, simplicity demands a high level of sophistication. As Einstein knew, one of the basic principles of science is that you should look to solve a problem by coming up with the simplest solution you can find. Simplicity is a way of understanding the world. It's an enlightened approach to a challenging environment. It helps untie the Gordian knot of complexity that often plagues start-ups. Finally, it's a kind of discipline. It helps you to do only what really matters and to do those few necessary things in the quickest possible way. The simple solution is the most elegant. Starting a new venture is like negotiating a minefield. There are hidden obstacles at every step; but if you have a simple map to guide you, you can avoid being blown away by the complexities of the terrain.

Start-ups must marshal six different components—offering, opportunity, organization, strategy, equity, and technology—each of which involves issues that are bewilderingly numerous and unfamiliar. Because of this complexity, perhaps it's not surprising that a hundred start-ups come and go for every one that succeeds. And those that do succeed are the few that act on the insight that the complexity of starting a new business can and must be made into a simple process.

Speed, Smarts, and Simplicity

In 2G you just had to be fast. In 3G you need to be fast, you need to be smart, and you need to keep things simple. These three fundamental principles are requirements today.

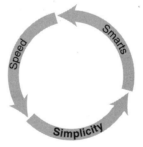

The spiral collapses if any one principle in the equation is missing. When these three parts merge in an organic whole, you can be sure that your start-up is targeted for the success zone.

■ SIMPLIFY YOUR OFFERING

By keeping it simple, you can develop your ideas faster and with fewer resources. Again, the example of Jeff Hawkins is instructive. When he left Palm to start Handspring, he had the idea for a PDA (personal digital assistant) that could double as a cell phone. He called this concept the "smart phone," and it became the Visor, a handheld with an expansion module that allows it to be used as a phone. As with the Palm Pilot, simplicity was the key to the Visor's success. Hawkins knew that his product would end up in the back of the drawer for many customers unless it "felt natural" and was easy to use. It wouldn't meet Jeff's criterion of simplicity if it required training sessions or consulting instructional manuals before it could be used.

eWeek described Jeff's way of working: "According to Hawkins, the price you pay to build a smart product is to risk looking stupid for awhile. . . . So he tried it himself with a block of wood. 'I'd go around the office answering phone calls on this block of wood,' [Hawkins] said. 'It felt OK . . . that's why the Visor has a microphone.'

'People had their doubts about the smart phone,' he said. 'But I already knew it would be OK because I tried it.' In the same vein, Hawkins believes voice-recognition software on handhelds will be a flop: 'I've tried pretending using voice recognition on a handheld and it doesn't feel right,' he said."

True, Hawkins's test group was a group of one, but he has the track record to justify his instincts. The point is that he fashioned his offering by focusing like a laser on what the customer wanted and how the customer would use the product. Anything that didn't support those simple goals was immediately abandoned.

Your offering must pass the simplicity test. By keeping your efforts customer-centric, you will likely create the best possible offering you can.

■ SIMPLIFY YOUR ORGANIZATION

By keeping the structure of your organization simple, you can move faster. The more complex your company, the slower it moves. If you keep it simple, communication is easier. So are implementation and follow-up.

Keep the company housed under a single roof if at all possible. Although e-mail makes communications faster, there is nothing as compelling and motivating to a staff as having a start-up housed together. Not only are you able to communicate quickly, but you can walk around and speak to the people who are making your start-up a success.

In the uniquely close and charged atmosphere of a start-up, a lot of important relationships develop on the fly between employees and across departments. An impromptu conversation can quickly turn into a meeting at which valuable information is exchanged. It's no accident that veteran employees of start-ups that have matured into established companies often lament the passing of "the old days" when they knew everyone in the company and could drop by anyone's office on the way to the kitchen and chat. Easy access prevents a lot of miscommunications.

A close and collegial atmosphere also fosters the spirit and the passion that are two of the greatest advantages a start-up has over more established companies. As soon as you start to divide your organization with multiple locations, too many departments, and too many layers of management, you introduce complexity and division that will undermine communication and morale throughout the organization.

Over time, organizations *inevitably* get bigger and more complex—you accumulate obstacles like a bulldozer. Of course you'll be a bigger company after two years than you were at two months—if you're doing things right. But you should always keep your organization as simple as possible even as it grows—in fact, especially as it grows. Where once you needed only one signature—or none at all—to sign off on something, now you need six. You want to avoid as many of the delays caused by organizational bureaucracy for as long as possible. By failing to keep your organization simple, you can easily gum up the decision-making process, add to its complexity, and create conflicts that might otherwise not have existed.

■ SIMPLIFY YOUR BUSINESS MODEL

Forget lengthy business plans that read like boring, turgid Ph.D. dissertations. If you can't describe your business in one paragraph, no amount of labored prose will either. According to Hans Severiens, the physicist and financier who founded Band of Angels, a consortium of Silicon Valley early-stage investors, Intel's first business plan was a half-page long. Think e-mail, not dissertation. A simple idea communicated quickly and with passion will get a VC's attention much quicker than a detailed, copiously written business plan will. One VC recently received a business plan (ironically, it was pitching an idea for software for creating business plans!), and the pitch was e-mailed as a gargantuan attachment. Needless to say, that's one file that never got downloaded. Remember, we are all running on Internet time. The model—and the pitch—must be simple or it probably won't get off the ground.

The business model that successful start-ups need to follow has to be based—as any marketing-savvy entrepreneur will tell you— on what the customer wants and needs. Do you pay companies to make your life complicated? Customers want simplicity. They prefer products—and even companies—that simplify rather than complicate their lives. This is what successful entrepreneurs like Jeff Hawkins intuitively understand. Palm Pilots outsell and outperform Microsoft's Windows CE devices because they are *simpler*. Tactically, a new product that boasts scores of features intimidates customers. A product with fewer features is actually more customer-friendly. Simplicity works. ClubMed became a dominant brand in the resort business because people wanted their vacations to be simple. The Internet had been around for decades as a network used by only a few thousand engineers and academics. It only became a mass phenomenon when, back in 1994, Netscape distributed the browser software that popularized the Web and made using the Internet so easy that even the proverbial grandmother could do it.

■ A GUIDE FOR THE SIMPLICITY-CHALLENGED

There are thousands of distractions in a 3G start-up that can throw you off track. Here are three ideas to help you stay focused:

- *Don't tackle impossible situations.* A business that requires the cooperation and coordination of a lot of other organizations or government agencies is not simple. Automating hospital or banking operations, for example, has proven difficult. If you want to succeed as a start-up, you should stick to more straightforward challenges.

- *Don't do multiple variations of your business.*
- *Focus on the real problems of making a business work,* such as developing products, attracting and retaining customers, and generating revenue. Take shortcuts that bypass time-wasting toll roads. If, for example, your start-up can obtain money from early investors but is having trouble figuring the appropriate valuation, simplify the process: structure a bridge loan. Then move on.

The Zen of Start-up Success

Zen works in business because it is essentially about balance. The balance inherent in simplicity is a core value. It's about keeping things simple and remaining open to whatever comes your way. Using simple Zen techniques, you can clear your mind and begin to focus like a laser on doing the things you need to cross the threshold of opportunity and find yourself in the success zone. When you hear a gifted athlete talk about being "in the zone," he or she is talking about essentially the same thing. If you master the fundamental, "simple" things you need to do, the effort becomes nearly unconscious. You will find yourself doing them without having to think about doing them. There is an organic or natural order in the world of start-ups, just as there is in the world at large. The actions you need to take are self-selecting and mutually reinforcing. If you stay alert and keep things "as simple as possible, but no simpler," you will find yourself in the success zone.

According to Eido Michael Luetchford, a Buddhist monk, effective action is:

- Rational and explainable.
- Realistic and in tune with the circumstances.
- Clear and strong, without hesitation.

- Following the evolutionary stream of events.

Some simple steps:

- Empty your mind of old ideas.
- Envision yourself in the success zone.
- Focus on a few well-defined goals.
- Be conscious of the business environment.
- Sense and respond to the market.
- Be ready to change course quickly if things change—go with the flow.

If we are too aggressive or too passive, our actions are out of balance. Action focused on goals and in harmony with the business environment is more powerful than an out-of-control ego. When we take action without considering the world around us, we often slip out of the success zone and fail. Failing to act at all is another trap. Sometimes even the "wrong" move turns out to be right if the alternative is inaction.

■ SIMPLIFY YOUR TECHNOLOGY

If your approach to business makes the customer's experience easier, it's usually because your approach is simple—and elegant in its simplicity. Basic customer-centric principles should guide even your technological decisions. It works for both online and offline ventures.

In the *New York Times*, October 30, 2000, Bob Tedeschi described how a leading online business made using its Web site simpler—and more effective. Taking a leaf from the pages of *Why We Buy: The Science of Shopping* by Paco Underhill (Simon & Schuster Trade, 1999), which had become a bible of merchandising for bricks-and-mortar retailers, Amazon.com sensed and responded to its customers when in late 2000 it rolled out a redesigned —and greatly simplified—site front door. Gone were the "tabs" that had overwhelmed visitors when they logged on, as well as the extensive use of graphics, links, and scattered bits of promotional copy that made the page cluttered and difficult to use.

Tedeschi noted, "The company succeeded nicely in the eyes of many analysts. Rebecca Nidositko, an analyst with Yankee Group, lauded Amazon's redesign in a recent report, noting that it was particularly welcome, since the new navigation system would be 'emulated by many other online retailers.'"

Another example of "simple" technology is Napster. It was a simple idea, and the technology itself wasn't particularly complicated; but the downloadable music site became a phenomenon that has resulted in nearly as much media attention as the moon landing. Napster's application allows users to search others' hard disks, allowing free access to vast libraries of MP3 music files that had been collected by millions of individual users. Napster didn't own the files—it just provided access to them. Napster's future aside, the implications for providing access to other types of data files are huge. How successful the Web sites that do this will be in commercial terms isn't entirely clear yet, but someone will make the idea extremely profitable—probably very soon. This will happen because of one simple idea: Napster opened up individual hard drives to the World Wide Web.

A valuable resource for helping you keep product design simple is the Web site Useit.com. Jakob Nielsen, Ph.D., makes his living preaching the value of simplicity and writes a biweekly e-mail column in which he addresses Web usability issues. He is also cofounder of the Nielsen Norman Group, a consultancy dedicated to helping companies design human-centered products and services. Nielsen has authored a number of books on the virtues of product simplicity. We recommend reading *Designing Web Usability: The Practice of Simplicity* (New Riders, 2000).

■ NOTHING SUCCEEDS LIKE SIMPLICITY

If simplicity is one of the guiding principles for entrepreneurs, the good news is that they usually don't have a choice. Resource-limited start-ups are compelled to do only a few necessary things and to do them simply. If they fall into the trap of trying to do too many things, they'll inevitably fail to complete them because they lack sufficient resources.

But simplicity succeeds, not simply because it's an unavoidable predicament, but also because it provides an unambiguous advantage. Simplicity is the quickest path to the speed and innovation that are the hallmarks of successful start-ups. Simplicity is the tool that start-ups use to outmaneuver the megacorporations and long-established industries that they take on.

The necessity of simplicity is well illustrated by the fate of a company that didn't understand simplicity's virtues. As discussed in Chapter 9, Boo.com, fueled by an extraordinary $100 million in capital, was in a position to do just about everything it wanted—and so it did. With a phenomenally expensive, technologically advanced, and aesthetically impressive Web site, Boo was hot. Its imaginative graphic design, extensive Web site functionality, offices in four countries, and aggressive promotion made it attractive to investors who were blinded by the buzz Boo got from the global business press—and all this before the site even launched. After a full year in development, the site debuted—and quickly bombed. Boo.com didn't understand the need for simplicity. It did too many things—and not many of them well. Boo forgot that customers want their purchasing experience to be simple and enjoyable. Buzz will get you on everyone's radar, but only satisfied customers will keep you there.

Boo.com's critically acclaimed graphics, it turned out, not only failed to impress customers but also slowed the response time on the Web site so much that they drove most of its customers away. The extensive features weren't ones that customers especially cared about, and the programming code was too complex for the company to quickly recast the features that did matter. The offices Boo opened in four countries made internal communication difficult and wasted its executives' valuable time on frequent plane rides. Worst of all, the aggressive promotion that succeeded in driving masses of prospective customers to a Web site left them with an insurmountably negative first impression. The lesson: Simplicity succeeds where even limitless money fails.

■ SIMPLICITY ISN'T ALWAYS EASY

As easy as simplicity might seem, it is difficult for human beings to achieve it. Often, it seems easier—and safer—to take a "throw everything at it and hope something sticks" approach than to take the effort to determine the single right action to take. The latter approach requires more thought and judgment. It also runs the risk that what you thought was the right choice could turn out to be wrong. Product managers and marketing departments load products with features, for example, rather than zeroing in on the *one* feature that captivates customers. They opt for nonstandard business practices, rather then merely cloning the time-proven best practices of industry leaders. Founders create equity structures that, ironically, not only undermine the value of equity but also create even more work downstream. They attack symptoms rather than the source. They try to hire around a weak CEO, instead of installing a strong one, which not only would solve an immediate problem but also would lift the entire company to an even greater level of performance and success.

In many cases, it may seem counterintuitive—complexity seems more impressive than simplicity—but the advantages of acting to cut to the chase, to solve problems in a simple and direct manner, are glaringly obvious, especially in retrospect. To become a successful start-up, learn the lesson of simplicity early, and your chances of finding yourself "in the zone" will increase. Indeed, making things simple is so obvious that it is often overlooked. The best practices of successful Internet companies are readily apparent, yet few entrepreneurs ever follow them. Most business plans, for example, naively project 50 percent or even 60 percent operating margins; a few mouse clicks at Yahoo! Finance will tell anyone that anticipating and counting on operating margins that large is totally unrealistic.

Meanwhile, start-ups with a tiny fraction of the capital of Boo.com have succeeded brilliantly. These start-ups didn't have the capital-induced luxury of doing everything, so they did the few things that really mattered to customers; and by focusing on these things did them very well. Similarly, they didn't have a year-long runway paved with limitless capital, so they launched their offerings in three or four months—with the invaluable result of instigating quick customer feedback that produced insights that no amount of forecasting could even suggest. And the financial necessity of packing everyone into a small, single location fosters not only communication but also an us-against-the-world culture that brings out the best in people.

Anyone can do simple things, but adopting a mindset that renders the seemingly complex simple is harder than it looks. The next great start-up will be launched with a simple idea—and it will likely make something that the rest of us perceived as hard easier than it was before. And it will be a simple idea with big consequences—like the Palm Pilot or Napster.

■ THE SIMPLICITY SPIRAL

Simplicity actually makes other things you have to do *simpler*.

Starting with nothing, the best start-ups create success from a smart sequence of steps that build on each other, creating a virtuous spiral to success. They innovate. They raise capital. They lure world-class employees—and fire weak ones. They change strategy when necessary. They learn from their customers. The start-ups that take the simple, smart steps the fastest win. Simplicity actually fuels its own success. Simplicity, for example, enables a start-up to get to market sooner. In turn, the start-up grabs market share while its competitors are still developing more complex products, and it sparks precious customer feedback. Then in turn, the start-up refines the product even more, getting farther out in front while at the same time capturing even more market share.

We'll say it again: simplicity makes things simpler. Making one thing simple makes many other apparently complex things line up— it synchronizes them. The recognition that the goal of a start-up is simply to raise the next round of capital tells engineering to develop only those features, sales to court only those customers, and management to recruit only those employees that will help the company reach its goal. All of the confusion wrought by complexity falls away; and without realizing it, you find yourself in the success zone.

■ **REFERENCES**

Palm inventor offers glimpse into his methods: *http://www.zdnet.com/ eweek/stories/general/0,11011,1017774,00.html*

Web Merchants Make Good on Hype: *New York Times*, October 30, 2000

Virtuous and Vicious Spirals

NEILISM: Small actions cause big consequences.

A virtuous spiral may sound like something from the lexicon of astronomy; but it's an apt description of the path that successful start-ups take to gain liftoff and to continue to soar through the stratosphere. Unfortunately, virtue has its counterpart in the vicious spiral, which occurs when a start-up causes its own plunge to failure by making self-destructive decisions.

■ THE VIRTUOUS SPIRAL

What makes a virtuous spiral? This type of spiral occurs when a business undertakes actions that, even if small to begin with, quickly compound to put the business on an upward trajectory to success. A key characteristic of a spiral, whether virtuous or vicious, is that once begun, it's hard to stop. Gaining momentum with each small action, the virtuous spiral continues to propel the start-up into the success zone. Virtuous spirals work in all areas of the start-up, from marketing to funding to hiring, as well as in nearly every key aspect of the company's overall business environment. For example, here's how being the first in a market category can put a start-up into a virtuous spiral:

- A start-up that gets the early presence in a marketplace can attract financing . . .
- Which makes it easier to attract and hire great employees . . .
- Which in turn enables the company to build and market better products . . .
- Which means it can attract more customers . . .
- Which means it can make a profit . . .
- Which enables it to attract and hire more great employees . . .

. . . and so on. Once started, the momentum is hard to stop—especially if you're a competitor in second place trying to overtake the front-runner.

Another example of a virtuous spiral occurs when a start-up hooks up with beneficial business partners. If a company develops a relationship with AOL, let's say, it attracts the attention of millions of people; the company quickly gets valuable customer feedback that helps it perfect its offering; other companies want to work with the start-up; the best employees want to hire on; and venture capitalists want to back it with more money and at a higher valuation. It's a nuclear chain reaction.

■ AVANTGO: THE VIRTUOUS SPIRAL IN ACTION

Think of the virtuous spiral AvantGo set off in February 2000 when one of the company's founders replaced himself with a seasoned CEO who was able to take the company public in just over seven months.

AvantGo, an authority in managing mobile information, recruited Richard Owen—at the time vice president of Dell Online. Owen's experience in helping create and execute Dell Computer's highly successful global Internet strategy had demonstrated his superior marketing and positioning savvy. Under his leadership, Dell Online generated about $30 million in revenue each day. Felix Lin, AvantGo's former CEO and cofounder, became chairman of the board and devoted most of his energy and talent to the company's tech side. It was Lin's willingness to take this step that helped initiate the virtuous spiral.

AvantGo's aggressive hiring strategy (and the key hire of a world-class CEO) also gained it the other high-level executives the company would need to reach its full potential, including a new CFO, a general counsel, and a vice president. AvantGo was obviously ready to spiral its way to success with a new management team that was entirely capable of taking the company to new heights. After the Nasdaq's free-fall in the spring of 2000, when even the promising wireless space was losing ground, it took a remarkable team with a remarkable leader to launch AvantGo's IPO against the tide. Hiring the right team made all the difference—and demonstrated how making the right small moves at the right time can spark big consequences.

■ THE VICIOUS SPIRAL

Unfortunately, not all spirals go up. A start-up can make bad decisions that initiate a downward slide toward eventual self-destruction. The bad choices a start-up makes are in the same areas as a virtuous spiral: hiring, funding, choice of business partners, timing, and so on. For example, a company that enters the marketplace second or third tends to get caught in a vicious spiral. As it lags behind the lead dog, the best it can do is to convince customers that it is better than the first entrant—a battle the market leader doesn't need to waste time and resources fighting. So the also-ran must spend more money in an effort to get the same sale that the start-up that was first to market did. While Amazon.com is a good example of the virtues of being the lead dog, it wasn't literally the first online bookseller; but it was the first to mount a serious business online, which enabled it to get significant VC funding to attack that market.

When a second-to-market company approaches a VC, it usually will have a harder time articulating its unique, differentiating value proposition. The VC says, "Well, you're second into the marketplace. Assuming I invest in you, the most I will do is give you less money at a lower valuation than your competitor." Getting funding is a snap if you own your space and can pull in revenue fast. BarnesandNoble.com and Borders.com, the second- and third-to-market online booksellers to get funding, are prime examples of followers caught in vicious spirals. Even the powerful brand names of the followers can't overcome Amazon's lead-dog advantage. The second entrant is fated to struggle. It must somehow carve out a piece of the market someone else dominates. Unless the leader stumbles, the odds against succeeding are long. There may be a place in a mass market for more than one player, but the competition is so fierce when you're playing catch-up that it's often impossibly difficult to get there.

The spiral is self-reinforcing. If you make smart choices early on, you will find yourself spiraling to success. If not, your company may end up as a case history for failure. The Lightspeed Economy—not just the Internet industry—is about rapid mobility. When a start-up slows down, it can't afford new hires, investors are gun-shy, and competitors begin to cut into market share. These are the characteristics of a vicious spiral. This is what happened to eToys, which in 1999 was thought to be a sure winner, yet closed two years later. Can anything be done when a start-up finds itself in the grip of a vicious spiral? In the feast-or-famine environment of the Internet economy, it usually isn't simply a matter of adjusting the throttle to stay on course. Like a doomed plane, the company usually goes straight down for a crash landing.

Here's your scenario: A successful company is riding high; people have hitched themselves to this shooting star; the stock is headed to the moon. Sooner than anyone expected, the stock crashes. By the time management can begin to think about fixing the problem, it's too late. Because the stock price plummeted, key employees start leaving, no quality replacements for them can be found, and the company suddenly finds itself sinking into mediocrity. The company has slipped into a vicious spiral that reinforces itself just as surely as virtuous spirals reinforce movement in the opposite direction.

■ POINTCAST: THE VICIOUS SPIRAL IN ACTION

PointCast was at the top of its game in 1996. Considered by many to be the killer app of the Internet, PointCast sent news and other information to users' desktops by aggregating and personalizing content from a number of information sources. This technology was termed *push technology*. But PointCast set off a vicious spiral in 1997 when it turned down an offer to be purchased by News Corp. for more than $450 million.

PointCast's management felt it could do better on its own and planned for an IPO. The company was caught flat-footed when the idea of push technology failed to gain acceptance as quickly as management had expected. By this time, the aura surrounding PointCast had begun to fade, and it was too late: The downward spiral had begun.

Events spun out of control so quickly that PointCast suddenly withdrew its long-planned IPO in 1998, just days before it was to launch its road show. Instead, it was forced to desperately seek new partners that would never be capable of bringing in even a fraction of the cash and connections that the News Corp. deal would have brought. The mistake of refusing a $450 million offer cost the founder of PointCast his job; and his successor couldn't reverse the damage. The company and its investors lost not only millions of dollars in returns but also the opportunity to survive until they could fix the problems—some of them merely technical—that had slowed the company's growth. By early 1999, in a humiliating end to an effort that had held so much promise, the company's assets were sold to Launchpad Technologies for less than $10 million. Once the vicious spiral begins, it's tough to stop.

■ PARTNERS PUT CHECK POINT ON A SPIRAL TO SUCCESS

The story of Check Point Software Technologies provides a particularly good example of a start-up spiraling into the success zone. Check Point started in 1993 with three guys in Israel; but in a few short years it became the leading worldwide provider of Internet security firewalls. How did Check Point make it deep into the success zone so quickly? It executed a smart business plan whose individual steps compounded into a virtuous spiral. The steps included being one of the first to market, attracting a VC that provided valuable contacts, finding great partners, creating an offering based on a simple but important idea, and moving fast to expand globally.

In an era when nearly every business large and small—even established bricks-and-mortar companies—depends on the Internet to do business, Check Point's firewall product was right for its time and quickly dominated its market niche. It wasn't the first company to offer a firewall, but Check Point created a shrink-wrap firewall solution—easy to install and implement—that could be immediately deployed as a quick solution to security problems. Its timing was great. In 1994, when the commercialization of the Internet was growing, concerns about security were also on the rise. People were—as they still are—terrified that sensitive business and personal information would be at risk.

Founded by brilliant engineers who came out of an elite military unit of the Israel Defense Forces, Check Point's virtuous spiral really took hold when its lead VC helped Check Point establish a nonexclusive, take-or-pay, multimillion-dollar licensing contract with Sun Microsystems. This one key deal meant that the company would never have to raise venture capital again. Another element in the spiral was the company's rapid growth. "Technology companies are born global from day one," said Bruce Taragin, partner at Blumberg Capital, one of Check Point's early VC backers, in an interview with the authors, "We introduced them to Mr. Shuji Sugimoto, now CEO of Asgent, in Japan." As a result of the deals with Sun, Japanese distributors, and later Hewlett-Packard, as well as other deals Blumberg Capital helped negotiate for Check Point, the new company garnered market share that made their IPO a slam-dunk.

The Check Point story is almost a textbook example of a virtuous spiral. Checkpoint got off to a fast start. Its technology was first-rate. A savvy VC stepped in with advice, funding, and contacts and helped the company negotiate the critical licensing agreement with Sun and foreign markets. And finally, Check Point went global at just the right moment to make it the market leader before anyone else could hope to catch up.

Today, Check Point is one of the most profitable software companies in the world, with gross profit margins approaching 92 percent. Initially, says Taragin, "you could have bought the whole company for $400,000, and today their market capitalization is more than $20 billion."

Acquisitions Are a Quick Trigger to a Virtuous Spiral

Sycamore Networks, a Massachusetts-based optical networking equipment maker, used an aggressive acquisitions strategy to create a virtuous spiral that put it on a track for huge success. By acquiring Sirocco Systems, and its key products, Sycamore opened up vast new markets for itself. The company introduced two Sirocco-designed products, the SN 3000 and SN 4000—formerly known as Typhoon and Tornado— aimed at switching data traffic on local metro networks and linking those smaller networks with larger regional ones. This allowed Sycamore to offer a technology set to the booming metropolitan networking market.

Customers previously beyond Sycamore's reach, like European telecommunications operator LDCOM Networks, now approached it because of the new metro switches that the Sirocco deal brought to Sycamore. This acquisition opened up a $17 billion market to the company, making Sycamore a player. The deal brought the company many other contracts it previously had no hope of acquiring. BellSouth and CoreExpress, for example, were lured by Sycamore's SN 16000.

After the acquisition Sycamore Networks reported earnings that exceeded analysts' expectations as revenue grew more than fivefold from the previous year. The strong revenue growth was based on the new customers and new products that the acquisition of Sirocco made possible.

The acquisition also raised Sycamore's profile to prospective hires who wanted to get in on the burgeoning fiber optics industry, where the future looked so promising. The right action taken at the right time can set off the virtuous spiral that will take you quickly into the success zone.

■ ELEMENTS OF VIRTUOUSLY SPIRALING COMPANIES

Luis Arjona and Vikas Agrawal, consultants with McKinsey & Company's e-commerce group, outlined the best practices of firms in the happy grip of a virtuous spiral:

- A clear path to sustainable profitability.
- A wide and increasing gulf separating the leader and the pack.
- Achieving success through discipline in key areas:
  - Aligning the value proposition and target segments.
  - Controlling extension into natural market opportunities.
  - Focusing on superior marketing functions—rifle shots rather than shotgun media blasts.
  - Exploiting market conditions—for example, seeing a depressed market as an opportunity.

■ HOW TO KICK OFF A VIRTUOUS SPIRAL: ANTICIPATE!

Acting quickly, smartly, and simply, you can anticipate the problems other start-ups have faced. One example is in dealing with equity and vesting issues early and in a serious way. By standardizing employee stock option plans, you can head off the inevitable employee revolt that would erupt if there were a perception of unequal treatment.

If there is a suspicion among employees that you're fungible, you will have employees trying to negotiate periodically. If the policy is clear from the beginning, not only will you be able to deploy equity in a way that is fair for employees and for the company's long-term future, but you will also create the perception that your company is disciplined and fair. The virtuous spiral will be underway—affecting your start-up's progress across the board.

Opportunity Won't Knock Twice: A Vicious Spiral's Predictable Consequences

Quokka Sports seemed poised to succeed when it received the contract to run NBC's official Web site during the 2000 Summer Olympics in Sydney, Australia. Not long after, the once-promising sports site began cutting employees and restructuring its offerings in a desperate bid to stay alive. How did this vicious spiral take hold?

It began with the disappointing performance of the Olympics both on TV and on the Web. Based on TV viewership numbers from previous Olympics, Quokka's management had predicted its site would attract 10 million unique visitors. Yet TV viewership ended up being drastically below estimates, and fewer than 6 million people ended up visiting the site. In the wake of the Olympics disaster, Quokka cut 217 employees—59 percent of its workforce. This followed an earlier layoff in which 90 employees had been let go.

The sports site lost nearly $150 million in 2000. By the end of that year, it had only $50 million left in the bank, and in 2001, it filed for Chapter 11 bankruptcy protection. Although it still attracts several million visitors per month, it trails far behind industry leaders CBS SportsLine and ESPN.com. It is always hard to catch up when you're not first to market. It's so often a matter of boom or bust.

■ REFERENCES

AvantGo Hires a Great CEO in Feb 2000: *http://avantgo.com/corp/news/ press_archive/2000/release01_25_00.html*

AvantGo IPO: CNET News.com, September 27, 2000: *http:// news.cnet.com/news/0-1006-200-2878404.html*

McKinsey: *http://www.mckinsey.com/articles/surviving_aftermath.html*

CNET News.com, October 19, 2000, and February 13, 2001: *http:// news.cnet.com/news/0-1004-200-3237514.html*

http://news.cnet.com/news/0-1004-200-4809470.html

Quokka Sports Lays Off 217 Workers: CNET News.com, February 12, 2001; *http://news.cnet.com/news/0-1005-200-4798113.html*

Scenario Analysis

NEILISM: Sometimes it's so obvious that everyone misses it.

Scenario analysis is an invaluable tool for plotting your start-up's path to the success zone. By going through the exercise of systematically evaluating the issues facing your company and then making choices, you narrow the seemingly wide range of possible courses of action by quickly sifting out the ineffective ones, eliminating extraneous factors from your field of vision, and focusing only on the actions and goals required to make your next milestones. This method is especially valuable in the Lightspeed environment, where change is a constant and new challenges continually arise. The need to make the right decisions—and at an accelerated pace—is daunting. How do start-ups deal with competitors? Customers? Venture capitalists? Lawyers? Potential partners? Employees? Faced with the need to make the right decision and to stay on course, what's an entrepreneur to do?

Scenario analysis gives entrepreneurs a structure for planning for the future by examining all the options available to them. In a loosely structured but highly focused environment, managers walk through a sequence of events by describing a range of possible outcomes driven by internal and external factors. At the end of the process of imagining alternative futures, entrepreneurs can make better strategic decisions about what they should then do.

There are a number of models available to use as your blueprint for scenario analysis, ranging from a quick-and-dirty assessment of the issues to a scientific analysis of factors utilizing masses of empirical and quantitative data. By now, you can probably anticipate where we stand on this: Since it takes speed, smarts, and simplicity to make a start-up succeed, we favor a stripped-down version of scenario analysis that allows you to think through crucial decisions while maintaining the speed necessary to thrive in the Lightspeed Economy.

Peter Schwartz's classic text on the process of scenario building, *The Art of the Long View* (Doubleday, 1991), provides an excellent guide. We recommend that you consult it in depth before beginning your own scenario analysis process. Schwartz, who founded Global Business Network, and before that developed scenarios at Royal Dutch Shell and Stanford Research Institute, sets out the major elements of scenario analysis in a book that has become standard reading in business schools. The principles of scenario planning have nearly replaced older corporate planning models, and these principles also have begun to be adopted in public policy, think tank, and nonprofit environments.

■ WHY DO SCENARIO ANALYSIS? WHAT IF?

While the range of issues you face may seem bewilderingly infinite, the choices are elegantly simple once you've done your homework. The best way to begin the scenario process is to ask yourself a basic question: What if? There may be five or six or even a dozen or more courses of action your new company could take. But once you follow each scenario through to its logical conclusion, you'll likely find that those dozen possible paths really come down to only one or two scenarios worth seriously contemplating. But it often takes walking down each of those paths—however briefly—to reach this conclusion. Asking "What if?" for each scenario can be critical for navigating the complex business environment any Internet-related start-up faces.

According to Kees van der Heijden, in *Scenarios: The Art of Strategic Conversation* (John Wiley & Sons, 1996), there is a good reason that scenario analysis has displaced corporate planning, the planning tool preferred by business consultants in the 1950s and 1960s.

It didn't work. These days most experts agree that the model that does work is scenario building. It's a method that allows a company to challenge its own assumptions, to think more clearly about choices, and to embrace uncertainty in vital ways. Just as important, it's a technique that focuses attention sharply on the company's surrounding environment so that nobody misses the obvious. And the obvious, as the Neilism that heads this chapter suggests, is not always so obvious to everyone.

We want to emphasize that scenarios are not predictions. Rather, they're a way of exploring potential outcomes. The process allows you to forge strategies that take into account the many alternative possibilities that may occur. Anyone who attempts to predict the future is going to be wrong in more ways than they will be right. On the other hand, periodic scenario analysis lets you adjust your thinking and actions to shifting circumstances. As the entire world learns to spin in new directions and as new data comes in, you must continually revise your scenarios. Plan ahead, but be ready to change your plans. In the Lightspeed Economy, change is the rule, not the exception. Scenario analysis is a way to stay nimble.

■ POSSIBLE SCENARIOS

How might scenario analysis work for your start-up? Scenarios can be constructed for funding, partnering, marketing, hiring, competing, developing products, or any one of the range of challenges your company will face. If the process is done correctly, issues will narrow and the choices will be easier to make.

➤ Business Concept

Do you have a start-up worth starting? This is the first, and arguably most important, scenario analysis you do. Do you have a compelling business concept that will enable the start-up to get the backing it needs, or will it struggle to survive at every step? While the scenario analysis process may consume some precious time early on, we believe it will speed your start-up's path to success if you carry it out before you make key decisions. In fact, if the scenarios show the company will dead-end at every turn, bailing out fast will save you and your company the time, money, and pain that come with complete failure. You'll save your resources and life's blood for a better opportunity.

➤ Marketing

Consider a start-up that wants to enter the U.S. and international markets. What's the best way to achieve this goal? Scenario 1 might be to focus exclusively on the domestic market first and to delay entering international markets. By not dividing its efforts, the company can claim a larger share of the U.S. market faster. A larger market share means the company gets a higher market cap. And with a higher market cap, it can more quickly acquire other companies to further build market share or to more easily find partners once it has dominated its market space domestically.

Scenario 2 might involve entering the U.S. and international markets at the same time. This will establish the company's presence overseas quickly; but it will take longer to really penetrate both markets simultaneously, and it will slow the company's progress overall. A competitor will surely come along and focus on just the United States, threatening to dominate the U.S. market. The start-up may have positions in both Germany and the United States, but it will lack a large customer base. Its market cap will be lower, so it will have a harder time attracting more customers, funding, top employees, and so on.

Scenario 3 offers a hybrid solution. Let's say the start-up feels it's critical to establish itself as a global company from the get-go. It could basically follow scenario 1 and concurrently begin to plant the seeds of an international presence by hiring engineers in, say, India, Singapore, or Ireland. The engineers could work from remote locations, a common enough practice today, and at the same time act as a beachhead the company could later use to expand its operation and move product in the countries once it has established itself sufficiently in the domestic market.

During scenario analysis, a horizon that seemed wide open with possible courses of action suddenly narrows to one or two clear choices. By discarding the unworkable choices, you may find that your final choice is in fact less a matter of choice and more the result of a process of elimination.

➤ Funding

When it comes to funding, entrepreneurs all too often create their own homespun equity arrangements without giving thought to the long-term consequences of their actions. In Chapters 6 and 16 on equity, we explain why such misguided deployments of equity are a recipe for disaster. But it's easy to see how a start-up can be tempted to cut unwise equity deals in order to attract funding or star employees, for example—especially in the early stages, when the start-up is hungry for funding. However, if entrepreneurs took the time to perform a scenario analysis before giving away too much—or too little—equity, they would save themselves and their start-ups from much pain down the line. Keep your equity structure simple, following the time-tested formula of other successful companies. But if you think you have a compelling reason to consider an alternative structure, use scenario analysis to put it through its paces.

One common funding issue is deciding whether to accept a round of funding right now based on a current valuation of your company or to hold out for the possibility of getting more funding in a future round based on a higher valuation. In other words, should you take less money now or wait for more money later?

In scenario 1, you postpone the funding round until you've had time to increase your market share and therefore the value of your company. That way, you'll receive more money in your next funding round. But will it be too late? Will you lose your market opportunity and key employees? If you set a low valuation, will it result in giving up too much equity in the long run so you and your employees lose the motivation to make it a success?

In scenario 2, you accept the funding offered right now, even though it's less than you would probably receive if you waited awhile. With that immediate funding, you have money to build your business, hire good employees, and increase market share. Even though you have less money to work with than if you wait, you move faster in executing your business plan and you'll reach your milestones more quickly. And who knows what the competitive landscape will look like then? You will probably have made your company more attractive to investors, so that in subsequent funding rounds you will succeed in getting more money at higher valuations.

This scenario analysis illustrates the point that over the life of a company equity is a zero-sum game: If you wait to raise money, you might raise a little bit more at a slightly higher valuation; but if you had raised less money at a lower valuation, you would then be able to raise the next round for more money at a higher valuation. When you total up the funding the start-up would have received a year or two out in each scenario and what it enabled the start-up to accomplish in that time frame, it will be clear that the best course of action is the one that opts for taking the immediate funding and using it to move your company ahead more quickly.

➤ Partnering

Here are some common issues regarding partnerships with other companies that you could use scenario analysis to help resolve. Should you choose partners for strategic reasons (companies that can complement your offering, let's say), or is it sufficient that they're the 800-pound gorilla in your market space and they're offering you money? Ideally, of course, you'd want a relationship that offers both financial and strategic advantages; but if you're struggling to gain visibility and credibility, a high-profile but nonstrategic partnership might be the smart course of action. Will a partnership that positions your company as a technological innovator bring you more customers, attention, and investors? Or should you forge alliances with companies that can provide you with a steady source of customers or revenue? A partnership with a large, entrenched corporation may offer you cachet value, but will the deal still be worth it if the corporation ignores you and drags its feet on matters important to your company?

➤ Advertising

Here's an issue that is not as easy as it seems at first. If you're trying to gain visibility and build brand awareness and if you have a limited advertising budget, should you commit most of it to a 30-second spot during the Super Bowl? Or should you spend your ad dollars on a series of smaller, lower-profile TV spots—or even on a mix of print and TV ads? Or should you focus your spending on areas other than advertising? To answer these questions, a scenario analysis that takes into account your environment at the moment could help you choose the best course.

For example, in 1984 Apple Computer shook up Super Bowl viewers with a powerful ad in which a lone heroine wielding a sledgehammer destroyed the symbol of an authoritarian, Orwellian-style established order. The commercial was a huge success, establishing Apple's renegade image and market position in the minds of a mass audience of viewers. In this case, the expensive, flashy Super Bowl commercial paid off.

Fast-forward to January 2000. That year's crop of Super Bowl ads jammed the airwaves with fledgling dot.coms trying to increase their brand's visibility in one high-stakes gamble. Did it pay off? Well, for some, it was a desperate Hail Mary pass that failed. Pets.com and Computer.com were among the losers; yet HotJobs, Etrade, and Monster.com all bought Super Bowl ads and their businesses grew. The difference between the winners and the losers? The companies that followed up their Super Bowl ads with supportive marketing campaigns had a markedly better success rate.

■ GETTING STARTED WITH SCENARIO ANALYSIS

Scenario analysis is a task that should involve the entire management team. Without multiple perspectives, you won't get much out of the process. And remember, even if your guesses are not always right, the process itself will ensure that you will be more prepared to meet future challenges than you would have been without the exercise.

➤ Scenario Time Frame

Choose a target date when the scenario will take place, then work backward. We recommend that start-ups keep the time frame limited—think in terms of months rather than years. While more established companies may plan 10 or more years out, business realities move too quickly for a leading-edge technology or Internet-related start-up to be able to plan that far out. Look at the driving forces of the business and the options that are likely to be available in the

months ahead. Be as unconventional as you like; there will be opportunities for building a number of alternative scenarios. Use the
brainstorming technique of refusing to consider any idea as being
bad or too "out there." Think the unthinkable.

➤ Scenario Questions

Fire away. Ask any question that addresses future possibilities and
how they may impact your business. Frame the analysis with the
lessons learned from other companies that initiated either virtuous
or vicious spirals as a consequence of the course of action they chose.
Keep asking, "What if?" and you will be on the right path. It's especially important to try to look past your own blind spots so that you
can see the future as it is likely to be rather than the way you wish
it would be. As long as your scenarios address real concerns, you
can range as freely as you choose. The process forces you to think
about what you will have to do to succeed, and it prepares you for
most any contingency.

Peter Schwartz, in *The Art of the Long View*, puts it this way: "You
can tell you have good scenarios when they are both plausible and
surprising; when they have the power to break old stereotypes; and
when the makers assume ownership of them and put them to work.
Scenario making is intensely participatory, or it fails."

➤ Build a Scenario Mindset

When you gather your team to work through scenarios, make an
effort to include people who think differently than most and who
can envision and articulate potential roadblocks and opportunities
most others don't see. In today's speeded-up business environment,
any plausible scenario must account for significant change to occur
on a routine basis; so people who are adept at anticipating the unexpected will be a great asset to the team. Similarly, encourage team
members to constantly challenge assumptions. "[In scenario build-
ing], you look for disconfirming evidence," says Peter Schwartz in
The Art of the Long View. "You look for those facts and perceptions
which challenge the facts." Schwartz recommends paying attention

to the topics that are actually on the spot and keeping track of new developments in science and technology, physics, biotechnology, computer science, ecology, microbiology engineering, and other key areas that affect your larger business environment, and cautions that you should be neither credulous nor incredulous of everything you find.

➤ **Steps in the Scenario Analysis Process**

Art Kleiner, author of *The Age of Heretics* (Currency Doubleday, 1996), is one of the pioneers in scenario building. He teaches scenario planning twice a year in New York University's graduate-level Interactive Telecommunications Program. These three steps in the scenario process are based on his teachings:

1. *Define the question.* Of course, it has to be the right question. For real learning to occur, you must address real, not imaginary, concerns.
2. *Define the driving forces.* What does the environment your company is likely to face look like? What are the predetermined elements? What are the critical uncertainties?
3. *Create subgroups.* Subgroups allow for a deeper probing of the story—one that asks why this particular scenario is significant and compelling.

➤ **Questions to Consider during Scenario Analysis:**

- Will it slow my start-up's progress or growth?
- Is it good for the business?
- How does it fit in this environment?
- Does this adhere to time-tested structures and formulas?
- Will I be able to make my milestones?
- Will I be able to hire?
- Where is it leading?
- What are my best options?

- How will I know it's coming?
- Does this product satisfy a real need?
- What if customers don't want it?
- What happens if I don't do it?
- What happens if I do it?
- What are the chain of events that brought my start-up to this outcome?
- How will it affect the company?
- Will current employees still want to work here?
- Will talented new people want to join?
- Will the company be cutting-edge, able to pull employees, marketshare, and media into its orbit?
- How diverse is the future?
- Will the idea work only in the United States? Will it work in Europe? In Asia? Elsewhere overseas?
- What have I not anticipated that could cause a shift in the company's thinking and planning?
- What is happening in the national economy? What about the global economy?
- What is happening to the market for technology?

Part Three

Equity Demystified

Chapter

14

The Arithmetic of Equity

NEILISM: When it comes to equity, NEVER sell more than 35 percent of your company in any one funding round.

The formula for raising money for a start-up isn't as mysterious as many entrepreneurs may think. As explained in Chapter 6, there is a system to equity that will take you through each stage of a start-up, from the very beginnings of your company to when you take it public in an IPO. A major component of the system is the equity budget, which helps you allocate how much of your company to sell—based on a standard range of percentages.

■ SUCCESS IN FUND-RAISING

There are infinite variations on how much money to raise and when to raise it, and of course it's your option to explore as many as you can stomach. But if you want to lessen your stress and increase your chances of successfully funding your company, follow the fund-raising sequencing system outlined in the following pages. This chapter explains in detail how much capital the start-up should raise at each stage and how much of the company should be sold and allocated to investors, employees, and founders. Although the system is not a guarantee that your start-up will be successful, adhering to it does guarantee that your financing is following in the footsteps of entrepreneurs from other successful start-ups who have come through the fund-raising process intact.

Capital is vital, and you will fail if you don't raise enough money. Raise too little and you can't achieve your goals: You won't be able to hire the employees to build and market your products, which means you won't be able to attract and retain customers, and that means you won't make your milestones. Raise too much money, and not only do you run the risk of not retaining enough equity to make working your tail off at your own company appealing to you, but you also could find yourself reliving the profligate history of Boo.com and PowerAgent—too much money made them complacent and slow. Both companies failed a result.

■ NEVER SELL MORE THAN 35 PERCENT AT EACH FUNDING ROUND

The amount of money you raise is based on a number of variables, the most important being the amount of cash you need at each stage. The second variable is the amount of equity to sell at each funding round. The rule of thumb is to sell no more than 35 percent at any one funding stage. Why 35 percent? It turns out that this is the number that the natural order of equity (in other words, time-tested experience) shows is required to keep the equity equation in balance so that all players in the start-up are sufficiently motivated to play their parts. Investors want the company to succeed, so the people who are making the company a success must have enough equity to share in the success of the company. If you sell more than 35 percent, there's a chance that the founders and employees won't have a big enough stake to make it meaningful to them. Sell too little, and you may not raise enough capital to survive until the next funding round.

Here's another reason why 35 percent is the rule of thumb: In the first funding round, no single outside entity should own more than 50 percent of the company so that the founders don't lose control. As the company issues equity in future funding rounds, the founders' share will of course get diluted, and the total amount of outside ownership will be more than 50 percent—but as long as no single entity controls more than the founders do, the founders remain in control. If a company sells 51 percent in the first round of funding, that amount will discourage future investors because they will fear that the founders won't be able to exercise control of their own company. Ideally, entrepreneurs should keep as much ownership of the company as they can, while at the same time deploying as much equity as they need to for the company to survive—and thrive.

Say an entrepreneur has a business idea for which the first stage of the company's launch requires $9 million. The entrepreneur has attracted prominent venture capitalists who want to back the company. But the VCs say, "Well, the risk profile here is such that we will value the company at $12 million. So we'll value the company at $12 million and we'll give you the $9 million." But that in effect requires the entrepreneur to sell two-thirds of the company (67 percent), and that is outside the band of success.

There are several actions entrepreneurs can take in this situation:

- They can take the deal at an unattractive valuation but with a firm that can help them get the company launched.
- They can shop the deal to other VCs in the hope of getting a higher valuation, more like a valuation of $28.5 million for a $10 million investment (although this VC firm may not be as helpful to the start-up in terms of advice, contacts, and guidance).
- They can reformulate the business so that it will require less capital.

But if it comes to this scenario, then the entrepreneurs have put themselves in a difficult position. While they can always agree to accept the lower valuation, if they had positioned their business correctly in the first place, VCs would actually be bidding up the valuation. By not making the start-up attractive enough to entice a number of VCs—in other words, by not making it a buyer's market—the entrepreneurs have made it a seller's market, where the VCs are in total control. When possible, entrepreneurs should tip the market in their favor so they have an opportunity to choose between a number of VCs.

Perhaps the more important lesson to draw from this scenario is that you probably don't have a viable start-up. If your business requires more than $2 to $5 million for its first round of funding, then something is probably wrong. As suggested earlier, either try to reformulate your idea so that it requires less capital, or ask yourself if it's a start-up worth starting. Certainly, some ventures will require more up-front capital than $2 to $5 million—for instance, a business that involves setting up a massive telecommunications infrastructure. But the vast majority of successful start-ups fall into the $2 million to $5 million range for their first funding round. Amazon, Yahoo!, and InfoSpace, to name a few, all started up with little or no money to begin with—and that was back in the heady second-generation days.

There's a range of equity to be sold at each round (see Table 14.1). If you're not within this range, then you should have a good reason.

If you sell 35 percent of the company at Series A, existing ownership gets diluted by 35 percent down to 65 percent. Sell an additional 25 percent of the company at Series B, and the founders' ownership gets diluted to 49 percent, while outside investors own 51 percent. Sell an additional 20 percent at Series C, and the founders' ownership is diluted to 39 percent, with outside investors owning 61 percent. When an additional 15 percent is sold to the public in an IPO, the founders' share gets diluted to 33 percent, and outside investors, including the public, own 67 percent (see Figure 14.1).

Table 14.1   Equity ranges.

Stage—Funding Round	Percentage of Equity to Sell
Stage 0—Founding	0—Raise money through a bridge loan.
Stage 1—Series A funding	30–35
Stage 2—Series B funding	20–30
Stage 3—Series C funding	15–25
Stage 4—Initial public offering	12–18

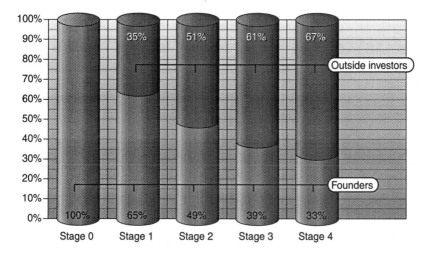

Figure 14.1 Founders' percentage of ownership gets diluted at each funding round.

■ VALUATIONS ARE DIFFICULT TO CALCULATE

Most professional investors, such as VCs or investment bankers, will determine your valuation based on the amount of money you need to build the business, rather than on a detailed financial analysis. Don't be alarmed if in a meeting with a VC you hear, "Your valuation analysis is meaningless." What's important to professional investors is how much capital you need to succeed. When a VC looks to invest in your start-up, the conversation may go something like, "Here's $3 million. We'll value the company at three times that. We don't know what your revenues are going to be, but we believe in you and your team."

A Range of Start-up Valuations

If you think valuations are really hard to figure out in a public company when many more factors are known, then you have to realize it's even harder to determine valuations of

(continued)

start-ups. There are so many unknowns about what the start-up market is and what the risks are.

So if you can't figure out the true valuation of a public company with 50 percent of the information available, how can you possibly figure out the valuation of a private start-up? The answer you'll get when you talk to VCs is a range of valuations. Different VCs will value a start-up within a two-to-one range. One VC may say it's worth $12 million and another will say $6 million. But the point is there's a range; not all VCs are the same and they all value differently. The valuation formula is nebulous, and every VC has a different formula.

—*Steve Kirsch*

■ DILUTION: GET USED TO IT!

There are some factors of financing that are hard to swallow. Many entrepreneurs have a difficult time accepting that fact that their percentage of ownership in the company will be diluted. Get over it! Companies constantly both sell and issue equity in order to run the business. From stock option grants for employees to equity incentives for business partners, a business issues equity each year of its life. So don't worry about it. In Chapter 6 we illustrated how the founders' equity in a start-up becomes more valuable even as the percentage of ownership decreases.

Another touchy issue has to do with the amount of control you as an entrepreneur have at each funding round. Each funding round affects the previous owners. In any one funding round, the new investor gets to set the rules. This means no matter what terms and stipulations are attached to each series of funding, from the seed stage to the IPO, the next investor that comes in can change those rules. Why? Because the start-up needs that potential new investor's money to continue operating, so the new investor has the bargaining leverage. For example, an early investor might insert a clause that stipulates that he gets to keep the same equity percentage that he originally purchased. Or he may demand to invest in the following round at an average of what he just paid and what the next round is going to be. But later, when prospective VCs consider whether to invest in the current funding round, they will probably view those types of clauses as undesirable and will write them out in the current round of funding. However, doing so incurs the risk that the previous investor will sue for breach of contract—exactly the kind of legal baggage investors hate. And if the entrepreneur protests, she runs the risk of alienating the new investors, who may then decline to invest in the company. So the last investor in gets to set the rules.

Get a Lawyer

If you're ready to begin discussions with VCs, be sure to hire an attorney who has represented start-ups. Don't try to become a budding lawyer yourself. You don't have the time, and you'll never be an expert. An experienced lawyer can assist you in structuring your corporate and financial documents and can advise you on information the VC will require.

The law firms that specialize in start-ups (most of which are in Silicon Valley) include:

Brobeck, Phleger & Harrison

Cooley Godward LLP

Fenwick & West

Morrison & Foerster

Pillsbury Winthrop

Venture Law Group

Wilson Sonsini Goodrich & Rosati

■ EQUITY DEFINITIONS

Investment bankers and VCs often seem to speak another language. The words and phrases they use, when discussing equity, are unfamiliar and not always clear. Here is a guide to some common terms.

Dilution. The percentage decrease in value of the original shares. Each additional share of equity issued affects every share that was issued before it. To calculate the dilution, take the total pool of shares after the previous funding round and divide that number by the total pool of shares after the new round. Then subtract that percentage from 100 percent, and you get the percentage of dilution.

Premoney valuation. The total value of a start-up before adding in the capital gained from the current funding round. Premoney valuation is often calculated *after* a funding round has been made; for example, if a start-up is given a $3 million investment for 33 percent of equity, the postmoney valuation is $9 million. So the premoney valuation is $6 million.

Postmoney valuation. Total value of the premoney valuation plus the proceeds of the funding.

Topping up. Adding more shares.

Option pool. Common stock shares budgeted for employee stock options.

Capitalization. The value of the company determined by multiplying all of the shares by the share value.

Ownership. The percentage of the company in the hands of the shareholders. Remember, there are only 100 percentage points of equity no matter how many shares you issue. Each additional share issued dilutes the overall ownership.

Preferred shares. The stock primarily granted to private investors. Each series of preferred stock typically comes with the right to assign a board member. It may have a liquidation preference, which means that if the company is liquidated, the holder has the right to recover his or her investment before investors holding common stock.

■ THE EQUITY BUDGET: DO THE MATH

OK, now for the nitty-gritty of the equity budget. Let's begin at the beginning of the start-up. An entrepreneur will raise money at every stage, beginning at Stage 0, the seed stage. At this stage the first sources of capital are cash and often credit card debt contributed by the founders. As the entrepreneurs begin to build the business, the next sources to tap for the seed money to flesh out the idea are friends, family, and angel investors. An entrepreneur will begin by raising anywhere from $50,000 to $1 million, depending on the size and needs of the offering. An optical networking start-up, for example, may require more cash to pay for expensive workstations and testing equipment than a software developer would. Most start-ups will need to raise about $200,000.

This is a time when entrepreneurs are in uncharted waters. They have an idea for a company or product that will set the world on fire, but they don't know how to go about it. They are unsure what valuation to give the company. They wonder if they should sell shares in their company, go to a bank for financing, or go directly to a VC. Whatever course of action they take, entrepreneurs should beware of accumulating baggage. Remember the Neilism: *No uncles on the board*. If you want money from a rich uncle, borrow it from your uncle as a loan.

Keep It Simple

During this bootstrapping phase, be careful not to harm the fledgling company by introducing complicated or unreasonable terms. For instance, if someone asks for 80 percent of the company in order to give you $100,000, clearly that is not an acceptable condition. If you can't get the money under reasonable conditions, then maybe it's not worth doing, even if it means your start-up is not going to move forward. And if someone is asking for clauses that will haunt you in the future, that is just as unappealing. For example, don't introduce a *ratchet*—an antidilution clause that states that if the start-up sells shares in subsequent funding rounds at a lower price, then the first investor gets to lower the cost of his or her shares (called the *strike price*) to the reduced price. You don't want the rules to change because you'll introduce unwanted trouble down the line.

Bridge Loan

The best, fastest, and simplest way to raise a significant amount of seed money is through a convertible bridge loan. For example, if you can get some money from friends, family, or wealthy individuals, don't try to figure out the valuation and then sell that formula to nonprofessional investors; instead, simply structure a convertible bridge loan. A bridge loan removes the inherent complications of any financing. If the bridge loan amount is $50,000, have it convert at one-half the valuation of the first professional round. That means that if the VC's shares are valued at $1.00, the investor's shares will be $0.50. The advantages of a convertible bridge loan are that you can transact it quickly, the investors have an implied future value, and you've avoided all the problems of trying to set a valuation. An arrangement like this is appealing to VCs as well because when they set a valuation for the company they can do it based on the merits of the entrepreneurs and the start-up itself and won't be bogged down trying to figure out what has been negotiated earlier.

While raising money during the seed stage, it's worth remembering these five guidelines from Chapter 8:

1. *Create a straightforward equity agreement.* Keep the loan documents uncomplicated.

2. *Don't promise any investor that he'll get his money first.* Keep all your options open and don't bet your entire company on one round of funding.

3. *Don't promise an investor more equity in the event the company misses its milestones.* Those clauses pit an investor's interests against a start-up's. You want everyone working together to meet all company goals.

4. *Avoid complicated debt.* Confusing financing arrangements are dangerous because VCs might shy away from a company that has too much baggage.

5. *Keep the number of early shareholders to a minimum.* Too many early investors can get unwieldy.

■ STAGE 0—BOOTSTRAP

This is the very beginning of the start-up, when it's just rising from primordial goo. The entrepreneurs are living off their credit cards, formulating plans in their kitchens or garages, and pulling ideas together (see Table 14.2). At the end of the bootstrap stage (see Table 14.3), the start-up will be capitalized in an uncomplicated way. And

Table 14.2   Business snapshot—Bootstrap stage.

Stage	0
Age	0–6 months
Genus	Bootstrap
Number of customers	0
Number of employees	4

the simplest way is always the best way. The goal is to raise the capital for the next stage; entrepreneurs need to do the things that allow them to raise the next amount of capital, because when they get the money they can do more things with the business.

Table 14.3   Capitalization snapshot—Bootstrap stage.

Stage 0—Seed Stage	Preferred Shares	Common Options	Total Shares	Ownership (percentage)
Founders			5,000,000	100.0
VC1				
VC2				
VC3				
Option pool				
Public				
Total shares			5,000,000	100.0
Ownership purchased in series				
Dilution of previous owners				
Price per share				
Premoney valuation				
Proceeds				
Postmoney valuation				
Cumulative capital				

Business Goals for Stage 0

- Assemble enough of a business to attract the first wave of investors.
- Attract two to four key employees.
- Run the business so that you attract the next round of funding for Stage 1.

In going for Stage 1, VCs will either step up and invest, or entrepreneurs must turn to other sources, such as to angel investors. In the meantime, while in Stage 0, entrepreneurs are assembling enough substance to convince people that they have a viable business. They are creating mockups of products and working to crystallize the business offering. They're spending all their resources doing fundamental research, cultivating references, and developing relationships with accountants, lawyers, and friends who can introduce them to investors.

Fundraising Goal for Stage 0

- By the end of Stage 0, raise $3 million based on a $9 million valuation. Raise the money from professional investors, such as VCs, to make the start-up attractive to customers, employees, and additional investors.

■ STAGE 1—PROOF OF CONCEPT

The proof-of-concept stage is a period of rapid organization. This is when you create the prototype product or service, attract the first customers, sell your promise, and hire a few crucial employees (see Table 14.4). The goal of this and indeed each successive stage is to raise your next round of capital. At the end of this six-month stage you'll have raised an additional $12.5 million in Series B financing that enables you to move to the next stage (see Table 14.5).

What is different at the beginning of this stage?

- The company raised $3 million and was valued at $9 million.
- The company issued 4,000,000 shares at $0.75 per share to raise $3 million.

Table 14.4   Business snapshot—Proof-of-concept.

Stage	1
Age	0–6 months
Genus	Proof-of-concept
Number of customers	1 or 2 enterprise customers or 1,000 consumer customers
Number of employees	30 by the end of 6 months

- A pool of stock options for employees was established with 3,000,000 shares.
- The founders' share of the company was diluted by 58.3 percent, with 33.3 percent coming from VC 1 and 25 percent from the Options pool

Table 14.5   Capitalization snapshot—Stage 1—after the Series A funding round.

Stage 1— Series A Funding	Preferred Shares	Common Options	Total Shares	Ownership (percentage)
Founders			5,000,000	41.7
VC1	4,000,000		4,000,000	33.3
VC2				
VC3				
Option pool		3,000,000	3,000,000	25.0
Public				
Total shares			12,000,000	100.0
Ownership purchased in series	33.3%			
Dilution of previous owners			58.3%	
Price per share	$0.75			
Premoney valuation	$6 million			
Proceeds	$3 million			
Postmoney valuation	$9 million			
Cumulative capital	$3 million			

- The company has $3 million to take it to the next funding round.

Business Goals for Stage 1
- Build a simple product for proof of concept.
- Gain requisite customers (enterprise or consumer).
- Spend the $3 million over 6 to 12 months.
- Attract a core group of key employees.

Fundraising Goal for the End of Stage 1
- Raise $12.5 million based on a $50 million postmoney valuation.

■ STAGE 2—DEFINING YOUR LEADERSHIP

In Stage 2 (see Table 14.6), you've taken the feedback from your customers to build a stable version 1.0 product. You've increased the number of customers, added employees, and, by the end of this stage, raised more capital to sustain you for the next year (see Table 14.7). You have identified the market opportunity, and you are offering this solution to the marketplace. The market is becoming more competitive, and the company is spending its resources to rapidly build the business and define its leadership in the market.

What is different at the beginning of this stage?

- The company raised $12.5 million and was valued at $50 million.
- The company issued 4,410,000 shares at $2.83 to raise $12.5 million.
- The pool of stock options for employees was topped up with 1,230,000 shares.
- The previous investors' shares of the company were diluted by 32 percent.
- The company has $12.5 million more to take it to the next funding round.

Table 14.6   Business snapshot—Market defining.

Stage	2
Age	7–12 months
Genus	Market defining
Number of customers	10–15 enterprise customers or 200,000 consumer customers.
Number of employees	60 by end of 12 months

Table 14.7   Capitalization snapshot—beginning of Stage 2—after the Series B funding round.

Stage 2— Series B Funding	Preferred Shares	Common Options	Total Shares	Ownership (percentage)
Founders			5,000,000	28.3
VC1	1,290,000		5,290,000	30.0
VC2	3,120,000		3,120,000	17.7
VC3				
Option pool		1,230,000	4,230,000	24.0
Public				
Total shares	4,410,000		17,640,000	100.0
Ownership purchased in series	25%			
Dilution of previous owners			32.0%	
Price per share	$2.83			
Premoney valuation	$37.5 million			
Proceeds	$12.5 million			
Postmoney valuation	$50.0 million			
Cumulative capital	$15.5 million			

Business Goals for Stage 2
- Turn prototype into stable, go-to-market version 1.0 product based on customer feedback.
- Scale up the number of customers.
- Fill out executive ranks.

Fundraising Goal for the End of Stage 2
- Raise $20 million in Series C funding from additional professional investors.

■ STAGE 3—EXPANDING TO PROFITABILITY

As in the first two stages, you continue with product development, but now you're aiming for profitability (see Table 14.8). The business scales to produce $3 million of revenue a quarter, and you're very close to turning profitable (see Table 14.9).

What's different at the beginning of this stage?

- The company raised $20 million by selling 20 percent and is now valued at more than $100.1 million.
- The first VC bought an additional 500,000 shares at $4.40 each.
- The second VC bought an additional 500,000 shares at $4.40.
- A new VC purchased 3,550,000 shares at $4.40.
- The option pool was topped up by 580,000 shares.
- The equity of all previous owners was diluted by 22.5 percent.
- The founders' equity was diluted to 22 percent.
- The company has collected more than $35 million in capital.

Business Goals for Stage 3
- Further develop product.
- Scale customer base to produce $3 million in revenue per quarter without stunting growth.
- Be profitable by end of stage.
- Expand distribution and market potential of an already established position; open more sales offices.

Table 14.8   Business snapshot—Expanding to profitability.

Stage	3
Age	13–24 months
Genus	Expanding to profitability
Number of customers	100 enterprise customers or 2 million consumer customers
Number of employees	150 by end of 24 months

Table 14.9   Capitalization snapshot—beginning of Stage 3—after the Series C funding round.

Stage 3— Series C Funding	Preferred Shares	Common Options	Total Shares	Ownership (percentage)
Founders			5,000,000	22.0
VC1	500,000		5,790,000	25.4
VC2	500,000		3,620,000	15.9
VC3	3,550,000		3,550,000	15.6
Option pool		580,000	4,810,000	21.1
Public				
Total shares	4,550,000		22,770,000	100.0
Ownership purchased in series	20%			
Dilution of previous owners			22.5%	
Price per share	$4.40			
Premoney valuation	$80.1 million			
Proceeds	$20.0 million			
Postmoney valuation	$100.1 million			
Cumulative capital	$35.5 million			

Fundraising Goal for the End of Stage 3
- Raise $60 million in an IPO.

■ STAGE 4—IPO

This is the stage you've been working your heart out for (see Table 14.10). Revenues will be growing faster than expenses. You'll introduce extensions to the product lines and have more sales offices. By the end of this stage, you'll be profitable, you'll have gone public, and you'll have a great company (see Table 14.11).

What's different at the beginning of this stage?

- The company raised $60 million by selling 15 percent and is now valued at about $400 million.
- 4,020,000 shares were sold to the public for $14.93 each.
- The equity of the previous owners was diluted by 15 percent.
- The founders' equity was diluted to 18.7 percent.
- The company has raised in excess of $95 million.

Business Goals for Stage 4
- Introduce a second product.
- Be profitable.

THE NATURAL ORDER OF SEQUENCING

These four stages reflect the natural order of sequencing a start-up, not some arbitrary sequence. For example, Stage 1 takes six months because one month is too short to develop a product, attract the initial customer(s), and raise funds. And a year is too long because the competitive and customer markets change too fast. The successful start-ups all fall within these ranges of development. Follow this sequencing, and you'll stay in the success zone.

Table 14.10   Business snapshot—Go public!

Stage	4
Age	25–36 months
Genus	Go public!
Number of customers	200+ enterprise customers or 2 million+ consumer customers
Number of employees	200
Capital requirement	$60 million

Table 14.11   Capitalization snapshot—beginning of Stage 4—after the IPO.

Stage 4—IPO	Common Options	Total Shares	Ownership (percentage)
Founders		5,000,000	18.7
VC1		5,790,000	21.6
VC2		3,620,000	13.5
VC3		3,550,000	13.3
Option pool		4,810,000	18.0
Public		4,020,000	15.0
Total shares	4,020,000	26,790,000	100.0
Ownership purchased in series	15%		
Dilution of previous owners		15%	
Price per share	$14.93		
Premoney valuation	$339.9 million		
Proceeds	$60.0 million		
Postmoney valuation	$399.9 million		
Cumulative capital	$95.5 million		

Snapshot of an E-tailing Casualty

Violet.com was one of the many e-tailing dot.com start-ups that were annihilated in 2000, but it wasn't because its equity was out of whack (see Table 14.12). Violet started up in 1998 as a promising e-tailer of specialty goods. The founders used their own money and persuaded friends and family to give them $200,000 more. In 1999 Violet received more than $3 million from a number of high-profile investors. But the environment for e-tailing turned hostile, the dot.coms began to crash and burn, and in April 2000 Violet closed down. The start-up did everything right—except anticipate that the market for e-tailing start-ups would implode. Sometimes, even when you win, you lose.

Table 14.12   Violet.com's capitalization after Stage 2.

	Shares	% of Equity
Founders stock	6,600,000	38.34
Angels	130,988	00.76
Stock options	10,579,064	22.36
Preferred stock—Series A	502,359	02.92
Preferred stock—Series B	6,131,115	35.62
Total	17,212,538	100.00

Sources of
Start-up Capital

NEILISM: Don't confuse easy money with a good business.

All investment capital is not created equal. Certainly, an entrepreneur can turn to many sources to fund a start-up: Friends, family, and even the proverbial rich uncle can all play an important part at various stages in the financing of a nascent business. Each supplier of capital has its own positive and negative attributes and should be utilized at different points during a company's lifetime. It would be so easy if all investment capital were equal. But who offers the money, when they offer it, and, most important, what they offer along with it have a big impact on the success of the start-up.

It's important to understand what each type of investor brings to the table—and what it doesn't—so entrepreneurs can make the right choices for their start-up at the right time. Once you know what strings are attached to the funding, you can negotiate from a position of understanding.

■ PROFESSIONAL VERSUS NONPROFESSIONAL INVESTORS

Entrepreneurs can choose from a broad spectrum of investors, from Mom and Dad to individual amateur investors, such as angels, to sophisticated professional venture capital firms to corporate investors. An individual, however successful he or she may be, is not usually a professional investor and may or may not be able to tell you whether you have a business worth pursuing and then help you formulate your business. Some individuals approach investing in a start-up as a once-in-a-lifetime opportunity they're pursuing because they happen to know an entrepreneur, perhaps a family member or a neighbor, with what sounds like a worthwhile idea. Other individual investors are wealthy people who invest somewhat more seriously, in that they're willing to fund entrepreneurs with whom they have no previous relationship. These individuals often have full-time jobs and invest extra money as a sideline pursuit.

Venture capital firms and corporations that take stakes in start-ups are considered professional entities. VC firms differ from individual investors in that VCs invest full time. Their business is turning start-ups into successful companies. The partners and associates at VC firms spend much of their time cultivating contacts and resources—such as potential customers, headhunters, consultants, leasing companies, lawyers, and partners—that can benefit start-ups. In short, VCs are paid a salary to spend their waking hours making the companies in their portfolios a success.

Angels and VCs are very different types of investors. Angel investors appear in abundance during prosperous times, when large numbers of individuals have had significant success in the stock market. The number of angels tends to decline during downturns in the economy, when they have less money to risk in start-up ventures. Because VCs are professional investors, they take a long-term outlook and invest during both good and bad financial times. VCs get the money to invest from funds that are committed years in advance, so VCs have the ability to make follow-on investments, meaning they can provide additional capital in subsequent funding rounds and do so in any economic environment.

■ A WELL-TRAVELED PATH TO SUCCESSFUL FUND-RAISING

The successful start-up's quest for capital generally follows this route: Initially, the entrepreneurs raise seed money from their own savings and credit lines. Next, they turn to family and friends. Then they widen their quest for capital to outside investors, either by pitching their idea directly to venture capitalists or by turning to angel investors to provide the early funding that will enable them to develop their business enough to eventually approach VCs for more substantial, longer-term capital investments. Another source to which entrepreneurs sometimes turn is a corporation whose own strategic interests dovetail with the start-up's. Finally, the entrepreneurs turn to the public equity markets in an initial public offering.

There are seven primary buckets of funding capital available to start-ups:

1. The entrepreneurs' own money.
2. The entrepreneurs' friends and family.
3. Single angel investors.
4. Organized networks of angel investors.
5. Venture capitalists.
6. Corporate equity.
7. Public equity markets.

■ CHARITY BEGINS AT HOME

The first source for capital is the entrepreneurs themselves. If the entrepreneurs believe in their idea, they will use every dollar at their disposal, from savings accounts to credit cards to taking out a second mortgage on a house. The next step is to tap friends and family (see Table 15.1).

Table 15.1   Friends and family snapshot.

Range of Investment	Up to $50,000
Professional investor	No
From a fund	No
Seed-stage investor	Yes
Early-stage investor	No
Late-stage investor	No
Resources and advice	No
Examples	Mom, Dad, rich uncles
What to expect	Cash, moral support
What not to expect	Resources and advice to help you build the business

■ INDIVIDUAL ANGEL INVESTORS

At this point your start-up may be cooking, and you may be ready to talk to professional investors such as VCs. But if VCs tell you that your idea needs more time to develop and ferment, the next source of capital you can turn to is an individual angel investor (see Table 15.2).

Individual angels are usually wealthy individuals who have

Table 15.2   Individual angel investors snapshot.

Range of Investment	Up to $500,000
Professional investor	No
From a fund	No
Seed-stage investor	Yes
Early-stage investor	No
Late-stage investor	No
Resources and advice	No
Examples	Rich uncles, wealthy neighbors
What to expect	Cash
What not to expect	Resources and advice to help you build the business

made a lot of money in the stock market (or at the race track), and they probably will invest in you because they know you. (Or sometimes they are wealthy individuals who put their names out with investor groups and lawyers with the message that they are looking for opportunities to put some money to work.) They've made enough money that they are comfortable risking $25,000 to $50,000 and sometimes up to $500,000 in you even though the investment will be illiquid and it may take them many years to realize any income from the investment, if they realize any income at all.

■ ANGEL CONSORTIUMS

The next level is a group, or consortium, of angel investors. These are prosperous people who want to regularly invest in start-ups and choose to invest with others in order to get into more and bigger deals and to spread the risk (see Table 15.3). The approach taken by consortiums of angels is to invest in a number of companies that happen to be start-ups. Unlike the friends-and-family type of investors, angel consortiums are often unfamiliar with the entrepreneur, so the entrepreneur has to pass certain criteria. The entrepreneur has to establish a level of credibility with the group and must convince them that the idea or opportunity has some potential before the group

Table 15.3 Angel consortium snapshot.

Range of Investment	Up to $1 million
Professional investors	Sometimes
From a fund	Sometimes
Seed-stage investor	Yes
Early-stage investor	No
Late-stage investor	No
Resources and advice	Some
Examples	Band of Angels, Angel Investors
What to expect	Cash, some advice, access to contacts, one-time investment
What not to expect	Active participation in your business, "due diligence" analysis of your business

will make an investment. Angel groups often make decisions quickly and spend less time than VCs do researching the viability of the opportunity—what VCs call performing due diligence. Organized angels can bring more than just money to the table: they have contacts with lawyers, VCs, and potential customers that can be quite helpful to start-ups.

■ CORPORATE INVESTORS

Another source for capital is a corporate investor. In most cases, corporations invest in companies that will help them advance their own corporate goals by expanding the current and future markets for the investing company's products. These are usually strategic investments where the host company can benefit from the start-up's success. Having a corporate investor brings cachet along with cash, but there is usually little in the way of hands-on advice and management. Intel is a good example of a company that makes strategic investments in start-ups. Intel invested in CNET in 1996 in order to foster the growth of high-bandwidth content that would encourage users to buy computers with faster processors in order to better enjoy the content.

To VC or Not to VC? That Is the Question

Say there are four start-ups that are all in the same general competitive space: Each develops B2B software for enterprise companies. But then Company A gets additional capital in order to turbocharge the business. The money allows it to hire more programmers, even though revenue based on their work is not expected for months. The extra programmers enable it to develop a more effective product; or the company can afford to make more in-person sales calls. As a result, Company A can attract and retain more customers; and all of a sudden, Company A becomes better known in the marketplace, makes more money, is able to spend more dollars on marketing, and can therefore increase market

---

share. The capital has allowed Company A to take small significant steps to beat their competition—namely, companies B, C, and D. Eventually two of the other start-ups see the success Company A experienced when it got VC money, and they decide to go that route as well. The start-up that doesn't gets left behind.

■ VENTURE CAPITALISTS

When a start-up is serious about pursuing a big opportunity, VCs are the best source of capital. Not only are VCs in the business of helping start-ups succeed, but they have access to large, dependable funds of capital. But money is only a part of the relationship. VCs provide insight, advice, leadership, and mentorship in the package (see Table 15.4).

VCs invest in businesses they think are viable. There isn't a minimum or maximum investment—VCs will invest in start-ups as small as two engineers in a garage. What VCs look for is a potentially big business opportunity and an innovative offering to attack

Table 15.4   Venture capitalists snapshot.

Range of Investment	Up to $50 million
Professional investor	Yes
From a fund	Yes
Seed-stage investor	Yes
Early-stage investor	Yes
Late-stage investor	Yes
Resources and advice	Yes
Examples	Accel Partners, Benchmark Partners, Kleiner Perkins, NEA
What to expect	Cash, hands-on advice, pressure to perform
What not to expect	Automatic success, an adversarial relationship

that market. The size of those investments happens to be in the range of millions of dollars, so VCs rarely make investments in the $200,000 range. This fact has led to a common misperception that VCs don't invest in start-ups in the very earliest stages. That, in fact, is the ideal scenario for a VC.

There are hundreds of VC firms, and they vary from seed-stage specialists to late-stage investors, while many invest at all stages. Some are small firms that work with tens of millions of dollars and others are gargantuan VC firms that have billions of dollars to invest. The large firms include Accel Partners, Benchmark Capital Group, Draper Fisher Jurvetson, Kleiner Perkins Caufield & Byers, Mayfield Fund, New Enterprise Associates, Oak Investment Partners, Sequoia Capital, and Softbank Venture Capital.

What's the Investing Threshold?

There's a common misperception that a VC won't bother with a company they feel warrants less than a $5 million investment. This is wrong—and more important, it misses the point. The more accurate way to look at it is that VCs invest only in businesses with a big market opportunity that offers the possibility of a substantial return on investment. When they find such a company they feel can succeed, they will invest whatever amount of money it takes to make that company successful—whether the start-up consists of two engineers in a garage or has evolved to a more developed stage. In the past few years, the average amount of capital needed to take a start-up from bootstrap stage to prototype stage is from $2 million to $5 million. Of course, it could be more if the start-up is building an infrastructure-intensive company.

▪ HOW VCs WORK

No matter the size, all VC firms operate the same way. A VC firm is most often a partnership, with two to six partners. Each partner has a large pot of money at his or her disposal to invest in start-ups. The amount of money ranges from $25 million to $80 million per partner. A three-partner firm, then, may have a fund of $75 million to $240 million to invest in start-ups, while a large firm with dozens of partners may have more than $1 billion to invest. The money that VCs invest, which is pooled into a fund (see Table 15.5), is raised from outside investors, called limited partners, such as insurance companies, pension funds, university endowments, corporate investors, and wealthy individuals. The money is not given to VCs in a lump sum but rather is collected as needed over a long period from the limited partners in what are termed *capital calls.*

VC firms return to the limited partners the money and any appreciated gains when there is a liquidity event. A *liquidity event* occurs when the investment, which has been used by the start-up to build the company, is in a form that can be resold, such as when the company has an IPO or when it is acquired or merged with another company and the VCs get cash or stock in the new company. VCs then distribute the proceeds of the investment to the limited partners, in the form of either cash or stock in the portfolio companies.

Because of the sizable stakes taken in a start-up, VCs have a very powerful incentive to make a company profitable and eventually liquid. Most VC funds call for a 10-year term that can be extended by a year or two after that. This means the capital is untouchable by the limited partners during the term.

You can look into how VC companies make money and read about internal rates of returns, net present value, and fund performances, but the math is actually quite simple. VC firms make money when the capital they invest increases in value. The partners get a fee called the *carry,* or *carried interest,* on the capital appreciation. For

Table 15.5 Snapshot of a sample VC fund.

Fund size	$100 million
Capital appreciation	$300 million
20 percent carry	$60 million
Amount returned to investors (includes the capital appreciation plus the initial investment, minus the carry)	$340 million

example, if you have a three-partner VC firm with a $100 million capital fund and the fund ultimately returns $300 million, the VC partners get a carry on the $300 million appreciation; the investors in the fund—the limited partners—get their original capital investment back plus the capital appreciation, minus the carry. The amount of the carry is typically 20 percent of the capital appreciation and is split three ways by the general, or managing, partner. Also, most VCs charge an annual management fee of a few percent of the capital committed.

■ VENTURE CAPITAL ECONOMICS

The venture capital business can be lucrative. A number of VC firms make sizeable profits, but most VC firms don't have dazzling returns year after year. Much attention is paid in the media to the returns of VC firms, and indeed 1999 turned out to be an anomalous year in which the average VC firm returned 143 percent of their committed capital to their investors. But according to Venture Economics, an industry research group, the average return of more than 1,625 venture firms from 1990 to 2000 was 29.5 percent. During that same period, the top performing mutual fund companies returned an average of 15.5 percent. Keep in mind that money invested in a mutual fund is far more liquid than that in a VC fund and can be easily moved from fund to fund. The money invested in a VC fund may be unavailable for up to 10 years and is invested in riskier companies than those in a mutual fund.

Table 15.6 illustrates the success rate of a typical VC firm. If the firm has a $100 million fund and invests $8 million in each of 10 companies, 2 of those companies may be exceptional successes and return 10 times the investment; 5 companies may return 5 times the investment; and 3 companies may be total failures. Keep in mind that these returns occur over many years—on average 5—and the investments are illiquid.

■ NO FREE LUNCH

Once you accept money from VCs, you also accept the added pressure to perform well. Entrepreneurs need to understand the expec-

Table 15.6 Success rate of a typical VC firm (fund = $100 million).

Number of Companies in Portfolio (out of total of 10)	Investment Amount	Rate of Return on Investment	Returns
2	$8 million per company	10×	$160 million ($80 million × 2)
3	$8 million per company	0	$0
5	$8 million per company	5×	$200 million ($40 million × 5)
Total return			$360 million
Initial investment			$100 million
Capital appreciation			$260 million
20% carry			$52 million
Amount returned to investors (capital appreciation plus initial investment, minus the carry)		30%	$308 million

tations. If a lucrative start-up opportunity arises, aggressive investors will fight to fund that start-up in order to profit from that opportunity. When a market sector becomes hot, that leads to a herd mentality among VCs, and that, in turn, raises the stakes of the game. Once the entrepreneur gets capital from a VC, the onus is on the entrepreneur to hire more people, to get more customers, and to build the business quickly. Because VCs are hands-on investors, entrepreneurs should look forward to active participation from the VC firm.

Entrepreneurs seek VC funding because they want to super-charge their business, and VCs are looking for entrepreneurs who want to build the next Cisco Systems. In the best cases, when entrepreneurs and VCs work together, there's an inevitable meeting of the minds—both parties clearly understand their responsibilities in the relationship. When approaching VCs for funding, remember the saying, "Be careful what you ask for, you just may get it." You may get the capital, but in return VCs expect you to grow quickly. That's the commitment that comes with accepting the money. The VC is involved to assist you in your quest, to help you make the tough choices, and to provide advice.

The money invested by VCs entails additional burdens for an entrepreneur in terms of growing faster. The capabilities of the investors directly influence the success or the failure. For example, if one start-up has access to world-class headhunters because of a VC's close ties and the other start-up doesn't, then the other start-up is at a disadvantage in hiring key executives. As a result, the second start-up will probably not have as strong a management team.

Receiving VC money and the smarts that come with it sparks faster growth in a start-up. After getting the capital, the business will have to draw on even more resources in order to grow. It will need the components that make it faster and more competitive, as well as the intangible contributions that VCs can bring—like contacts with business partners, heightened publicity, and a positive reputation. The benefits entrepreneurs get from the incremental value of a good VC is directly proportional to the success trajectory of a start-up.

Put on the Path to Success by VCs

VCs have a direct hand in quickly putting a start-up on a trajectory toward success. A good example is When.com, which approached 21st Century in 1997. The founders' idea was to replicate the Microsoft Outlook Calendar software as a Web service. Of course, the Outlook calendar is complicated, with a sophisticated group scheduling feature, and it had a very loyal installed base. We as VCs saw an opportunity in calendaring, but we knew that it would take a year or two to develop the technology for Web-based group scheduling. Instead of funding the original offering, we helped the company come up with a strategy for a centralized event service where a user could subscribe to a number of events, such as baseball games, and the user's calendar would be automatically updated. We effectively turned the original offering into a media business with advertising. (When.com was sold to American Online in 1999.)

When AvantGo came to us in 1997, it wanted to provide client software for the Palm Pilot. In 1997 creating client software seemed like a good opportunity, but it became obvious over time that client software wasn't a great business. We as VCs knew that a more lucrative opportunity would be to develop software on the server side. The founders were capable entrepreneurs and quite knowledgeable about a specific market area. But their specific approach was not on a success path. So we ripped up the business plan that called for client software that ran on Palm Pilots and instead convinced the founders that the real opportunity was to provide server software that allows companies to manage their Palm Pilots. And that's AvantGo's business today. (AvantGo went public in September 2000.)

—*J. Neil Weintraut*

■ TOUGH LOVE

Despite the dot.com meltdown of 2000, there are boatloads of dollars to invest in viable start-ups, and VCs are complaining that they don't have enough good companies to invest in. Because they have funds with millions of dollars and because VCs only make money when start-ups succeed, VCs are constantly on the lookout for viable opportunities. If they are under the gun to find fundable companies, why do they pass on yours? There is a message in a VC's rejection. If you make a presentation to 10 VCs and they all pass on the opportunity, the message is that your start-up is not viable. So learn from what they tell you. If your business plan doesn't change from one VC presentation to the next, then you're not absorbing what the VC is counseling. And it just may be that you are not a start-up and you won't get backed. That's the tough love lesson from VCs.

An example of a company that learned quickly was Compaq Computer. When it made its pitch to Kleiner Perkins in 1982, the business plan called for Compaq to market hard disk drives for IBM's recently released desktop PC. The Kleiner Perkins partners decided to pass on the idea but backed Compaq when it returned with a new plan to develop a portable IBM-compatible PC. Compaq went on to become a huge success.

Then again, VCs aren't always right. As the Neilism states, "Don't confuse easy money with a good business," which means that just because you're getting funded, you shouldn't believe for a minute that your business idea is a slam-dunk.

Recall the lessons learned from the glut of online pet supply stores in 2000:

• Pets.com launched in November 1998, and within a year it had taken in more than $100 million in VC funding from Hummer Winblad Venture Partners, Bowman Capital Management, Amazon, and others.

• Petsmart.com formed in February 1999 and launched its site in June 1999. Petsmart.com received a $50 million investment in July 1999, filed for an IPO in early 2000, but pulled it in late 2000 because of lack of interest.

• Petopia.com was formed in late 1998 and began selling pet supplies online in August 1999. It got a $66 million investment in

July 1999, filed for an IPO in March of 2000, and was out of business by 2001.

• In 1999 Petstore.com received more than $90 million in cash and marketing services from Discovery Communications. It was out of business in 2001.

In 1999 more than $300 million was invested in online pet supply stores. Virtually all of the money went down the drain, and most of the companies that received the cash are closed. In hindsight it's easy to say that online pet stores are not a great business; but in 1999 thousands of people thought otherwise, including VCs. They were wrong.

■ CHANCES FOR SUCCESS

If you get funded by VCs, your chances for success are quite good. While not all of the companies that VCs fund will go public, or even survive, there is a track record of success for companies funded by VCs (see Table 15.7).

■ VCs SLEEP LIKE BABIES

The goals of VCs are easy to grasp: They want to make money, and they want to have fun in the process. There's a common perception

Table 15.7   Venture capital–backed IPOs from 1995 to 2000.

Year	Total IPOs	Venture Capital–backed IPOs	Percentage
1995	583	204	35
1996	873	278	32
1997	636	137	22
1998	397	78	20
1999	572	263	46
2000	453	239	53

Source: ventureeconomics.com

of VCs (sometimes less-than-fondly referred to as "vulture capital-ists") as ruthless browbeaters of hapless entrepreneurs, whose only interest is squeezing every last dollar out of a struggling company and whose idea of a fun day at the office is fighting with founders of start-ups stuck in a vicious spiral. In truth, VCs would much rather work with a successful founder than insist on changes from a failing founder. The number of jokes about VCs are few and far between—maybe because so many people fear that VCs *really are* "vulture capitalists." But this joke popular in Silicon Valley paints a truer picture: Even with all their high-risk investments, VCs sleep like babies. That is, they sleep for two hours, wake up crying, sleep for two hours, wake up crying, sleep for two hours, . . . VCs wish that all their start-ups would be stress-free successes.

Working With VCs

When searching for capital, keep these guidelines in mind:

- There two types of investor: professional and nonpro-fessional. Professional investors, like VCs, make it their business to make start-ups successful.
- The capabilities of the investors directly influence the suc-cess or the failure of the company.
- Take your idea to a VC if you want to supercharge your start-up.
- Be prepared to accept hands-on assistance from VCs.

■ REFERENCE

http://www.ventureeconomics.com

Chapter 16

Putting Equity to Work

NEILISM: Beware of equity missing in action.

By now it should be clear that equity is one of a start-up's most powerful tools. Because start-up equity offers such a potential for dramatic returns, a start-up can use it as a surrogate for money. It can be traded, assigned, bartered, and used both in lieu of and in partnership with cash.

Equity is a resource the entrepreneur must utilize in a systematic manner to be successful—from the very beginning when a business is being bootstrapped to long after it has gone public. If the equity is used well, the value of everyone's share increases. If the equity is squandered or used incorrectly, then the equity's value is debased, and the company will almost certainly fail.

Many entrepreneurs fear that by giving away equity they dilute their control, so they're hesitant to deploy equity. But by hoarding equity, entrepreneurs can deal their company a mortal wound just as easily as they can by deploying it indiscriminately. Successful entrepreneurs walk a fine line between issuing too little equity and too much.

What's the value of your equity? When you first launch your

start-up, the equity doesn't really have any intrinsic value—but it does have enormous upside potential. It's that upside that people want to latch on to, so you need to understand the power and the value of the equity you're distributing. The value of the equity depends on a number of factors, one being how well you deploy it. The actual dollar value of it will be determined by professional investors, such as venture capitalists and investment bankers. And that concrete dollar amount can be used when you're negotiating how much equity and cash to pay for outside services. But it's the lure of a potentially big upside in value that can work most to your advantage.

■ FORM AN EQUITY BUDGET

Equity is ownership; and when equity is used correctly, it aligns every owner's motives and goals with the best interests of the business. Equity can help you attract people and resources that you couldn't lure with cash alone. For example, issuing equity to employees gives them a powerful incentive to help the company succeed—if the company does well, then the value of their shares increases. The same is true for strategic investors; the advice and counsel they impart is not just for the company's benefit, but for their own as well. This same principle holds for consultants and third-party contributors, such as attorneys, headhunters, and public relations agencies. Strategic business partners also may be motivated by equity and should not be overlooked.

Taking Equity in the Poster Child of the Internet

When Yahoo! was just beginning, William Ryan, chairman of the public relations company Niehaus Ryan Wong (NRW), Inc., knew the start-up was something special. "We wanted Yahoo!'s business, but Yahoo! didn't have very much cash," he explained. "They had a limited budget, yet we felt they needed a lot of PR. We felt that the Internet itself needed a voice, it needed a spokesperson, somebody to evangelize the

Internet, because it hadn't yet crossed the chasm—it hadn't gone mainstream. The Internet's old guard—the Vint Cerfs, Tim Berners-Lees—they were all older and they were academics. We thought Jerry Yang and David Filo had the opportunity to be positioned as the poster kids of the Internet at that moment in time. So we took a large portion of our fee for our work with Yahoo! in stock. At that time it was an innovative thing to do.

"As an agency we've never done a stock-only deal; we've done stock plus cash. We've taken as little as 15 percent of our fee in stock and as much as 50 percent. Over time, as a start-up gets more funding, it's no longer advantageous for that company to give equity for services that it can pay for with cash.

"As with Yahoo!, as more cash came into the company we started taking less stock. We've also had similar arrangements with Software.net, which became Beyond, and Zapme, now called rStar. We lost money on Open Horizon.

"Having stock in the early stages of a start-up is subtly motivating. It motivated us to make sure [that] we always had the best team on Yahoo!, and that Yahoo! received the appropriate amount of partners' time. Also, we could directly benefit from Yahoo!'s success.

"We will consider doing a stock swap on a case-by-case basis. The intention is to build a long-term relationship, and the advantage is a lot of vested interest. Here's how we think about it. When NRW takes stock in a company, that money comes out of our profits. It's like asking the principals of an agency to function like venture capitalists. So any investment in lieu of cash becomes a personal investment that comes out of the profit of the business. So it is in the best interest of the owners to make sure they get a return.

"When the deal is being structured, start-ups need to see this as similar to making a deal with angel investors. So we'll ask the same tough questions: 'What percentage of the com-

(continued)

pany are we getting? Do we believe in the idea or this is just another dogfood.com? Does the management team have what it takes to turn this into a winning company? What's the path to profitability? What are the chances that this company will be able to go public in the future?' We see a 'great idea' a day, so it's not hard for us to spot a winner."

—*Christopher Barr*

Because each share of equity affects all the other shares, entrepreneurs must have a big picture view of equity as well as a granular understanding of where each share is being allocated. As a result, one of the most important duties an entrepreneur can undertake is to deploy the equity in a disciplined manner. And as discussed in earlier chapters, the best way to be disciplined is to have an equity budget. This allows you to carefully plan to whom you want to give equity and how much to give them, and it also helps you evaluate whom *not* to give equity to. By taking the time to create an equity budget, you will establish a system that helps you preserve equity for only those players who contribute in an ongoing way to your company's success.

In Chapter 6 we outlined a system of equity distribution that included founders, investors, employees, and others. The "others" category is the small percentage allocated for consultants and service providers. What's important about equity is the percentage of ownership, not necessarily the number of shares or the price per share. In the first stages of a 3G start-up, the equity budget typically breaks down into these ranges:

Founders: 20% to 50%

Investors: 30% to 50%

Employees and others: 20% to 30%

Remember, there are only 100 percentage points of equity, and the total of the portions issued to all the constituents never exceeds 100 percent.

Third-party resources and service providers are motivated by

Table 16.1 Small amounts of equity can become quite valuable.

Funding Round	Price per Share	%	Shares	Value
Bootstrap	$ 0	3	157,250	$ 0
Series A	$ 0.75	1.3	157,250	$ 117,938
Series B	$ 2.83	0.9	157,250	$ 445,720
Series C	$ 4.40	0.7	157,250	$ 691,209
IPO	$14.93	0.6	157,250	$2,347,743

owning a vested interest. The 3 percent allocated to outside consultants may seem like a pittance, but in fact it turns out to be substantial, as shown in Table 16.1. Using the same valuations illustrated in Chapter 14, the value of the shares increases dramatically at each stage of the funding process, even as the shares are diluted. For example, if 3 percent of the equity translates into 157,250 shares, then the value increases from $0 at formation to more than $2 million when the company has an initial public offering, even though there has been a steady dilution in the percentage of ownership at each funding round.

■ WHO GETS EQUITY AND WHO DOESN'T?

How should you divvy up this potentially lucrative equity pie? It's your job to sift through the demands for equity and to deploy it only where it helps you attain your goals. There are clearly certain parties whose help and assistance are vital to the start-up's success, and there are others who may demand equity but should not get it. Because equity is used to align goals and to motivate, founders and entrepreneurs should think through the ramifications before issuing any equity. For instance, if you issue stock warrants with a vesting period to consultants and other third parties, they may be holding illiquid stock for possibly three to five years. Make sure you choose people with whom you want to have a long-term relationship and who share your business goals.

Test-Drive a Long-Term Partnership First

Melody Haller, owner of the public relations firm Antenna Group, has a lot of experience in partnering with clients in exchange for a piece of the company—and has gained much insight into what makes a successful partnership.

"The most sterling relationship I've had is with WebEx," she says. "When we started working with WebEx, Subrah Iyar, WebEx's CEO, wouldn't agree to give us stock without knowing how compatible our two organizations were. Iyar suggested we work together for a couple of months to see how the relationship developed. He felt that if Antenna Group were to have stock in his company, then that would make us his partner. Regardless of the amount of stock, he wanted to make sure that both of us wanted to be in this together. Sixty days went by and he said, 'I'm loving this, and I want you to be our partner.'

"You can tell a lot about a company's viability by how they treat their vendors and consultants and the people who are helping them achieve success. Integrity flows through WebEx's organization, and the way they treat their partners is indicative of how they treat their employees and customers."

—Christopher Barr

Ask yourself the following questions before issuing equity to third parties:

- *How will the person/company be motivated by the equity?* It's in every owner's best interest to have an incentive to move the company forward and reach its goals. For example, equity issued to employees will motivate them to perform, whereas the equity given to a landlord will not serve to motivate a landlord—once you've signed a lease, the landlord performs no ongoing function for the company. Make sure the equity you distribute is motivational and encourages a long-term relationship.
- *Does the person/company share your business goals?* Ownership

in a company usually aligns the interests of all the owners, no matter what the size of each stake. Make sure the person or the company receiving the equity has the same expectations and goals in mind.

• *Will issuing this equity help get you to the next funding milestone?* Your job as entrepreneur is to get to the next funding round. If issuing the equity puts you at odds with your short-term goals, then keep the equity and find another way to compensate the other party.

• *Will issuing this equity make you more successful?* Equity is more valuable than gold and should be issued only when it's absolutely necessary. If the equity is not going to contribute to the start-up's success, then you shouldn't issue it. It's too valuable to waste.

• *Will these consultants add value to the business?* Just as there are some investors who contribute in an ongoing way to your start-up's success by providing advice and insight, so too should consultants who accept equity. As mentioned, in most cases landlords do not provide any additional value to your company and therefore are not appropriate candidates for equity. However, there is occasionally the case where a business deals with customers face-to-face and requires an impressive-looking office to make the business succeed. In this case, the start-up may grant equity to the landlord if it's deemed necessary to fulfill a strategic objective.

• *Can you have a long-term business relationship with these people?* The timeline to an IPO has increased significantly in 3G start-ups, so it may be many years before equity holders have any opportunity to sell their shares and see any income. That means you may have a very long association. Make sure these service providers are entities you want to work with for a while. You should avoid issuing equity if the consultant is doing a project that will take less than 9 to 12 months.

• *Will the equity cement a beneficial rapport?* As an entrepreneur you should feel comfortable calling on your stakeholders for advice and guidance, and as owners they should want to help you grow. Only use equity where you feel there will be open, supportive communication.

• *Is it a strategic relationship?* You'll waste equity if you use it to get your hands on, say, networking server hardware, because acquiring hardware—basically a one-time investment—does not constitute an ongoing strategic relationship. You should issue equity only when it can pay dividends over time, such as when sealing a distribution deal or sharing core technology information.

- *Is now the right time?* As in much of life, timing is everything, and it's also an important factor when issuing start-up equity. Because equity is so valuable and because each share of equity issued affects every other share, you should be certain that you're bringing in the right equity partner at the right time. The first service provider you'll likely bring in is a lawyer, because you'll need legal advice when you are setting up your business and when you first start to work with VCs. Public relations companies and marketing partners usually come second.

The answers to the previous questions will help you determine which people can help the business, and they will also help steer you away from service providers who don't add value over time. The key is to put equity to work in a smart and simple manner.

At the height of the second-generation dot.com boom in the late 1990s, it was customary for start-ups to issue equity to every Tom, Dick, and Mary who asked for it. The glut of Internet start-ups meant that consultants had dozens of companies begging for their services by offering stock that held the possibility of great future wealth. Lawyers, landlords, advertising agencies, headhunters, and public relations agencies often accepted equity in lieu of or in combination with cash payments.

Of course, with the dot.com crash of 2000, many of those people who had accepted stock in ultimately failed companies were damaged by the write-downs of those assets. The pile of worthless stock certificates from the end of the second generation of start-ups could have towered over the Empire State Building. Both parties to any equity agreement need to do their due diligence or suffer the consequences.

Due Diligence Cuts Both Ways

Antenna Group owner Melody Haller has accepted equity from a number of start-ups with win-win results. Clients

Digimarc, WebEx, AskJeeves, and Bamboo (which merged with Ipix) all went public. Another client, Alexa Internet, was bought by Amazon; and AllApartments.com, which became SpringStreet, was bought by Homestore. In each case, her equity stake paid off.

According to Haller, "Our product is our time, as it is for all PR agencies. I can put a price on the time we spend and what we deliver. Our contracts with start-ups specify the dollar amount of what I'm contributing and what the company will pay us in both cash and equity. I make sure that I get a document that says I'm earning so many shares. I avoid hidden surprises as well as restricted stock that has lockups structured longer than the other early investors. The shares vest each month as we earn them, but the price is set at the price of the last funding round. We're not in the business of telling entrepreneurs what their company is worth."

This isn't to say Haller hasn't made some mistakes in structuring equity agreements. Early on, she had an arrangement with a client in which the value of the shares changed each month, depending on a complicated formula devised by the entrepreneur to protect his share of equity. As the company's stock price declined, so did Haller's share. The stock ended up being worthless. Admits Haller, "I learned the hard way."

Now, says Haller, "I avoid warrants and options and go for straight common shares. It's a dollar out of my pocket, and I don't think I should have to pay to exercise it. I'm already paying salaries and overhead for my own company, so I'm funding this machine just as if I were an angel investor."

Haller advises start-ups to be wary of a PR firm that routinely takes more than a third of its fees in stock. Any company that does so pushes its risk profile to extremes, and that means you're partnering with a company that has made a big gamble in one area; if it loses, then that's going to affect the company's ability to deliver for you. Warns Haller, "You

(continued)

want to be sure that the consultant or agency that you're partnering with is engaging in prudent business practices."

But overall, Haller says she's come out ahead. "We began accepting as much as a third of our fee in equity many years ago, and we've had a number of successes. Theoretically, if a company took a third in equity from every client and didn't get any of it back, it wouldn't be able to meet its operating expenses and payroll, let alone partners' salaries. In the PR business, we have a success formula that's similar to a VC's; we'll make our money back on half the companies we accept equity from; we'll have a huge success with 20 percent, and a total loss on 30 percent."

And her experience has made her a tougher negotiator. "I had one client who lectured us on how privileged we were to have equity in his company," she says. "That company's equity turned out to be worthless. I'm getting to where I can look them in the eye and say, 'I know you have a wonderful vision, but this is a high-risk venture and I'm sharing your risk. In exchange for sharing your risk, I should be sharing your upside.'"

—*Christopher Barr*

Among the groups that can provide ongoing value are public relations companies, executive recruiters and search firms, marketing consultants, advertising agencies, and attorneys. Other types of third parties should be looked at with a gimlet eye—and then looked at again. These include landlords, office equipment vendors, and technology outsource services.

Equity Enhances Strategic Partnerships

To see how stock can be allocated to a third party for the purposes of growing the business, look at CareerBuilder. In 1998 the recruiting site established a close relationship with ADP, the payroll processing services company. CareerBuilder created an agreement whereby ADP resold CareerBuilder services through ADP's expansive distribution network. In one stroke, this arrangement increased CareerBuilder's sales team from a dozen to more than 500 salespeople throughout the United States. ADP was motivated to sign the deal because it saw online recruiting as a service that was a natural extension of its business: ADP was already dealing with the human resources departments of large companies, and job posting was another product they could offer their customers. Besides, ADP viewed the Internet as being strategic to its business—so much so that they thought about acquiring CareerBuilder outright, although they decided instead to take a sizable stake.

ADP invested in CareerBuilder and had warrants to buy additional shares based on sales revenue milestones. As ADP produced additional sales of CareerBuilder services, the warrants would vest and give ADP the ability to buy more stock in CareerBuilder. This is an example of how the business objectives were mirrored in the equity structure. ADP was incentivized to perform because the more revenue ADP generated, the more stock it could own in a company that was increasing in value. CareerBuilder was incentivized to have ADP perform because the more revenue ADP generated the more valuable CareerBuilder stock would become. CareerBuilder was acquired by the Tribune Company and KnightRidder.com in 2000.

—J. Neil Weintraut

■ HOW TO STRUCTURE THIRD-PARTY EQUITY

No matter how you structure the shares that go to long-term consultants, third parties, and service providers, it always translates into a percentage of the business. Whatever the form of equity you grant—warrants, preferred stock, stock options, or common stock—when the company goes public, these all convert into the same thing, common stock. So don't waste your time engineering who gets preferred, who gets options, and who gets warrants. Hire a lawyer to work out those issues, and spend *your* time running the business.

How does the 3 percent of equity get allocated to the various parties requesting equity? You want to give enough stock to motivate but not so much that you regret it if the service provider drops you as a customer the next day. Remember that any shares you issue to one group reduce the budget available to others, so don't blow it on one opportunity.

The parties who will be motivated by equity include business partners, public relations firms, law firms, and long-term consultants, such as executive recruiters. Law firms and public relations firms may accept a percentage of their fees in equity. At most, it works out to approximately a third of the fee. Keep in mind that the firms accepting equity have fixed costs they need to cover, such as payroll and rent, so they can't accept the entire fee in equity. Lawyers and PR companies are less likely to demand and accept equity from 3G start-ups because of the losses incurred in the 2G dot.com era.

Executive recruiters have a standard rate. When they recruit an executive, these firms get one-third of the annual salary of the executive and one-third of their first year's stock option grant. So if you recruit a CEO who gets an annual salary of $180,000 and 10 percent of the equity of the company (on a four-year vesting schedule), then the recruiter would receive $60,000 and 0.833 percent of the company's equity. Keep this toll in mind if you plan to use executive recruiters to hire your senior staff!

Board members and advisers should all get small percentages of stock, and these shares should fit easily within the equity budget. There are exceptional cases when you may need to exceed your budget, for instance, when you work with big strategic partners. In those cases, you may end up issuing up to 10 percent of the company to strategic partners that make a significant impact on the performance of your business.

Captain Kirk and Whoopi Goldberg: Gambling on the Upside

When Priceline.com was looking to make a big splash, it attracted William Shatner, best known for his portrayal of

Captain James T. Kirk of the starship *Enterprise*. To get Shatner, in April 1998 Priceline gave him warrants for 100,000 shares of Priceline stock. Since it would be more than a year before Priceline had an IPO, Shatner was clearly taking a chance.

It was a chance that paid off for both Shatner and Priceline. Priceline was able to attract a celebrity around whom to create a memorable ad campaign, which helped publicize Priceline. Shatner was able to bring attention to Priceline that helped send the stock soaring, thereby increasing the value of his holding dramatically. A truly motivated spokesman, Shatner made Priceline a household name while cashing out with millions. (Of course, you have to give Shatner credit for timing it right and cashing out before the stock tumbled with the rest of the dot.com herd in early 2000.)

Whoopi Goldberg, unfortunately, wasn't nearly as successful. In September 1999, in exchange for cash and equity, e-commerce company Flooz signed Whoopi Goldberg as its spokesperson. While Flooz concedes that Whoopi increased consumer awareness of the site from virtually zero to more than 50 percent, Whoopi has been unable to cash out because Flooz has never gone public. According to Flooz's CEO, Whoopi owns less than 10 percent of the company.

—*Christopher Barr*

■ RULES FOR ISSUING EQUITY

Before you issue equity, think through the ramifications, then follow these guidelines:

- Create an equity budget for third-party consultants and service providers.
- Determine the people with whom you want to have a long-term relationship to grow your business.
- Keep it simple—don't create arcane formulas and complicated arrangements when issuing equity to third parties.

Chapter 17

How to Tell Your Story

NEILISM: Entrepreneurs often ask, "What's the best way to raise venture capital?" Wrong question!

The biggest key to a start-up's early success is an entrepreneur's ability to communicate what the company is all about. Whether it's during a search for financing, customers, or employees, if entrepreneurs can't put into words the wonder of their creation, they will have a tough time convincing anyone to fund it, use it, or join it. A 30-page business plan is not the best path to success in the Lightspeed environment. Although a 30-page business plan may be an appropriate tool to gather metrics and may provide a thorough analysis of an opportunity, you will strike out if you ask time-constrained venture capitalists to plow through 30 pages of overmassaged data. It's time to ditch your business proposal and start outlining how to tell your story.

The right business plan to win the favor of VCs isn't a business plan at all, but a great start-up story. You will attract the attention and possibly the backing of VCs through a simple eight-topic story that identifies the diamond-in-the-rough potential of your start-up and explains how you will turn this potential into a success story.

The entrepreneurs who have mastered how to tell their story in three or four sentences are the ones who will land not only investment money but also employees and eventually customers.

Thirty-page business plans are a good exercise for collecting your thoughts and testing your assumptions, and they may have been the best tool to profile your business a decade ago; but it won't work for 3G start-ups. Opportunity-rich and time-constrained venture capitalists get thousands of pitches each week and just don't have the time to wade though massive business plans. Even if they did, oversized business plans with reams of financial projections are rendered obsolete by rapid fluctuations in the Lightspeed marketplace. Volumes of well-engineered data actually hamper an entrepreneur's ability to frame a business that is predicated on pivotal details, improvisation, and expertise. Venture capitalists are more concerned about the reality of, say, landing an experienced VP of engineering in a technology start-up than they are about business models or spreadsheets.

Venture capitalists are captivated by start-ups with the prerequisite *right stuff* of a great business that is articulated to them in a story with clarity, focus, and swiftness. When they ask an entrepreneur, "What's your business?" they want to know that the entrepreneur is on top of the business and has mastered the skill of delivering the start-up's essence on a silver platter. Rather than plow through aggregated data, the VCs want to hear what it is in just a few crisp sentences. If the entrepreneur can't effortlessly articulate what his or her business is about, ironically, the more they speak, the less they impress. To VCs, the lack of a concise vision statement means the entrepreneur has yet to master the business. VCs dismiss thousands of business plans weekly with nothing more than a form letter, even though they are flush with money they are eager to deploy—all because the entrepreneurs failed to articulate their business idea.

That's the Wrong Question!

Entrepreneurs attend conference after conference trying to crack the code on how to raise venture capital. When I'm asked that question—and I get it all the time—my response is always the same: You're asking the wrong question. It's not about raising venture capital; it's about being attractive to venture capitalists. Make your company attractive to capital, and it will find you.

Here's the secret code:

• *Go after a big market opportunity.* If you're going after a market opportunity that's small or if you're going after it late, you can't attract venture capital. It doesn't necessarily mean that you don't have a good idea for a successful business; it just means you're not venture capital material. The opportunity must be big enough to make it worth the VC's while.

• *Recruit A-team players.* If you have a good story, then you'll be able to attract great people to work with you. Besides, if you have a clear vision of a winning idea and the ability to convey it with passion, you can hire the best people on terms more favorable to you than if you had to woo them. As with attracting venture capital, make your business attractive and the A players will find *you*.

• *Get a reference.* Have someone contact me on your behalf. What I'm looking for is a demonstration that you can attract other people. And if you can't attract someone who thinks you're worthy enough to be referred, then either you don't have the internal drive or you're not a person who can attract others. Either way, I don't want you. So don't respond to that rejection by simply writing a longer business plan; get a reference.

• *Be clear about your business.* I get spreadsheets and business plans that outline a start-up's financials by month; so there are 18 columns covering revenue, hiring, and research and development (R&D) and I can't tell what that means about the business. I don't dispute any of the numbers, but these actually haven't provided any useful information. Instead, I want to know that you've mastered the business. I'd

(continued)

> prefer that you said, "We think that to be successful we need to have one million customers in this time frame. To do that, we need a sales and marketing budget of $10 million, and we'll need 30 employees."
>
> Make yourself attractive to capital, and everything else will follow.
>
> —*J. Neil Weintraut*

■ PREREQUISITES: THE RIGHT STUFF

Start-ups that warrant billion-dollar valuations and create headline-grabbing revenues must have a big market to attack, a breakthrough idea, and the wherewithal to execute on the opportunity. To win the favor of venture capitalists, your success depends on the degree to which your story has these attributes:

- A big opportunity that will support a billion-dollar-plus stock valuation.
- A first-to-market position to claim customers, partners, and employees before the other three or four early movers enter the market.
- A knock-your-socks-off benefit to customers (otherwise, why should they care?).
- A growth-within-costs infrastructure and company strategy. You must be able to thrive in the fast-eat-the-slow, big-eat-the-small reality of the 3G environment.
- Steely founders who can make all of this happen. Through their leadership they attract more great people to make more happen, they fully "get" and fit their environment (and change with it), and they listen to the market cues to intuit where to go next.
- Baggage-free company where the equity, the board of directors, the location, and other structural components help rather than stymie the success of the company.

Not all start-ups have a full complement of the *right stuff*, so your odds of attracting a backer go up exponentially if you have a full quiver. So if you can formulate the 3G start-up equivalent of nirvana, which is early entry into a big market with a viral offering executed by capable entrepreneurs, then you can expect VCs to be trying to win *your* interest, rather than you having to win theirs. Doers rather than wishers are essential, and armchair entrepreneurs need not apply. But if you go out and make things happen: identify a big market before others, quit your job, team up with others, throw together a mock-up, and somehow convince a first customer to give you the time of day, then the odds are in your favor that you'll be receiving a wire transfer from your new venture capitalist within three months.

■ ARTICULATING YOUR BUSINESS

When you make a formal presentation you should have eight components: (1) business case, (2) customers, (3) solution, (4) alternatives, (5) entrepreneurs, (6) accomplishments, (7) company, and (8) numbers. Using these components you'll need to develop three different presentations: a 10-slide presentation, a verbal "five-floor elevator pitch," and a three-page e-mail.

➤ Your Story

Here are the eight components of your story:

1. *The Business Case*
   This states the reasons that customers care if your business exists. Your success in the opportunity-rich Lightspeed environment is predicated on your focusing on doing just a few things, doing them well, and doing them quickly. In a business case, you want to give a complete overview and explain how it all comes together, including the demand and the road to market. Here you explain how you will turn the *right stuff* into a grand opportunity, by extracting the pivotal details and connecting everything together into a tight, doable strategy with clear actions.

2. *Your Customers and Why They Need Your Product*
   Profile your customers, and identify the potential number of them. Of the myriad customer needs, describe in some detail the

handful that are very important yet easy to implement. These distinctive needs provide the rationale on which you'll launch your business.

3. *Your Solution*

Your offering is your solution to the customers' needs. It's the value proposition of your company. Explain why your offering is so compelling by outlining the "secret sauce" that will draw millions of customers and the strategy that gets you to market quickly. With a special focus on how this fits into the external environment, explain why customers care about it and how that makes for a good business. In the solution section, both identify what about your offering will knock customers' socks off and develop the strategy that will enable your start-up to succeed!

4. *Alternatives to Your Product*

Provide a comprehensive assessment of every alternative to your business, whether a direct or an indirect competitor. And remember, one of the alternatives is that the customer takes no action at all. Describe each alternative's different value proposition and unique circumstances. Based on your insights about the customer, describe how the customer will respond to each alternative offering—and how your company will respond to that competitive challenge. Although it's a natural instinct to avoid discussing your competitors' strengths for fear that they undermine your story, including them in your pitch tells your audience that you thoroughly understand your market and your competitive landscape and that you have the confidence to compete successfully. Ironically, it gives you more credibility, not less.

5. *You and the Other Founders*

Highlight your role and your background, as well as the roles and the relevant backgrounds of the other founders. Investors want to feel confident that they are backing a solid and experienced team.

6. *Your Accomplishments*

These are the accomplishments, related to your business, that you've achieved to date: for example, business partnerships, first customers, and other head starts.

7. *Your Company Info*

Describe your location, equity, board of directors, founding date, contact information, and other key company facts. Include this info because it paints a fuller picture of your business, of course, but also because it helps you convey more subtle messages about your company—for instance, how baggage free it is. And on a more practical note, you'd be amazed at how many people send their business plan without identifying who they are or where they are located!

8. *Numbers*

And finally, outline your projections for product development, staffing, and customer acquisition costs, and include a time line describing when you need the cash to reach each milestone—for example, to ensure that you purchase the necessary equipment to support a million customers *before* you actually acquire them.

There you have it: eight topics, five sentences each on average. That's it. Give the right amount of information, but no more. Don't try to impress VCs with reams of data because that is as counterproductive as is giving too little. The more specific and punchy you make your story, the better. Make a clear, credible case for how your start-up will get big faster than the competition, and your business will be more likely to out-sing the 10 or more stories a VC considers each day.

➤ PowerPoint Presentation

Keep your slideshow to 10 slides, and have them illustrate the eight components of your start-up. Avoid complicated or busy slides, and get to the problem you're solving right away. Be prepared to answer questions like:

- What's the key concept?
- How quickly can you scale?
- Who are your customers? Advisers?
- What are the factors affecting your success?

➤ Five-Floor Elevator Pitch

Why a five-floor elevator pitch? In an elevator you have one chance to make an impression, and it takes about 30 seconds to go five floors. Your elevator pitch needs to be the purest distillation of what your business is all about. Keep the elevator pitch broad, explaining the opportunity size, the customer needs, your solution, and the benefits of your start-up. Close with a call to action: "Would you like to hear more?" Be sure to keep it clear, concise, and jargon-free.

➤ **It's All about You**

Keep in mind that your goals in telling your story are twofold: (1) to identify the *right stuff* that your start-up has, and (2) to explain how you will turn this right stuff into a 3G success story—the leader in a big market. The approach you take in telling the story enlightens venture capitalists about the centerpiece of the right stuff: you.

So approach it constructively, conveying an appropriate degree of paranoia about all the external factors that can affect your business and a mastery of your market opportunity to show that you have a clear vision to lead your team to do the few critical things very well. Make sure your presentation is smart and reality based. You undermine your credibility, for example, if you project ridiculous operating margins that can be achieved only by the most monopolistic companies in the best of circumstances. You can save yourself from such embarrassments by going to, say, Yahoo! Finance and performing a simple reality check of your projections of your market opportunity, your competitors, and your potential domination of that market.

One last note: Be willing to listen to the feedback you get when you tell your story. That doesn't mean you have to accept it; but you are talking to people whose life's work is helping to turn fledgling start-ups into big, important, successful businesses. Chances are they have some valuable things to tell you. And if you get the same kinds of responses from several people, consider the feedback carefully and change your story accordingly.

Storytelling Dos and Don'ts

- *Do a detailed mock-up.* A mock-up will vastly boost your effectiveness in capturing attention and conveying your message. Besides, the process of creating a mock-up itself helps you hone your story.

- *Do initiate contact through a reference.* Start-ups that can't even get a reference rarely develop the drive and the ingenuity to succeed. Top-tier venture capital firms simply decline unreferenced solicitations.

- *Don't send generic or unintroduced proposals.* Be sure to get an introduction before you send a proposal. An unwanted pitch will be ignored.

- *Do know your audience.* Learn about the venture capitalist that you are contacting or visiting—look up its portfolio companies.

- *Do a reality check of your conclusions.* It's easy to synthesize numbers and assumptions that are wrong. Check them with a few mouse clicks at Yahoo! Finance, Moneycentral, or other readily available sources of financial information.

- *Do listen to feedback!* The people you are contacting may offer informed insights or advice. Even if you disagree with it, listen! Most likely the feedback reflects the same thoughts in other VCs' minds. Be sure to address the feedback in future presentations. One good test: If you haven't changed your story after interacting with the fifth VC, you aren't listening!

- *Do send your story in an impassioned e-mail.* The convenience of electronic information overshadows the gloss of paper documents.

- *Do send your slide presentation to a universally accessible e-mail account,* such as Hotmail or Yahoo! Mail. Most venture capital firms have large monitors hooked up to computers. By sending your presentation to a universally accessible e-mail account, you avoid the risk and the hassle of having to connect your personal computer to the VC's slide projector.

(continued)

> - *Do practice.* Time yourself and videotape your presentation. Count the "uhs" and "you knows," and eliminate them. Perfect your pacing and timing.
> - *Don't wait!* In the Lightspeed Economy, no good idea goes unpunished, and the odds are that when you thought of your idea, so did five or 10 other would-be entrepreneurs.

➤ **Impassioned E-mail**

Have an e-mail version ready that you can send to VCs before you make an in-person presentation. It will incorporate the same eight components. Here is an example of an actual letter written by an entrepreneur. The names have been changed to protect the privacy of the people involved.

To: VC firm

From: Entrepreneur

Re: RedLadder.com – The Contractor's Place on the Web

RedLadder – a leading vertical portal for midsized construction contractors – is seeking to raise $25 million in venture funding to market its free Web-based tools and services to construction contractors nationally.

RedLadder has just released the killer application for the construction industry – a free Web-based organizing tool that helps contractors solicit bids from trading partners before procuring supplies and services.

RedLadder has made the most of its initial round of funding obtained through 21st Century Internet Partners by

- Building a company of over 45 people, including 90 years of domain expertise.

- Completing three popular releases of our Web-based service over the past 60 days.
- Designing and implementing a strategy for lightning-quick market penetration.

The centerpiece of the RedLadder toolset is a communication tool that invites subcontractors and suppliers to bid and that tracks responses to bid invitations. This tool solves a longstanding industry problem (a thorn in the side of all construction cost estimators) that revolves around the ability of getting sufficient subcontractor and supply bids to assemble a competitive estimate on bid day. This tool is, at the same time, a vehicle for lightning-fast adoption of the RedLadder system.

Please let me know if you would like to learn more about RedLadder and the midsized construction contractor that we serve.

Best Regards,

Entrepreneur
President & CEO
RedLadder.com

Here's how the letter *should* be written:

Jeff,

Hi, per ___ (*insert name of person who referred you*), I would like you to consider the possible match of RedLadder with your firm.

RedLadder is a portal for construction contractors that presently serves more than 600 contractors with thousands of projects totaling more than $1 billion, after only three months of operation.

We now have the system, a critical mass of projects and contractors, and the organization to scale geographically as well as functionally into the commerce side, which of course requires further board-level skills and capital to go to this next level. And hence this e-mail. I'm hoping that we'll prove to be a match.

Our approach to the construction space—namely as a portal—not only distinguishes us from the exchanges and project-management offerings, but more important is also instantly valuable, easy, and desirable to contractors. As a result, we are attracting contractors at a high rate—and one much higher than the other, more complicated or less contractor-centric vendors. We are also becoming positioned as the first, and potentially last, stop for contractors on the Internet.

Today we provide contractors all of the technology and information for launching projects, culminating in an eVite-like system; but where eVite gives consumers a way to arrange events between multiple parties, we offer contractors a mechanism for bidding construction projects among multiple parties. Our offering today features a directory of more than 600 currently active projects; a yellow pages of 20,000 directly validated contractors and subcontractors; a library of fresh information, ranging from prices on toilet rentals to different types of finishes; basic e-mail; and affiliate links to blueprinting, permit-submission, and other downstream services. Most important, we have an "invitation-to-bid" system that brings all of these components into a project-centric console, which reflects the contractor's view on the world. Additionally, the invitation-to-bid system, which we are publicly launching April 15, is the one process in the contracting life cycle that is inherently viral—as well as at the front end of the contractor's experience—and hence, we are using this feature both to accelerate our user growth and to capture those users long before downstream services do, thereby putting us in a dominant and front-end position to participate in all of the revenue flows, from sponsorships to B2B commerce.

To date, we've grown from 3 founders to 45 people since November, with $3.1 million from 21st Century Internet and

Camp VI. The executive team includes me [*entrepreneur*]; Mark H, Director of Operations; Dan B, VP of Contractor Acquisition; and Drew P, Director of Product Development. I have extensive experience as a contractor, which is resonating well with customers (some other technology-industry-originated competitors aren't perceived by customers as "getting it"). I also have experience in the technology industry, notably in the JavaSoft Division of Sun. Our Director of Technology has done a superb job of getting a Unix/Oracle-based system up and running, as well as the invitation-to-bid program and all of the associated components. However, as we move to the next level, we plan to install best-in-class VPs in engineering, marketing, and business development; searches are active for them presently.

Regards,

Entrepreneur

■ BIGWORDS: TELLING THE STORY

BigWords is a company that started up in January 1998 and offers a good illustration of how to craft an effective business story.

➤ Business Case

BigWords is an e-merchandiser aimed at the collegiate market. Aimed at filling a need for college students' most visible and necessary product—textbooks—BigWords offers college students an electronic store to get the products that they need with an experience that they want. The ultimate win is turning BigWords into a brand to which college students look for fulfilling a wide range of their merchandise needs.

Through a variety of specialized merchandising features, including the ability to search for books by college-class title as well as book title, the ability to buy and sell both new and used books, a supply-chain designed specifically for the seasonal purchase spikes inherent in the semester lifecycle, and a brand with the right attitude, BigWords differentiates itself from other e-merchants, especially general-purpose online booksellers, while catering to the college student's unique needs and tastes.

➤ The Market for College Student Merchandise

There are 20 million college students in the United States (a number that's growing 3 percent annually), and they account for an estimated $20 billion of annual purchasing power for textbooks, clothes, computers, music, and similar products. College students spend more than $10 billion annually on textbooks alone.

Meanwhile, textbook sales involve unique requirements. First, unlike mainstream books, which involve one-way transactions (selling) of one type of item (new books), textbooks sales entail two-way transactions (the ability to sell *and* buy) of two types of items (new *and* used books). Similarly, the supply chain involves unique characteristics: textbooks are typically purchased in a three-week surge at the start of each semester or quarter. This is a particularly acute supply-chain problem because textbook sales involve small volumes of a large range of books (say 1,000 copies each of 10,000 different titles), rather than a large volume of a small number of books as is the norm in the traditional book publishing industry. In addition, textbooks are specified by class rather than name.

Finally, college students are a large demographic group that is very attractive to companies ranging from credit card services to automobile manufacturers. These companies know that college students are tomorrow's most attractive consumers and that many retain the product or brand relationships established during college for the rest of their lives. As a result, they are motivated to reach this audience.

➤ Why to Buy at BigWords

BigWords provides college students with the products they need and like, and it does so in a convenient e-commerce platform that lets users order online, compare prices, search on a variety of criteria, and select from a wide range of products. BigWords offers an experience students enjoy, a brand with which they identify, and the product availability and fulfillment that addresses their unique needs.

BigWords provides:

- E-commerce benefits of convenience, price, and selection.
- Capabilities unique to college textbooks, notably, both the buying and the selling of new and used books and locating books by class rather than title. In every shipment, for example, BigWords includes a preaddressed box for returning used books. Through a combination of on-campus representatives, parties, and giveaways, as well as by engaging professors to promote BigWords in classes by empowering professors with control of their books on BigWords' site, BigWords adds value to the student's life on a variety of levels, while fostering word-of-mouth marketing.
- A reliable, responsive supply chain. The three-week surges inherently overstress the current supply-chain systems, leading competitors' Web sites, for example, to accept orders when in fact the third-party distributor is out of stock. By operating its own supply chain, BigWords has full control over its fulfillment and can stockpile books in anticipation of demand.

The strategy is to start with, and build on, books as the primary draw of customers and the major revenue stream. From that foothold, we will build the collegiate brand and expand into other product categories and partners, becoming the premier conduit for numerous other companies seeking to connect with this fickle but important demographic.

➤ Alternatives

- *Off-line*: college bookstores with multimonth lead times. On the upside, bookstores provide instant gratification—assuming the student finds the desired book. On the downside, in addition to all the drawbacks to offline bookstores described previously, professors don't like the offline process. It limits the selection of books that stores can stock, and it requires longer planning.

- *Online:* Evarsity, eCampus, direct collegiate, general e-commerce ventures (especially Amazon.com), and collegiate portals, which are both partners and competitors.

➤ Accomplishments

In the first 10 months of the company, we have attracted a $100,000 investment from Bell Canada, hired six employees, established retailer relationships with the top 50 book publishers, created an NT-based Web site, promoted the company at eight California universities, and sold $50,000 of textbooks to students at over 150 colleges nationwide.

➤ Entrepreneurs

Matt Johnson, CEO. Before founding BigWords, Matt was director of online services at In-touch Survey Systems, where his clients included the Gap, Holiday Inn, McDonald's, and American Airlines. Prior to In-touch, he was cofounder and VP of technology and strategic marketing at Tierra Communications, an information-filtering software company. He was also an analyst at BC Capital, the venture group of Bell Canada. Matt first thought of the concept of buying textbooks online when he was a student at the University of Ottawa. Matt left college because he couldn't afford the textbooks. He doesn't like paying too much or standing in line, and he doesn't think anyone else does, either.

John Gates, VP of Making Things Happen. Prior to joining BigWords, John was director of business development and technology evangelist for Skunk Technologies, a Santa Monica–based Java developer. Prior to working at Skunk, he was director of online services for Virtual Vegas, the first online entertainment Web site in the dot.com domain. John also cofounded RadioNet, the first and longest-running radio show with a home page. John graduated summa cum laude from the Honor Collegium at UCLA.

➤ The Company

BigWords was founded in January 1998 and is located in San Francisco. The company was capitalized with a $100,000 investment from Bell Canada. Matt Johnson and John Gates are BigWords' two board members. The company's legal counsel is Fenwick & West. The company's Web site is at www.bigwords.com; the company's phone number is (415) 543-1400; and Matt Johnson's e-mail address is matt.johnson@bigwords.com.

➤ Numbers

To achieve our goal of more than $100 million in annual sales, we require $20 million in order to hire and support 200 employees, to create a state-of-the-art distribution center, and to expand our sales and marketing efforts.

■ ONLY THE BEGINNING

Finally, packaging and telling your story to venture capitalists is not the end but rather the beginning of your story. As every entrepreneur soon finds out, he or she will pitch the story hundreds of times over to recruit every employee, every business partner, every service provider, and every reporter. So the better your story, the better the employees, partners, and providers that you'll attract, and the better the news stories that will be written about your start-up. Additionally, the challenge of telling your story to others prompts you to refine it at every opportunity, perhaps turning it from a close second to the hands-down winner.

So what's your story?

Part Four

Sensational Start-ups

Chapter

Survive and Thrive

NEILISM: Get out in front and run like hell.

We're not saying that building a start-up will be easy. In fact, most start-ups will fail because they can't overcome the admittedly daunting challenges to success. Not only do you have to create the technology or the product, but you actually have to get customers to buy it. And if you're looking at a brand-new idea or market space, you must establish a demand for the product. In the second generation of start-ups, fledgling companies hardly had to concern themselves with these issues in order to get funding to pursue their dreams. Not so in the third generation. But even though the environment has changed drastically from the giddiness of the dot.com craze, opportunities abound.

Not only is technology here to stay, but it's becoming an ever more integral part of daily life the world over. And new technologies will create new products and new market opportunities we can't even envision today. As populations grow, the number of technology users will scale, which means there will be an ever-increasing demand for hardware and software to support their use. For example, the demand for bandwidth and storage seems insatiable, and so there will be growth in broadband communications as well as in the underlying broadband infrastructure. Business models that have technology as a key component will continue to be invented and deployed as market forces and innovations continue to march forward.

Investors and employees will continue to be attracted to compelling start-ups. Venture capitalists flush with money carry on in their relentless tasks: Find passionate entrepreneurs with great ideas, great teams, and great technologies, and then support them with investments.

■ "THE FOOT BONE'S CONNECTED TO THE LEG BONE . . . THE LEG BONE'S CONNECTED TO THE KNEE BONE"

Successful start-ups all share the same fundamental "body parts". These body parts include a great opportunity, the right offering to make the most of the opportunity, and a top-flight, no-baggage organization that's assembled into a thriving, constantly evolving organism. The component parts are supported by sound strategy, straightforward equity, and industry-standard technology. This organic whole is united by a mindset that uses speed, smarts, and simplicity to set the whole thing into motion and propel it to success.

The parts connect in an organic manner. Just like the song "Dem Bones," where the knee bone is connected to the thigh bone, all the parts of a start-up must work together. For example, you should target a big market opportunity because:

1. To succeed, you need to attract great people to staff your company.

2. To attract great people, you need an opportunity big enough to enable you to reward them accordingly.

3. To get millions of dollars to compensate a large number of people, you need a company that's worth at least a billion dollars.

4. To build a company that's worth a billion dollars, you must target a multi-billion-dollar market.

So it needs to be a big market. This same concept of interrelated parts working together in an organic whole, where small actions compound into big consequences, holds true in virtually every aspect of a business. In your organization, for example, if you don't hire the CEO early enough in the start-up's lifecycle, then you won't have the person in place to attract the vice presidents who will execute the vision. And if you don't have the VPs in place, then you can't build an effective organization. And so on. If one body part fails to function as it should, it impacts the whole organism.

Another example is with fundraising. If your overall goal is to be successful, then your only goal is to raise enough money to make it to the next funding round, for several reasons: (1) If you raise the money then you stay in the game and have the time to continue to do the things that will make you successful; (2) it just so happens that the things you need to accomplish to raise the money are also the essential things you need to do to succeed with your business; and (3) even if you're unsure of what you need to do next, raising the next round of capital keeps you alive until you figure it out.

Your equity structure is another key body part in the organism, as are the technologies you choose, the strategies you adopt, and the scenarios you decide on. If any of these parts don't work smoothly with the rest, you'll find building your business more painful, and you run a much greater risk of failure.

■ KEEP IT SIMPLE AND SMART

The goal of every start-up is to succeed, and the way to succeed is to do certain activities that lead to your success. Because there are often so may different choices open to an entrepreneur at any given point, the best strategy is to do the simplest, quickest thing that will get you to the next step in the sequence.

For example, getting back to the first major goal of fundraising, the first step in that sequence is to raise the next round of capital. So to do that, you need a product that works and a customer who has paid you to use it so you have hard evidence that somebody thinks it's valuable and that the product works. Take these few simple and smart actions, and you will then be on the path to your next goal: attracting a management team. Every member of the team doesn't need to be recruited by then, but you're clearly on that path. And the further down the path you are, the better off you are.

The sequence is important to focus on, because if you don't do any of those steps, then you probably won't raise the next round of capital. You want to keep your focus because circumstances shift so quickly and there are so many issues that you only have time to do it right once. In the end, all the components of your start-up will converge to a natural order anyway, either into a cohesive whole or else into a jumbled mess that can't be fixed. It's your choice.

■ INNOVATE YOUR OFFERING

There's a natural order, a right way, to build a start-up. For example, try as you might to come up with an outrageously high operating margin percentage, the factors in a free market economy, in which competition lowers the cost of products, will drive operating margins down to within a certain range. You can look at a start-up and divide it in two parts: what the start-up has, and what it does. For example, product design and marketing are things a start-up does, whereas equity is something that a start-up has. Both halves work in a Darwinian fashion, so that start-ups that have the right components will survive, while the start-ups that lack key parts—or whose parts don't function together—will fail.

Even if you come up with a variation on equity, organization, strategy, or technology for your start-up that deviates from the norm, you have effectively lowered your odds of success more than a start-up that is structured in a straightforward manner. The customer doesn't know that you have, say, a complicated equity structure. But if your nonstandard equity structure causes key employees to quit, your organization and offering will suffer, and the customer will surely feel the impact. When it comes to success, all that matters is getting as many customers to buy your product for as high a price as possible. To increase your odds of being successful, save your innovation efforts for your product offering, and stick to the time-tested models for the other parts of your business.

■ START-UPS ARE NOT IDEAS AND INNOVATIONS; THEY ARE ORGANIZATIONS FIRST

The acumen of the entrepreneurs behind the start-up is more important than ever. The single most important component in a company is its management team. When VCs evaluate whether a business is an attractive opportunity in which to invest, they're asking themselves whether the founders can attract other talent. If your start-up could attract a Jim Barksdale, then you're onto something.

Make sure you have the right employees. Start-ups require the leadership skills of many different individuals, from chief executive officer to chief technical officer. A common flaw of many entrepreneurs is to think they can play all the leadership roles in a start-up. While as a founder you may have the vision and the passion that launched the business, you may not have the skill set to be CEO and run the organization. Test yourself. Look in the mirror. Would you join this start-up? Would you join a company where you're CEO? If your answer is anything other than unqualified yes, then maybe you should think about attracting a CEO other than yourself. The success of your start-up will probably depend on it.

■ WHAT BUSINESS IS YOUR BUSINESS LIKE?

If you're starting a business, the first thing you should do is sit down and ask, "What kind of business do I want this business to look like?" Then from there, you find out all sorts of things. Using comparisons to existing businesses, you can understand more about your own business. You can see what they did to become successful, and you can avoid costly mistakes. You can get an idea of margins, product mix, marketing strategies, and market size and opportunity. You can look at their organization. You can examine the price points of their products, since yours will likely be similar. Then, during the comparison, you may find that this company has world-class managers who are perceived as leaders, yet the company's operating margins are only 20 percent. Now you can set reasonable goals for *your* business.

In performing one of these comparisons, you may actually discover your business is not a good business to start! If so, consider yourself lucky. The real worst-case scenario is the one where you and a lot of other people spend your time, money, and life's blood chasing an opportunity that's doomed to fail. For example, if you want to create a clicks-and-mortar drugstore chain, you may want to compare yourself with Eckerd or Rite Aid Corp. Go to Yahoo!

Finance, and look up a publicly traded drugstore company. Why look at Rite Aid and not Cisco? If you're selling aspirin, you will look more like Rite Aid than Cisco. You may happen to use Web servers and routers to sell your products rather than the salespeople and cash registers you'd find in a bricks-and-mortar store, but you're still selling aspirin.

As you build the comparison to Rite Aid, you discover that even if you do all the things that Rite Aid does and you secure relation-ships with a thousand different suppliers and have 20 million cus-tomers and generate more than $1 billion of revenue, you'll only be worth $200 million, and it's going to take 10 years to do that! That's not a good business. So guess what? You shouldn't even waste the VCs' time approaching them. Proposing an e-tailing business that must struggle to be worth $200 million in 10 years is not a business you should even consider.

Comparing your start-up to other businesses is a useful exercise for other reasons, too, such as recruiting. For example, if you're re-cruiting a world-class VP of marketing, the pitch boils down to a battle over whether the candidate wants to work at Cisco and then have stock options that might one day be worth $10 million or to work just as hard at Rite Aid and have stock options that might one day be worth $100,000. Where do you think that person is going to go? It's the same with investors and VCs. A VC can put $50 million in Cisco, and then it will be worth $1 billion in 10 years; or it can put that money into Rite Aid and maybe in 10 years it'll be worth $100 million.

A VC succeeds by producing multibillion-dollar companies that offer returns on investments of $50 million to $100 million. While an entrepreneur who creates a great small company that winds up generating $5 million is successful—and that's clearly a life-chang-ing number for the entrepreneur—$5 million to a venture capitalist is called "going out of business."

Where do you think the VC's money is going to go?

■ **END NOTE**

If you follow enough of these time-tested models, you will fall into a zone where you actually create your own success. After a while, the small successful actions you take will begin to compound and take on their own momentum, setting off a virtuous spiral of success. Success comes from leadership, and if you have a passion to succeed, and you take risks rather than waiting for opportunities to come to you, you'll be a leader whom others will want to join. Seize the opportunity!

Appendix

Further Sources

■ **CONSORTIUMS OF ANGEL INVESTORS**

Alliance of Angels
Seattle, WA
tel 206.389.7258
e-mail: *info@allianceofangels.com*
www.allianceofangels.com

Band of Angels
www.bandofangels.com
The deal flow considered by Band of Angels comes from its membership. Entrepreneurs should not submit their proposals directly to the Band administration or to the Band Fund managing directors. Band of Angels is generally interested in early-stage high-technology deals located in Silicon Valley.

TechCoast Angels
23011 Moulton Parkway, Suite F-2
Laguna Hills, CA 92653
tel 949.859.8445
fax 949.859.1707
e-mail:
techcoastangels@earthlink.net
www.techcoastangels.org

■ VENTURE CAPITAL FIRMS

There are thousands of VC firms. Here is a sampling of the top companies:

21st Century Internet Venture
Partners
Two South Park, 2nd Floor
San Francisco, CA 94107
tel 415.512.1221
fax 415.512.2650
www.21vc.com

Accel Partners
428 University Avenue
Palo Alto, CA 94301
tel 650.614.4800
www.accel.com

Benchmark Capital
2480 Sand Hill Road, Suite 200
Menlo Park, CA 94025
tel 650.854.8180
www.benchmark.com

Draper Fisher Jurvetson
400 Seaport Court, Suite 250
Redwood City, CA 94063
tel 650.599.9000
www.dfj.com

Kleiner Perkins Caufield &
Byers
2750 Sand Hill Road
Menlo Park, CA 94025
tel 650.233.2750

fax 650.233.0300
www.kpcb.com

Mayfield Fund
2800 Sand Hill Road, Suite 250
Menlo Park, CA 94025
tel 650.854.5560
www.mayfield.com

New Enterprise Associates
2490 Sand Hill Road
Menlo Park, CA 94025
tel 650.854.9499
fax 650.854.9397
www.nea.com

Oak Investment Partners
525 University Avenue, Suite
1300
Palo Alto, CA 94301
tel 650.614.3700
fax 650.328.6345
www.oakinv.com

Sequoia Capital
3000 Sand Hill Road, Bldg. 4,
Suite 280
Menlo Park, CA 94025
tel 650.854.3927
fax 650.854.2977
www.sequoiacap.com

Softbank Venture Capital
200 West Evelyn Avenue,
Suite 200
Mountain View, CA 94043
tel 650.962.2000
www.sbvc.com

Index